Fulbright Papers

PROCEEDINGS OF COLLOQUIA

SPONSORED BY THE
UNITED STATES — UNITED KINGDOM
EDUCATIONAL COMMISSION:
THE FULBRIGHT COMMISSION, LONDON

Volume 13

Controlling broadcasting
Access policy and practice
in North America and Europe

EDITED BY MERYL ALDRIDGE AND NICHOLAS HEWITT

This volume assesses the transformation of broadcasting currently taking place in Europe, where deregulation coupled with advances in satellite, cable and video technology promise consumer choice on an American scale.

The contributors, from the UK, France, the US, and Canada explore the paradoxes of the new era in broadcasting. Competition from more channels is leading to less diversity in programming; ensuring a voice for minority groups and interests is requiring elaborate regulation; and the creation of a free market in the EC is spawning a bewildering array of inconsistent statutes. The writers also show how broadcasting remains political; governments strive to keep control, particularly over television, because of its assumed importance in forming public attitudes. Whatever the rhetoric, images of elections, of war, and of terrorism will be tightly managed.

The Fulbright Programme of Educational Exchanges, which has been in operation since 1946, aims to promote mutual understanding between the United States of America and other nations. It now operates in more than 130 countries, with forty-six bi-national commissions involved in its administration. In the United Kingdom the Commission aims to offer qualified British and American nationals the opportunity to exchange significant knowledge and educational experience in fields of consequence to the two countries, and thereby to contribute to a deeper mutual understanding of Anglo-American relations and to broaden the means by which the two societies can further their understanding of each other's cultures. Amongst its activities the Commission promotes annual colloquia on topics of Anglo-American interest; the proceedings are published in this series.

Controlling broadcasting

Access policy and practice in North America and Europe

edited by

MERYL ALDRIDGE

and

NICHOLAS HEWITT

MANCHESTER
UNIVERSITY PRESS
IN ASSOCIATION WITH
THE FULBRIGHT COMMISSION, LONDON

DISTRIBUTED EXCLUSIVELY IN THE USA AND CANADA
BY ST. MARTIN'S PRESS

Published by Manchester University Press
Oxford Road, Manchester M13 9NR, UK
and Room 400, 175 Fifth Avenue,
New York, NY 10010, USA

Distributed exclusively in the USA and Canada
by St. Martin's Press, Inc.,
175 Fifth Avenue, New York, NY 10010, USA

British Library Cataloguing-in-Publication Data

A catalogue record for this book is available from the British Library

Library of Congress Cataloging-in-Publication Data
Controlling broadcasting : access policy and practice in North America
   and Europe / edited by Meryl Aldridge and Nicholas Hewitt.
      p.   cm. — (The Fulbright papers : v. 13)
   'This volume records the proceedings of the Fulbright Colloquium on Broadcast
Media in Britain and the US: Access and Control which was held at the University
of Nottingham from 18 to 20 September 1992'—Foreword.
   Includes bibliographical references.
   ISBN 0–7190–4277–1
   1. Broadcasting policy—United States—Congresses.   2. Broadcasting policy—
Europe—Congresses.   I. Aldridge, Meryl.   II. Hewitt, Nicholas.   III. Fulbright
   Colloquium on Broadcast Media in Britain and the US: Access and Control
(1992 : University of Nottingham)   IV. Series.
HE8689.8.C63   1994
384'.068—dc20   93–37271

ISBN 0 7190 4277 1 *hardback*

Phototypeset by Intype, London
Printed in Great Britain
by Biddles Limited, Guildford and King's Lynn

Contents

Part Three

Part Four

Part Five

Tables and figures

Contributors

MERYL ALDRIDGE, Senior Lecturer, School of Social Studies, University of Nottingham

DAVID L. ALTHEIDE, Regents' Professor, School of Justice Studies, University of Arizona at Tempe, USA

RICHARD COLLINS, Head of Department of Communications and Music Technology, London Guildhall University.

JOHN CORNER, Senior Lecturer in Politics and Communications Studies and Deputy Director, Centre for Media and Public Communications, University of Liverpool

RICHARD V. ERICSON, Principal of Green College, Professor of Law, and Professor of Sociology and Anthropology, University of British Columbia, Canada

MARJORIE FERGUSON, Associate Professor, College of Journalism, University of Maryland at College Park, USA

NICHOLAS HEWITT, Professor of French and Director of the Institute for Modern Cultural Studies, University of Nottingham

JOSHUA MEYROWITZ, Professor of Communication, Horton Social Science Center, University of New Hampshire, USA

JAMES MICHAEL, Director, Centre in Commerce and Information Law, University College, University of London

DAVID MILLER, Research Fellow, Media Unit, University of Glasgow

GRAHAM MURDOCK, Reader in the Sociology of Culture, Department of Social Sciences, University of Loughborough

RALPH NEGRINE, Lecturer, Centre for Mass Communications Research, University of Leicester

MICHAEL PALMER, Professor of Communications Theory, Centre for Research on Information and Communication theory in Europe, Université de Paris III – Sorbonne Nouvelle, France

Jean-Claude Sergeant, Professor, Institut du Monde Anglophone, Université de Paris III – Sorbonne Nouvelle, France

Robert P. Snow, Professor, Department of Sociology, University of Arizona at Tempe, USA

Foreword

This volume records the proceedings of the Fulbright Colloquium on Controlling broad-casting: access, policy and practice in North America and Europe which was held at the University of Nottingham from 18 to 20 September 1992. The issue of freedom versus control of the media, a subject central to the effective working of democracy, is a matter of continuing debate – with the recent expansion in the number and type of outlets available to the media fuelling fresh arguments and anxieties. The initiative of the Institute for Modern Cultural Studies at the University of Nottingham in bringing together specialists in the broadcast media from both sides of the Atlantic to discuss this important subject was timely and welcome and one to which the Fulbright Commission was pleased to lend its enthusiastic support.

In meeting its aim of promoting Anglo-American cultural understanding, the Commission sponsors at least one, and sometimes two, colloquia each year on subjects of mutual interest and importance to the United States of America and the United Kingdom. These meetings of distinguished scholars and practitioners in specialists fields augment the Commission's traditional awards of studentship, scholarships and fellowships to British and American citizens for study, teaching, research or work experience in the other's country. Over 11,000 such exchanges have been supported in this way by the Commission since it was established in 1948.

The colloquium at Nottingham used case studies to illustrate broad principles affecting access to and control of the media; and participants, who included representatives from Canada and France as well as from Britain and America, were able to assemble documentary evidence from a wide range of different sources in formulating their views and reaching their conclusions.

The opinions expressed are, of course, personal to the contributors and do not necessarily reflect the views of the Commission. Nevertheless, the Commission believes that publication of the proceedings will be greatly valued by all those concerned with how the broadcast media in democratic countries can and should be controlled. The subject is vital to the health of both Britain and America and the Fulbright Commission is pleased to have been able to contribute to its discussion at this time.

John E. Franklin, *Executive Director*
United States-United Kingdom Educational Commission
The Fulbright Commission, London

Acknowledgements

The editors would like to express their thanks to the Fulbright Commission for their generous support of the conference which forms the basis of this volume and, in particular, to Captain John E. Franklin for his help and advice during the preparation of the manuscript. They would like to thank the Warden and staff of Rutland Hall at the University of Nottingham, where the conference was held, for their unfailing help and courtesy, and extend particular thanks to Mr Leslie Hill, Chairman of Central Television, for providing the keynote speech on the first day of the conference. Thanks are also due to students in the School of Social Studies for their assistance in the organisation of the conference and to Mrs Judith Hayes and Ms Fiona Hayes for their work in the preparation of the final manuscript.

Meryl Aldridge
Nicholas Hewitt

Preface

'Competition, choice and quality' – the sub-title of the UK government's major broadcasting policy document (Cm 517 1988) perfectly captures the expected transformation of United Kingdom and European broadcasting that began in the 1980s. The mood was optimistic: technical change and deregulation would revolutionise the opportunities both for consumers and broadcasters. More terrestrial channels, and the expansion of satellite and cable would enable many more voices to be heard; competition would guarantee quality. Consumers would at last have the range of choice available in North America. Community television was eagerly discussed. Camcorder and cable would, between them, ensure that broadcasting could no longer be the preserve of the professionals. This was the context in which we proposed a Colloquium on broadcasting to the Fulbright Commission.

Yet the concepts both of access and of control abound with complexity and contradiction. In a recession more channels may limit the range of programming as broadcasters search desperately for the mass audience; cumbersome state controls may be the prerequisite for reflecting cultural diversity; opening up a free market in Europe is producing a mountain of potentially conflicting regulations. Even where the technology is there, lack of resources may limit non-professional broadcasters to bland mainstream subjects. However large the number of channels, what becomes news will be limited by sources and formats (as during the Gulf War) and by the working habits of newsgatherers, with their reliance on institutional contacts, official documents, and their intense professional reflexivity.

As the chapters in this volume show, participants took full advantage of the perspectives revealed by the new contours of broadcasting in the United Kingdom and in Europe to examine its political, legal and sociological dimensions. Taken together with the observations of the North American contributors, drawing from an apparently more diverse and open arena, the paradoxes of control and access in broadcasting are vividly illuminated.

The volume begins with an institutional and economic analysis of the issues of access and control in Western broadcast media by Graham Murdock, followed by a more theoretical discussion by John Corner, making use of access within the British documentary tradition. Part I is then completed by a chapter by Robert Snow on the role of broadcasting as a necessary part of the fabric of everyday life.

In Part II, Ralph Negrine and David Miller continue these theoretical discussions, but concentrating on two specific areas: Negrine on journalistic coverage of the British Aerospace takeover of the Rover company, and Miller on British and American television coverage of Northern Ireland.

The case-studies continue into Part III, with Joshua Meyrowitz' analysis of the 1992 Presidential campaign of Larry Agran, who was comprehensively denied national media coverage, and Richard Ericson's study of institutional control over access to the media, illustrated particularly through police and court reporting in Toronto. This is followed by David Altheide's discussion of 'postjournalism' through a detailed examination of the television treatment of the Gulf War.

In Part IV, Marjorie Ferguson compares access in American and Canadian television, and Richard Collins sets the British and North American discussions on access and control in a European context.

The European dimension concludes the volume, with James Michael's analysis of European legislation on broadcasting, Michael Palmer's examination of the role of the lobbyist in European broadcasting, and Jean-Claude Sergeant's discussion of the pervasive role of central government in the French broadcasting system.

Abbreviations

ABC	American Broadcasting Corporation
ACT	Association of Commercial Television
AIDS	Acquired Immune Deficiency Syndrome
AM	Amplitude Modulation
ANPA	American Newspaper Publishers Association
AP	Associated Press
ARG	American Research Group
BAe	British Aerospace
BBC	British Broadcasting Corporation
BCCI	Bank of Credit and Commerce International
BET	Black Entertainment Television
CAB	Canadian Association of Broadcasters
CAEJ	la Communauté des Association des Editeurs de Journaux
CBC	Canadian Broadcasting Corporation/Société Radio Canada
CBS	Columbia Broadcasting System
CCC	Citizens Communications Center
CIA	Central Intelligence Agency (USA)
CNCL	Commission nationale de la communication et des libertés
CNN	Cable Network News
CPB	Corporation for Public Broadcasting
CRTC	Canadian Radio-television and Telecommunications Commission
CSA	Conseil supérior de l'audiovisuel
DC	Washington DC
DOD	Defense Department (US)
EAT	European Advertising Tripartite
EBU	European Broadcasting Union
EC	European Community
EEC	European Economic Community
EPC	European Publishers Council
ETN	European Television Networks
FAIR	Fairness and Accuracy in Broadcasting
FCC	Federal Communications Commission
FIEJ	(International Federation of Newspaper Publishers)
FM	Frequency Modulation
GATT	General Agreement on Tariffs and Trade
IBA	Independent Broadcasting Authority
IRA	Irish Republican Army
ITC	Independent Television Commission

ITN	Independent Television News
ITV	Independent Television
LA	Los Angeles
MADD	Mothers Against Drunk Driving
MCC	Maxwell Communication Corporation
MP	Member of Parliament
MPAA	Motion Picture Association of America
MTV	Music Television
NAB	National Association of Broadcasters
NATO	North Atlantic Treaty Organisation
NBC	National Broadcasting Corporation (USA)
NCTA	National Cable Television Association
NFL	National Football League
NPA	Newspaper Publishers Association
NWICO	New World Information and Communication Order
ORTF	Office de radiodiffusion et télévision françaises
PBS	Public Broadcasting System
PR	Public Relations
RTF	Radiodiffusion et télévision françaises
RUC	Royal Ulster Constabulary
TF1	(French television channel)
TV	Television
TVNC	Television Northern Canada
TWA	Trans-World Airlines
UHF	Ultra High Frequency
UN	United Nations
UNESCO	United Nations Educational, Scientific and Cultural Organisation
VCRs	Video Cassette Recorders
VNRs	Video News Releases
WHSTV	W. H. Smith Television

PART ONE

Corporate dynamics and broadcasting futures

GRAHAM MURDOCK

BROADCASTING AND THE POLITICS OF REPRESENTATION

Recent years have seen an intensified debate about the nature and scope of rights in complex democracies coupled with an interrogation of established notions of citizenship. As these arguments have unfolded it has become increasingly clear that questions about communicative rights – rights in relation to the production and circulation of public knowledge and public culture – are central to any definition of full citizenship in a complex democracy. In order to address these issues however, we first need to work through a thicket of difficult issue to do with the politics of representation.

Questions of representation always involve debates about communicative power as well as cultural form. It is not enough to ask how far the diversity of social experiences, viewpoints, demands and aspirations are presented in the major institutions of public culture and whether the available range of aesthetic forms fosters open debate. We also need to ask who orchestrates these representations? Who is licensed to talk about other peoples' experience? Who is empowered to ventriloquise other peoples' opinions? Who is mandated to picture other peoples' lives? Who chooses who will be heard and who will be consigned to silence, who will be seen and who will remain invisible? Who decides which viewpoints will be taken seriously and how conflicts between positions will be resolved? Who proposes explanations and analyses and who is subject to them? These questions require us to confront the dynamics of social delegation and to interrogate the institutional structures and rationales that underwrite current structures of representation.

As the central public arena for organising complex societies' conversations with themselves, broadcasting, and more particularly television, has become a major focus for the politics of representation. During the 1970s however, it became clear that the established ways of managing this politics were no longer adequate to the emerging situation. The tectonic plates which had clamped the field of public representations together were moving apart. Cracks were appearing, boundaries were shifting, suppressed forces were re-emerging and new pressures were gathering force. The result was a deepening crisis of public represen-tation. Demands were being made that couldn't be accommodated comfortably within the established programme forms and institutional routines and which directly challenged the rationales that underpinned the historic projects of public service broadcasting.

This crisis of representation coincided with broadcasting's accelerated incorporation into the corporate system. The growing momentum of privatisation not only enlarged the market sector within the television industries by promoting commercially-funded expansion in cable and satellite service, it increasingly pulled the public broadcasting organis-ations into its orbit, both institutionally and ideologically. This chapter sets out to explore this shift and to suggest that corporate dynamics have prompted responses to the crisis of representation that are less and less able to guarantee the communicative rights required for full citizenship.

CITIZENSHIP AND COMMUNICATIVE RIGHTS

The problem is that 'citizenship' is subject to competing definitions, some of which are positively unhelpful. There is, for example, the narrow definition which equates citizenship with participation in the formal political process. This leads to claims that the major links between broadcasting and citizenship are to be found primarily (or even exclusively) in those areas of programming that deal with the political process, most notably news and current affairs, leaving drama and entertainment to be subsumed under the signs of 'culture' or 'quality'. Then there is the definition enshrined in John Major's Citizen's Charter which equates citizenship rights with consumer rights. Over and against these attempts to delimit its scope, I want to insist on a general definition of citizenship which identifies it with the right to participate fully in existing patterns of social, political, and cultural life and to help shape their future forms. (This right also carries responsibilities, but my focus here is on rights.)

Following the schema first outlined by T. H. Marshall in the immediate post-war period, and subsequently extended by later writers, we can identify four major clusters of rights that are constitutive of full citizenship.

First, there are civil rights, rights in relation to freedom of action within civil society and freedom from undue coercion by the state. These cover a wide range from freedom of assembly and freedom of belief and religious worship to freedom from arbitrary arrest, detention and torture.

Secondly, and most familiarly, there are political rights. These centre around the right to participate in the formation and application of the laws under which one consents to be governed, which are underpinned in social democracies by the universal franchise and the jury system.

Thirdly, there are social and economic rights, rights in relation to centres of economic power, employee rights and consumer rights for example, coupled with welfare rights in the areas of health, housing, benefits and pensions.

And finally, there are information and cultural rights.

Just as social and economic rights are crucial to guaranteeing the minimum material basis for the exercise of basic civil and political rights, so information and cultural rights play a central role in securing the symbolic and discursive resources for full citizenship.

Information rights can be usefully divided into two sub-sets. First, they require public provision of the full range of information that people need in order to make considered judgements and political choices and to pursue their rights in other areas effectively. In particular, they entail access to comprehensive information on the activities of governmental and corporate agencies with significant power over peoples' lives. But information, in itself, is not enough. To convert it into knowledge that can form the basis for strategies of action requires the availability of the broadest possible array of arguments and conceptual frames through which it can be interpreted and evaluated and its implications traced.

Cultural rights also have a dual character. They clearly involve the right to have one's experiences, beliefs and aspirations represented in the major fora of public culture. As Alberto Melucci has pointed out, this right is fundamental to the construction and reconstruction of social identity since the 'freedom to belong to an identity and to contribute to its definition presumes the freedom to be represented' (Melucci 1989, p. 258). This implies, in turn, that democracy in complex societies requires cultural spaces 'which enable individuals and social groups to affirm themselves and be recognised for what they are or wish to be' (Melucci 1989, p. 172).

These rights of representation are what Melucci calls 'rights of every-day life' in the sense that they relate to social identities that cannot be neatly subsumed within the master-categories of 'citizen' and 'consumer'. As Elizabeth Jacka has argued, 'allowing these voices of difference to be heard is the true meaning of the words "pluralism" and "diversity" that are bandied around so blithely by the proponents of the free market' (Jacka 1992, p. 22). Or rather, one of the 'true meanings'. For cultural rights also involve the negotiation of difference through the provision of communal spaces in which the competing positions and claims of specific communities of interest can be brought together and a workable conception of the public good hammered out. This involves challenging prevailing stereotypes and cherished assumptions coupled with a questioning of habitual grids and a willingness to look from the point of view of the 'other'.

Given these definitions it should be clear, even from this very cursory account, that information and cultural rights can only be guaranteed by open discursive spaces based on certain basic institutional prerequisites.

First, such spaces must be relatively independent of both state and government and major corporate interests to ensure that the field of public representations is not unduly commandeered by either official discourse or commercial speech. Secondly, since questions of representation involve social delegation there must be robust systems to ensure adequate accountability and participation. Thirdly, since different forms of expression allow different people to speak, about different things, in different ways, and with differing degrees of visibility and legitimacy an open system must support a diversity of forms and be actively committed to the creation of new ones. And fourthly, since the aim is to create a generalised public space for the exploration of difference it must be universally accessible.

BROADCASTING, IDENTITY AND DIFFERENCE

Public broadcasting's special relationship to the politics of citizenship and the constitution of information and cultural rights was built into the basic fabric of its organisation from its foundation in the 1920s.

This was a decisive moment in which capitalist democracy was shaped by the intersection of two major movements; the emergence of a mass consumer system and the consolidation of a particular notion of citizenship built around the political rights conferred by universal suffrage and the struggle to secure a range of social and welfare rights. These shifts offered two overarching identities, those of 'citizen' and 'consumer'. Both liquidated other identities, one in the imagined community of the nation, the other in the shared experience of the marketplace.

Broadcasting's efforts to situate itself within this emerging field of forces generated two major solutions; the corporate form developed most fully in the United States and the public service form forged by the BBC in Britain (Murdock 1992a). The first constituted broadcasting organisations as private companies who made profits by packaging audiences for sale to advertisers and beckoned their viewers and listeners to join the democratic community of consumers. The second operated with a public corporation, funded by a licence fee, which didn't take advertising and which addressed audiences as members of a national and imperial community. It advanced a highly selective version of national culture as the symbolic cement binding citizens together in a shared structure of feeling which transcended the allegiances of locality, class and ethnicity. During the thirty years of its monopoly the BBC invented the 'sound of Britain' whose

> function was to make people feel not simply uplifted but patriotic about the Hallé Orchestra or the voice of Laurence Olivier or the Glasgow Orpheus Choir. Such sounds merged with other, more formally national noises: a King fighting his stammer to make his Christmas broadcast, a roar of engines passing overhead at an airshow (Ascherson 1992, p. 21).

With the arrival of television, images were added to these sounds to create a very particular way of looking and of locating oneself, a perspective which reached its height in the reverential tones of Richard Dimbleby's commentary for the live television relay of the Queen's Coronation. Commercial television, which was introduced a few years later, in the mid–1950s, was a half-way house, a quasi-corporate model. The ITV companies were privately owned, they took advertising, and they set out to make profits, but the full force of corporate logic was interrupted by the imposition of extensive public service requirements, by the stringent controls on advertising, and by the fact that each company was a regional monopoly with exclusive rights to sell advertising in their franchise area.

This peculiar structure generated a specific kind of populist ethos which was more sympathetic to American styles and to the new consumerism, less inclined to defer to cultural and political authorities, more disrespectful, more engaged with popular experience, more responsive to the emerging cultures of youth. Where the BBC's sense of itself was built around notions of national unity and cultural inheritance, ITV enlarged the spaces for voices to speak with the accents of region, class and generation and to speak to the contemporary experience of dislocation and change.

CONTESTED REPRESENTATIONS

As the 1960s gave way to the 1970s, however, it was clear that this revised map of social differences and identities was less and less adequate to an emerging politics of identity in which a range of groups were staking claims for greater representation within the broadcasting system.

The women's movement was challenging the conventional boundaries separating the personal from the political, the private from the public, and pressing for a redefinition of citizenship rights that included rights in relation to the body. Struggles over public representation were at the centre of these debates as feminism sought to dislodge entrenched notions of femininity and a woman's 'place'. Other groups too – the disabled, the elderly and the young – were pressing for greater representation and attention to their claims and interests. But the most important assault was on the core notion of 'national culture' and on its intimate but suppressed connections with the experience of empire and colonialism (Said 1993). National minorities within Britain insisted on their cultural distinctiveness with renewed vigour, whilst the jagged transition from imperial power to multi-cultural polity forced a confrontation with plurality and difference which re-drew the mental map of the globe underpinning received notions of national heritage. Reorganising this map, with its divisions between centres and peripheries, metropole and margins, high and low, was a primary focus for the emerging battles around representation. These revolved around three main issues.

The first centred on questions of visibility and legitimacy, on whose lives and interests were shown and talked about within the broadcasting system and how, and foregrounded issues around stereotyping, sexism and racism in language and imagery. The second strand in the debate focused on whether the available forms of expression could accommodate new demands for representation or whether novel forms were needed, whilst the third confronted the issue of social delegation. This last concern generated a number of proposals. Some argued for widening the basis of recruitment into professional production through concerted initiatives on equal opportunities and positive discrimination. Others called for producers working outside the major institutions to be given greater access to the schedules as a way of widening the range of perspectives in play. At the same time there were mounting demands that programme makers, whatever their base, become more responsive to the constituencies they sought to represent by providing spaces for comment and criticism on screen. Others took the case for greater access a step further arguing that more people should be encouraged to make programmes which spoke to their interests and experiences directly, drawing on the facilities and expertise of professionals, but retaining editorial control.

These demands are not unique to Britain. They are signals of a generalised crisis of representation which has confronted the broadcasting systems of a number of complex democracies. But a comparative study is beyond the scope of the present chapter. My purpose here is more modest. I want to show how, in the case of Britain, responses to this crisis have been shaped and circumscribed by the concerted shift towards corporate models of televisual enterprise.

ADDRESSING DIFFERENCE: SOCIAL INTERESTS AND NICHE MARKETS

The lack of fit between the existing institutions of broadcasting and the proliferating demands for representation was a central theme of the Annan Committee's report on the future of Broadcasting, published in the spring of 1977. They broke with imagined unities of national culture and embraced a vision of Britain as a fractured cultural formation. In their view: 'Our society is now multi-racial and pluralist: that is to say, people adhere to different views of the nature and purpose of life and expect their own view to be expressed in some form or other. The structure of broadcasting should reflect this variety' (Cmnd 6753 1977, p. 30).

The question was: how? One powerful lobby presented the multi-channel possibilities of cable systems as the best solution. They argued that by abolishing spectrum scarcity and enabling television to move towards a publishing model they opened up multiple spaces for the articulation of interests. One of the most forceful advocates of this solution was the ex-Treasury official, Peter Jay. For him, and other enthusiasts of 'electronic publishing' the crisis of representation arose from the difficulties

 . . . of allocating scarce publishing opportunities between competing interest groups, whether established institutions, financial vested interests, worker vested interests, evangelical producers, Scotsmen, Welshmen, Irishmen, divines, educationalist, ethnic minorities or any other form of man-in-his-organisations as against man-in-his-home-wanting-to–sit-in-his-armchair-and-watch-the-telly (Jay 1984, p. 234).

Provide enlarged 'publishing opportunities' and the crisis dissolved.

The Committee accepted the definition of 'broadcasting as a form of publishing' (Cmnd 6753 1977, p. 24) but remained sceptical about the immediate prospects for significant growth in cable systems. Whilst they recognised the future potential of the new transmission technologies, they felt that they were unlikely to develop on a substantial scale until the 1990s. Moreover, they argued strongly that cable television should develop primarily as a local service addressing demands for greater access and representation at community level and not (as the cable lobby was urging) as a subscription service offering additional general channels. They therefore turned their attention to what could be done on a national basis in the immediate term (Cmnd 6753 1977, p. 381).

The struggle to enlarge broadcasting's sphere of representation rapidly focused down on the fate of the vacant fourth channel. There were two major proposals. Predictably, the commercial television lobby argued that it should be given to the ITV companies to match the two channels commanded by the BBC and restore a level playing-field in the competition for viewers. In contrast, the counter-proposal engaged directly with the emerging politics of representation. It recommended that the channel be a broadcaster commissioning programmes from a wide range of groups and individuals and financed by an annual sum taken from advertising revenues, topped up with monies from programme sponsorship. The Committee embraced this option enthusiastically on the grounds that it would not be a simple 'addition to the plurality of outlets, but a force for plurality in a deeper sense. Not only could it be a nursery for new forms and new methods of presenting ideas, it could also open the door to a new kind of broadcast publishing' (Cmnd 6753 1977, p. 235).

They hoped that by separating production from distribution and challenging the established structures of representation – both social and aesthetic – it would act as a catalyst for change within existing channels, moving the whole system closer to a publishing model.

This proposal carried the day and a version of Annan's organisational sketch provided the blueprint for the new channel. It was constituted as a non-profit-making corporation not a private company. The bulk of the schedule was to comprise programmes commissioned from a range of independent producers, supplemented by material bought in from overseas. Commissioning and purchasing decisions would be guided by a distinctive remit which emphasised the need to address constituencies of interest who were under-represented in mainstream terrestrial programming and to maintain a positive commitment to innovation and experiment with programme forms.

At the same time, it was to be financed by advertising revenue not by public funds. This positive endorsement of advertising finance represented a decisive break with the hostile stance of the previous major enquiry into broadcasting (the Pilkington Report) and introduced a permanent tension into the way the channel addressed the construction and representation of difference. The remit clearly works with a conception of social interests whilst advertisers work with a map of market niches.

This tension did not go unnoticed within the Thatcher government. In his account of his time as the channel's first chief executive, Jeremy Isaacs recounts how he was buttonholed at an embassy dinner by Norman Tebbit, a senior member of the Prime Minister's inner circle:

> 'You've got it all wrong, you know' he said, 'doing all these programmes for homosexuals and such. Parliament never meant that sort of thing. The different interests you are supposed to cater for are not like that at all. Golf and sailing and fishing. Hobbies. That's what we intended' (Isaacs 1989, p. 65).

Tebbit's opinion chimed neatly with the views of advertisers, who saw the channel as an opportunity to reach specialised markets that had proved difficult to access through ITV. There was a growing consensus, both inside and outside the industry, that targeting was increasingly important in a 'post-Fordist' consumer system in the process of moving from mass to niche markets, from emulation to segmentation, from 'keeping up with the Joneses' to constructing personalised lifestyles. To many commentators, Channel 4 offered an ideal promotional vehicle for the new times (Murray 1989, p. 43).

In the Channel's first decade, these marketing pressures, though clearly present, did not operate unchecked. Their logic was attenuated by the fact that the channel did not deal directly with advertisers. Air time was sold by the ITV companies who kept the proceeds in return for paying an annual subscription to fund the channel. This created a buffer between the commissioning process and the advertising industry.

Despite Annan's lukewarm response, arguments in favour of expanding cable television were gathering influential support. By the time Channel 4 went on air in November 1982, the Committee's cautious evaluation of the industry's prospects during the 1980s, and their resolute rejection of the operator's arguments in favour of subscription services had already been overtaken.

At the beginning of the year, the Information Technology Advisory Panel (which had been set up the previous summer to advise the government) had published a report on cable systems urging significant expansion at the earliest possible date. They argued that although cable's long term potential lay in the provision of new telecommunications services 'we have to accept that systems will go through an initial period when their attraction will be based on "entertainment" considerations' (Cabinet Office 1982, p. 48). In other words, the requirements of business users would be funded by 'revenue from additional popular programming channels' sold to the general public (Cabinet Office 1982, p.48). For 'this strategy to work however, new channels would either have to provide more of what people already liked and were prepared to pay extra for (sports and recent films for example) or cater for niche markets that were under-served by terrestrial services and attractive to targeted advertising (such as young people or major ethnic minorities). This necessarily ruled out any requirements to cater for a diverse range of minorities.

The Government's White Paper of April 1983, laying out its plans for the sector, welcomed the impeccable corporate logic of this position, arguing that because cable systems

> should not be seen as a further instalment of public service broadcasting but as something different from it . . . it is not necessary, or even appropriate, for [them] to be required to achieve in their programmes a wide range and balance [or to abide by] specific obligations to provide services for minority or specialist interests (Cmnd 8866 1983, p. 55).

Although when considering bids for cable franchises the new regulatory body, the Cable Authority, was 'required to take account of the range and diversity of the services proposed and of the arrangements for community programmes and local access' (Cmnd 8866 1983, p. 55) nobody expected promises in these areas to be anything other than cosmetic, useful for public relations purposes but continually vulnerable to financial exigency. The Authority conceded as much in its first *Annual Report and Accounts* arguing that although they hoped 'to see local services developing steadily, this must be undertaken in a properly cautious way consistent with the *need not to jeopardise the main business on which they will inevitably depend*' (Cable Authority 1986, p. 19. My emphasis).

The later development of cable is addressed elsewhere in this volume but so far there is little sign that it is likely to provide a viable way of addressing the current crisis of representation. Community programming remains marginal and precarious, a concession not a right, whilst minority channels continue to be defined in terms of niche markets rather than social interests. But even if cable operators had been required to address the politics of difference in a more wholehearted way, two major problems would remain. First, by its nature 'narrowcasting' constitutes its audiences as specific targeted groups. Channels are designed to appeal to their specific interests. This provides spaces in which groups can explore their communality and negotiate internal disagreements, but it does not bring differences into confrontation with each other or contribute to the development of new conceptions of the public good based on the negotiation of shared and sectional interests. Added to which, cable and satellite services are only available to those who can afford the subscriptions and other charges levied by the operators. In a situation where fiscal policies have combined with cuts in welfare provision to produce a steadily widening gap in income inequalities, this inevitably means that many constituencies are permanently barred from representation by their poverty (Murdock and Golding 1989). These dynamics make the fate of the main terrestrial channels all the more crucial, since it is here that we need to look for services capable of addressing the crisis of representation in its full complexity.

DISMANTLING PUBLIC BROADCASTING

In advancing the case for cable, the authors of the ITAP report were eager to emphasise that they saw 'no reason why the introduction of cable systems should necessarily lead to a reduction in the range and quality of programme services on the public broadcasting network' (Cabinet Office 1982, p. 48). In a strict sense they were right, since for most of the 1980s cable (and later) satellite channels made only modest inroads into the revenues and audience shares of established terrestrial services. But the indirect impact was considerable. Cable policy broke the public service consensus that had structured debate until then and offered an alternative model of commercial television built unashamedly around corporate rationales. This vision proved increasingly attractive to the Thatcher governments as the decade wore on and they became increasingly eager to apply it more generally. Separating programme production from packaging and distribution; the enthusiasm for subscription systems; the advocacy of 'light touch' regulation, and the retreat from public service requirements, all came to play a prominent part in debates about the future of ITV and the BBC.

In the spring of 1985, a committee of enquiry was appointed to look into the future financing of terrestrial broadcasting. It was chaired by Professor Alan Peacock, a vocal supporter of free market mechanisms, and included another prominent enthusiast of the 'hidden hand', Samuel Brittan, the *Financial Times* columnist. Although its main task was to review options for funding the BBC, it soon widened its brief to take in the commercial sector. Its final report, published in July 1986 (Cmnd 9284 1986) made three key suggestions for the immediate reorganisation of the ITV system.

The first, and by far the most radical, was the proposal that in the next round of licence allocations, franchises should be awarded by competitive tender and should usually go to the highest bidder, providing that their programme plans had passed an initial test of minimum quality.

Secondly, they argued that over a ten-year period, the ITV companies 'should be required to increase to not less than forty per cent the proportion of programmes supplied by independent producers' with the aim of increasing competition and encouraging multiple sources of supply (Cmnd 9284 1986, p. 142). This publisher-broadcaster model, whereby a channel assembles a schedule but commissions or buys in most of its programming from outside suppliers, was already in operation within Channel 4 and the cable industry. However, whereas Channel 4's remit directed it to cater for interests not well served elsewhere in the system, cable channels were free to purchase whatever they thought would maximise interest among audiences and advertisers.

Finally, in a bid to integrate Channel 4 more fully into corporate logic, the committee recommended that it 'should be given the option of selling its own advertising time' (Cmnd 9284 1986, p. 144). This was a direct response to advertisers' long-standing complaints about the ITV companies' monopoly rights over advertising space within the terrestrial system, and their accusations of over-charging and lack of responsiveness to their needs.

Although, overall, the Peacock Report had a somewhat uneven reception from the government (see Brittan 1991) the proposals for ITV were largely successful in setting the legislative agenda for the subsequent White Paper, entitled *Broadcasting in the 90s: Competition, Choice and Quality*, published in November 1988 (Cm 517 1988). The proposed changes would be administered by a new regulatory agency, the Independent Television Commission (ITC), which would replace both the Independent Broadcasting Authority and the Cable Authority and oversee all commercial television services regardless of how they were delivered. The ITC was to operate with a 'light touch', extending the market-driven regulatory regime developed for cable and satellite services to the ITV (renamed Channel 3). The White Paper justified this shift by arguing that 'as viewers exercise greater choice there is no longer the same need for quality of service to be prescribed by legislation or regulatory fiat' (Cm 517 1988, p. 20). Accordingly, it would be left to 'the operators to decide what to show and when to show it', subject only to the general provisions of the law and some very residual public service requirements (Cm 517 1988, p. 22).

The ITC's first major task was to preside over the auctioning of the ITV franchises. This proved to be a highly contentious process, with a chorus of disapproval greeting both the arrangements for bidding and the eventual outcome (Murdock 1992b). Advocates of the original idea of a cash auction were disappointed that incumbents had retained twelve of the sixteen franchises on offer, and that of the thirteen that had been contested, only five had gone to the highest bidder. Supporters of public service ideals within ITV were dismayed that Thames Television (the weekday contractor for London and one of the most respected companies in the system) had been displaced by Carlton Television. And the letter that Mrs Thatcher wrote to Bruce Gyngell, the chief executive of the nationwide breakfast channel, TV-AM, commiserating on his defeat by the Sunrise consortium, amounted to a repudiation of the whole process by the person who had pressed hardest for its institution. As she admitted: 'I am only too painfully aware that I was responsible for the legislation. When I see how some of the other licences have been awarded I am mystified that you did not receive yours, and heartbroken'.

Looking at the outcome of the franchise auction overall we need to ask whether it has created a system that is likely to address the crisis of representation by sustaining and extending the diversity of programming. The answer is almost certainly 'no'. As two prominent business economists argued in 1989, when the debate about the auction process was at its height: 'no amount of regulation . . . can change the fact that the auction method of allocating television franchises will, by increasing the priority given to profit maximisation, make it very difficult to impose non-commercial programme obligations on licensees' (Cheong and Foster 1989, p. 121).

Certainly the very substantial annual sums that a number of companies have to return to the Treasury under the new system, coupled with the projections of relatively flat advertising revenues and increasing competition from satellite and cable services, are a massive discouragement to diversity. And in the absence of any clear statutory requirements to produce politically-challenging programmes or to provide space for minority experiences and viewpoints, the Channel 3 companies are free to jettison 'difficult' productions altogether. As Anthony Smith has argued, they 'have been placed within a structure so flimsy . . . that the constant temptation will be and is already to offer a narrower, safer range of material, much of it bought in' (Smith 1992, p. 47).

In this situation corporate rationales necessarily take priority. As Paul Jackson, director of programmes for Carlton Television (which needs to return twenty-nine per cent of its projected advertising earnings to the Treasury each year) has admitted: 'Given the commercial realities, we won't have the latitude in future to find excuses for programmes that don't earn their keep. Programmes will not survive in the new ITV if they don't pay their way' (Henry 1992a, p. 3).

For many senior programme makers who had grown up in the old ITV system, such as the journalist Michael Nicholson, this statement is typical of the new style of executive who care 'nothing for its past reputation' and are 'bereft of public duty and any public concern beyond their shareholders' (Henry 1992b, p. 6).

The ascendancy of corporate rationales has been aided by the shift in the regulatory regime. At first sight, the ITC appears to have more sanctions at its disposal. Whereas the IBA's only option was to revoke a company's licences if it broke its programme promises or overstepped the rules (something it was understandably very reluctant to do) the ITC can issue warnings, demand apologies on-screen and impose fines of varying severity before moving to cancel a franchise. But, unlike the IBA, it can only use these disciplines after the event. It no longer has the power to approve Channel 3 programmes and schedules in advance. This withdrawal of prior approval greatly increases the companies' room for manoeuvre and confines the Commission's primary role to damage limitation. As one Channel 3 company director has conceded, given the political and financial realities of the current situation, 'The ITC can't stop the companies doing what they want' (Douglas 1993, p. 23).

Moreover, where the ITC has taken a more pro-active role, the effect has generally been to extend the scope of corporate influence on programme making. One of the Commission's first major acts on assuming responsibility for Channel 3 was to publish more permissive guidelines on programme sponsorship giving advertisers access to all programmes except for news and current affairs and those dealing with industrial controversy or current public policies (ITC 1990, p. 5). This marks another import of the 'permissive' regime developed for cable into mainstream terrestrial broadcasting and one with significant implications. Despite the ITC's insistence that funders must not seek to influence editorial decisions, the greater hospitality to sponsorship is widely seen within the industry as indicating 'a fundamental change in television culture' (Carter 1991, p. 20). By providing a considerably enlarged space for commercial speech – speech produced by and for the major corporations and designed to promote their products and images – the new rules represent a substantial retreat from the ideal of public service broadcasting as an open, imaginative and discursive space (Murdock 1992c).

Concern has also been expressed about Channel 4's ability to sustain its commitment to diversity and experimentation now that it has to sell its own air-time and the commissioning process is subject to the full force of advertisers' demands. In this situation there is bound to be increased pressure to build programming strategies around market niches rather than social interests. As the distinguished programme-maker Roger Graef, one of the original campaigners for the Channel, has put it:

> If the channel's remit matters, selling its own airtime moves it in precisely the wrong direction. From the commission and transmission of a distinctive service, Channel 4 now moves into a new business: delivering viewers to advertisers. This is in direct conflict with the essential element of innovation and experiment; trial and error (Graef 1991, p. 22).

Commercial television's increasing capture by corporate rationales makes the maintenance of a strong BBC, concerned to address the current crisis of representation and ensure that all its programming remains universally available, of central importance. Whether these ideals will survive the bruising political battles around the renewal of the Corporation's Royal Charter in 1996 is debateable however. Whilst it makes no firm proposals, the government's consultation document on the BBC's future, published at the end of 1992, includes options that would significantly alter the balance of the Corporation's activities (Cm 2098 1992).

It gives a sympathetic hearing to the Peacock committee's view that in a multi-channel environment public service broadcasting is best used as a back-stop, compensating for the gaps in commercial provision, arguing that 'with greater choice now available to viewers, the BBC could concentrate on programmes which are unlikely to be broadcast by other organisations' (Cm 2098 1992, p. 18). These would be of two main kinds, those 'which reflect the British way of life, history and culture' and 'more programmes for minorities of all kinds, including ethnic minorities and people with special interests' (Cm 2098 p. 18). The evident tension in this view, between a view of the BBC as a force for conserving 'national' culture and as an arbiter between proliferating claims for representation also marks the Corporation's own outline of its future role, *Extending Choice*, published in the same week as the government's document. Here too we find a commitment 'to portray a multiracial, multicultural society and to respond to the diversity of cultures throughout the UK' coupled with a promise 'to give special prominence to artistic, sporting and ceremonial events that bring the nation together' (BBC 1992, p. 19–20). How exactly the competition between the claims and identities offered by the imagined community of the nation on the one hand and the multiple constituencies of differ-ence on the other will be managed, in terms of programme budgets, expressive forms and social delegation, is not addressed. Nor is there any recognition that the unities of national culture have been secured by repressing the claims of cultures rooted in class, region, gender and ethnicity or that the presentation of 'national heritage' cannot be uncoupled from an engagement with the imperial past. It is not enough to provide room for a diversity of cultures alongside a celebration of heritage. It is necessary to work through the problematic relations between them.

There is a significant degree of consensus too on questions of finance. Whilst the government's consultation document presents a generally critical review of the arguments in favour of the BBC taking spot advertising, and cautiously endorses the continuation of the licence fee, it follows the Peacock Committee in presenting a positive evaluation of subscription services as a way of 'reducing the BBC's dependence on the licence fee' and introducing a direct relationship between the Cor-poration and its customers (Cm 2098 1992, p. 34). The BBC's dismissal of advertising is more comprehensive and its defence of the licence fee more adamant but it, too, argues strongly 'that the BBC should partici-pate in the development of a subscription television market' to 'enable the creation of new specialist services, primarily on satellite' (BBC 1992, p. 65). It could hardly do otherwise since it has already responded to government demands that it exploit the commercial potential of its assets more effectively by establishing a series of scrambled services for specific groups using its terrestrial network at night, when public services have closed down, and by launching a satellite-delivered general entertainment channel, UK Gold, in partnership with Thames Television. These developments are defended on the grounds that they generate revenues that can be used for programming on the main channels. At the same time, there is no doubt that they mark a sharp break with the BBC's historic commitment to universality and the introduction of a two- or three-tier service. *Extending Choice* claims that 'It is entirely consistent with the BBC's public service role for it to supply programming to satellite channels, which supplement and deliver greater depth than is possible on the core licence fee-funded services' (BBC 1992, p. 49).

But this is a far cry from John Reith's original promise that 'There need be no first and third class' and that public service broadcasting would provide 'nothing which is exclusive to those who pay more, or who are considered in one way or another more worthy of attention' (Reith 1924, p. 218).

The gulf between these statements is a measure of how fully the BBC's strategies have already been shaped by corporate rationales. If this process continues there will be very little chance of developing a public broadcasting system that is capable of addressing the current crisis of representation and contributing the symbolic resources required for the exercise of full citizenship in a complex democracy.

2

Mediating the ordinary: the 'access' idea and television form

JOHN CORNER

A small puncture in the rotating machinery of television, through which fairly ordinary people can catch glimpses of fairly ordinary other people without the interposition of a mind exterior to either.

The notion of 'access' is an important one in respect of many different aspects of broadcasting. In this chapter, it is the use of the term to indicate a particular kind of project – the giving to ordinary people of a chance to 'have their say' – with which I will be most concerned. And within this project, broadly conceived as an attempt to increase the democratic character of broadcast services, it is questions of communicative form which provide my primary topic. For it is *how* 'ordinary people' appear and speak on television, within particular programme formats, which determines both the character and the success of 'access' socially and politically. This has a pre-history in the ways in which social documentaries have represented ordinary people through a variety of visual and verbal devices, some of which have been projected as providing 'direct' renderings of ordinary views and ordinary life. It also has a future in which, at least in Britain and probably in the United States too, the development of new genres of non-fiction television, including formats extensively drawing on home-shot camcorder material, will increasingly change the terms on which the ordinary is perceived by television audiences.

In the first part of this chapter, I want to explore some of the principles behind the 'access' idea and to look at the different ways in which they have been applied to television. I then want to explore some of the questions of form which still present a challenge to all those who wish to see the development in the public media of a more democratic order of representation.

'Access is the newest word in the onward march of broadcasting'. So commented broadcaster/writer Frank Gillard in *The Listener*'s lead article of 6 July 1972. Although Gillard might well have known that plans were under way for a regular BBC 'access' slot to start the following year, his article was principally concerned with the American model of public access television. In particular, he discussed the success of the Boston nightly half-hour programme *Catch 44*, which he considered 'the nearest thing yet to genuine citizen's television'. His citation of the *Boston Globe*'s own comments on the innovatory series, as 'a small puncture', provides my epigraph above. This campaigning sense of access, precisely as 'citizen's television', was grounded in a feeling by the *Catch 44* workers that the broadcasting industry was increasingly getting out of touch with 'views, life-styles and community backgrounds' different from those of the broadcasting professionals themselves'. In Britain at roughly the same time, the people behind the planning of the BBC's pioneering national access programme, *Open Door*, had come to a similar conclusion. One of them, Mike Fentiman, subsequently to become a key member of the BBC's access team (the Community Programmes Unit), tells of a decisive moment in the development of the idea:

> I was involved in the conspiracy that created public access. And it was a conspiracy, it had to be a conspiracy otherwise it probably wouldn't have happened. On the evening discussion programme *Late Night Line Up* in 1972 we did a few things that were started by an interview done by Tony Bilbow with some workers from the Guinness factory. These workers, when asked questions by a very sympathetic interviewer, said they were being manipulated and 'that's the trouble with television, television manipulates us. You know how to do it. We work with our hands, you work with words and you'll take this film back and you'll edit it to what you want, and you'll shorten this and change that and you can make it do what you want it to'. So we brought it back to look at it and because we'd shot it on two cameras, other than tidying it up, the whole thing went out. Every single word, including the clapper board shots, went out unedited. So what we had was workers saying you're going to take this back and edit it and it all went out unedited.

The Community Programmes Unit went on to produce an often

controversial strand of BBC programming which, however marginal in budget and in audiences (when judged by the national ratings lists), succeeded in accessing to the screen groups, individuals and issues of a kind then heavily under-represented on television (see Oakley 1990 for a brief historical account). The main method, first of all limited to live, studio broadcasting but subsequently extended to location shooting and recorded material, was the provision of directorial and technical aid to 'accessees' who had been judged as having something interesting and/or important to say on national television. The accessees had editorial control over the content and form of the programme within the limits of the regulations affecting broadcast output. In the topic areas which were selected for treatment, the programmes often contributed substantially to wider debate. A decade later, the launch of Channel 4, with a specific commitment to minorities and to the correcting of imbalances of representation across the other three channels, put the access project a little more firmly on the institutional agenda of British broadcasting.

I shall return to some aspects of the social history of access later; as we can see, it is a history of expressed dissatisfaction with conventional practice, with the exclusive sweep of institutionalised 'professionalism', and with the relegation of ordinary people to being simply the raw material of 'human interest' stories. But the access idea is one which raises (and sometimes begs) fundamental issues about public representation and it is these issues which I now want to explore further.

PRINCIPLES OF 'ACCESS'

First of all, it might be useful to attempt a working definition of the access idea in broadcasting. Among other things, this has the merit of suggesting immediately how politically and socially contentious – and how difficult to *implement* – it may be. Without aspiring to categoric perfection, we can say that access is the avoiding or the correcting of imbalances in broadcasting's representation of politics and society by the articulation of a diversity of 'directly' stated views from different sections of the public and by the reflection, again 'directly', of the real diversity of cultural, social and economic circumstances, particularly those which require attention and action.

Such a definition connects access ideas to the political principle of equality. And it is worth pointing out that, given the way in which national broadcasting services have developed, it is nearly always the case that access projects have emerged as partial remedies for perceived *in*equality. Access is in this respect most often a *corrective* idea, a point

I shall return to. My definition also suggests that access is a broader, more socialised notion than that of 'Right of Reply', itself a campaigning slogan for media reform. Whereas the latter idea has, as its core, the citizen's individual opportunity to respond to misrepresention, the former concept works more with the idea of the accessee as speaking for a misrepresented or under-represented *group*. Moreover, and relatedly, whereas in 'Right of Reply' the 'Reply' is generally understood to be a quite specific act of correction or response, access projects have sought to offer a *general* corrective to what is seen to be a systematic imbalance in social and cultural power. Within the terms of access therefore, specific items have had the freedom to take on a socially pro-active rather than reactive character; they have not needed to be framed as 'replies'.

The 'socialised' nature of the access idea means, as I have indicated, that access is also a quite directly political project, implying theories about the nature of the political system and about the extent and scale of social inequality of which communicational inequalities are but one aspect. In placing its corrective emphasis on the disadvantaged and the marginalised, the access project has politicised both itself and its versions of 'ordinary people' in a way which has sometimes proved controversial in its degree of explicitness and in the strategic imbalance of its own representations. Again, 'Right of Reply' has available to it a defence of the rights of the individual citizen which is nowhere near as politically contentious. Indeed, 'Right of Reply' is a project quite compatible with a political viewpoint in which generalised and systematic inequalities are not admitted to exist at all.

Within these general terms of conceptualisation, we can see access initiatives as being put forward principally on one or other of *three* different levels within the broadcasting system.

1   As a mainstream principle of broadcasting policy and programming, institutionalised into practice. According to such a principle, news, current affairs, documentary and special interest programmes would draw on a diversity of 'ordinary' sources as a routine part of their production and structure. McQuail (1992) discusses how access is a fundamental concept in the formulation of a democratic broadcasting system.
2   As an ongoing alternative to mainstream networking and the major broadcast and narrowcast options. This manifests itself most obviously in the idea of the 'public access' channel, in Britain an idea related to the development of cable systems. The 'localism' of most projects at this level (clearly indicated in the philosophy of the Community Media

movement, but often technologically unavoidable given available means of distribution) often raises the question of the adequacy of a local remedy for a national ill. The British Channel 4 model has provided a distinctive precedent for alternative programming at national level, but this is essentially grounded in a pluralism of independent professional production and of audience-interest groups, not in access programming as such.

3 As a regularly scheduled opportunity on a channel mostly devoted to other kinds of output. This is 'access as slot' or, in the terms of my epigraph, as 'small puncture'. However, as I shall discuss later, both its identity as a marginal genre of television and the scope it offers for self-representation have been transformed recently as a result of the use of camcorder technology.

I have suggested that it is at levels two (e.g. the fight for 'community cable') and three (the developing genre of 'access slots') that access projects have been most active. Of course, much of this activity would not have been necessary had provision at level one been anything like satisfactory.

ACCESS AND DOCUMENTARY FORM

It is within the documentary tradition of broadcasting, whose practices refer back to the longer history of documentary cinema, that what I have earlier called the 'pre-history' of access can be traced. This 'pre-history' has had implications for discussion about access at all three levels outlined above. It has also provided influential precedents for ideas about the kinds of communicative 'directness' which can be achieved by public access communication and about the methods for producing it.

In documentary, a level of the accessed ordinary is an integral part of the project of critical social revelation and social inquiry. This is particularly so in the British tradition of the 'social documentary', within whose visual and aural discourses it is, routinely, aspects of the 'ordinary' which are brought into 'official' public view, either with the intention of affirming the integrities of work, trust and community which they exemplify or of exposing inequality and hardship, or perhaps both. A key communicative component of this investigative and representational practice has been the *interview*.

The interview has a 'dual' character not only insofar as it is devised as communication with an audience (devised, that is, as *public* communication) whilst being usually set up in terms of communication between two people (that is, as a form of *conversation*). It is also 'dual' in its accessing function. Through the interview, audiences are accessed to particular themes and problems, whilst particular interviewees are accessed to the public, and have their views, feelings and experiences widely disseminated. However, the terms of this double accessing cannot but be unbalanced. For no matter how minimal a role the film or programme-makers wish to give themselves in the project, it is impossible for the accessees of documentary inquiry to be placed other than in a position of relative objectification before the initiating activities of the researchers, reporters and crew members whose job it is to make public communication happen. If this is true in the planning and shooting stages of documentary practice, it is even truer at the post-production stages. Here, decisions about the editing of interview sequences and their deployment within the finished text according to different strategies of visual and aural combination and in relation to other materials, inevitably have the effect of further 'objectivising' the accessed speakers. Paradoxically, some of the changes introduced at this stage (for instance, the editing out of interviewers from the visuals and perhaps of their questions from the soundtrack too; the 'lifting' of interviewee speech from the shot interview and its placing over other visual material) may have the effect of 're-subjectivising' the speakers, giving their speech the appearance of unsolicited testimony, of 'direct', self-initiated utterance.

I want to take a few examples from what I termed earlier the 'prehistory' of access in order to explore in more detail questions concerning the televisual representation of the ordinary. The examples I shall choose are all ones from documentaries in which a key part of the overall communicative design is an accessing of 'ordinary people', an accessing which is self-consciously foregrounded in the film or programme's structure as an element of its formal or thematic originality. Such documentaries are thus different in their mediation of the ordinary from those many others that display a more routine use of interviewees to pursue their inquiries, a use more conventionalised than innovative and therefore not as marked or self-conscious.

My first example is the classic, 1935 documentary *Housing Problems*, often cited as the film from the British documentary cinema movement which had the most influence upon post-war developments in television. Directed by Edgar Anstey and Arthur Elton and produced by John Grierson with the sponsorship of the Commercial Gas Corporation, this twenty-minute film looks at slum clearance schemes by using a before-and-after structure which gives a central place to the 'slum dwellers' themselves. In what at the time was a strikingly original use of location sound, a number of people speak about their conditions of living from interior settings in both the old tenements and terraces and the new blocks of flats. In the sense that the film is a promotional vehicle for the Gas Corporation (which is involved in providing cooking and heating appliances for the new housing schemes) the film might better be called *Housing Solutions*. Certainly, its emphasis is very much on progress achieved, upon a problem solved. Yet this emphasis does not reduce the communicative force of the 'ordinary' accounts, where the details of squalor and deprivation are presented with a directness and resonance of testimony which finally escapes containment or appropriation by the commentary's upbeat message. By the conventions of today, the mode of speech and of visual depiction is quite extraordinary (for recent critical assessments, see Higson 1986 and Miles and Smith 1987). The speakers are filmed in 'direct address', looking straight into the camera. The static shots usually take in most of their standing or sitting body and enough of their rooms to register a degree of 'environmental/ domestic' detail (e.g. a mantelpiece with collected ornaments; a patch of peeling wallpaper; cooking utensils; a bed). Some sense of the way the speakers are framed by the commentary of the film, and yet are given considerable communicative space for description of their own experiences, can be found in this extract from the film's first 'access' sequence:

COMMENTARY. And now for the people who have to live in the slum. Here is Mr Norwood.

MR NORWOOD. These two rooms I'm in now I have to pay ten shillings a week for and I haven't enough room to swing a cat round. I've also five other neighbours on the side of me who are in the same predicament as I'm in myself. And I'm not only over-run with bugs, I've got mice and rats as well. With the washing, my missus has to send out every little bit of washing there is, every drop of water we have to go out to the yard for, to fetch in. . . . And as far as cooking, we have to use the gas stove alongside the bed, where we sleep. . . .

Students viewing this film today register the awkwardness of the non-professional direct address involved, the self-consciousness of posture in front of the fixed camera and the uncertain patterns of stressing and pauses in the prepared (but apparently not scripted) speech. Such lack of spontaneity and informality can be read as indicative of *inauthenticity* but we also need to take into account the sense in which these segments are acts of *public speaking*, explicitly projected as such. That they are not organised by shooting and post-production into the naturalistic flow of a modern interview sequence, one which only indirectly registers the existence of the audience, should not count against their integrity. Indeed, the film's very technological limitations in this respect seem to be the ground of its strength as access cinema. Moreover, the simplicity of style is by no means all a product of early technology. Anstey has commented about the film's making:

> We narrowed ourselves down in *Housing Problems* to a very, very simple technique, which was open to us, at that time nobody had done it, and we gave the slum dwellers a chance to make their own film. This is why we kept all the aesthetics out until the very end. . . . What we felt was 'this is their film not ours. We don't want any directorial intervention. Their story is strong enough by itself' (in interview with Roger Graef, *Arena*, BBC2, 9 March 1982).

Precisely this approach to 'direct' communication was applauded in Graham Greene's review of the film carried in *The Spectator* (19 October 1936). Expressing what would subsequently, in television criticism, be a familiar point of comparison between access projects and more mainstream, professionally-managed accounts, he noted: 'Compare the characters in *Housing Problems* with the frightened, ironed-out personalities with censored scripts whom the BBC present as documentary.' Now, of course, it is clear that the film is not a film *made* by those ordinary people who feature so strongly within it. This is an over-statement by Anstey, and one which needs to be recognised as such. Nevertheless, it is an over-statement made from a real sense of being involved in a radical breakthrough both in public communicational form and in the social relations of form.

I have spent some time discussing *Housing Problems* because it seems to me to raise a number of problems about the direct mediation of the ordinary, and about the specific modality of that mediation through image and speech, which are still on the agenda of access. Moreover, what now seems to be the film's curious and even disturbing formality may have been, as I have indicated, an entirely appropriate acknowledgement of the gap between accessees and audience, an acknowledgement of the real social context of the communicative act being performed.

The subsequent history of *television* documentary, though largely a history of developments in the televisual means of professional journalistic inquiry (e.g. effective 'visualisation' of issues, and the use of 'ordinary' interviewees to provide data for a programme's own descriptive account and judgements), is in part also a history of stages in the development of access communication.

When, in 1955, the commercially-financed ITV system began broadcasting in Britain, a re-thinking of the terms for depicting the ordinary in current affairs and documentary programming was the result of the imperative to be popular. This often meant an attempt to distinguish programme formats from what was regarded as the 'stuffy, middle-class' attitudes dominant in the BBC schedules, at levels ranging from the social perspectives informing programme ideas through to the particular styles of behaviour and speech of those who were most often invited to appear. A number of ITV programmes tried to achieve a more popular (and, some might say, populist) appeal by working hard at 'meet the people' formulas, in which a television presenter would go out on location and encounter ordinary people in the business of their everyday work. These people would then be interviewed, often in lengthy sequences of question-and-answer shot in a workplace setting. Unlike the direct address conventions of *Housing Problems* (and of early BBC series like *Special Inquiry* – see Corner 1991a) which gave interviewees a discrete, individualised, 'access slot' within the programme structure, connected to others by presenter links, the newer formats both socialised and dramatised the very terms of access as a *meeting* between the 'television world' (represented by the reporter) and the 'ordinary world' (represented by the interviewees). Access was organised as a narrative episode, often one appearing to have the open-endedness of happenstance. One of the most interesting features of this type of programme is the way in which any ostensible *topic* quite often becomes secondary to the interest which the interviewees hold for the programme as 'ordinary people'. So, for instance, whilst an interview might start with inquiries about the details of a particular trade, the novelty of this kind of casually accessed ordinariness is seen to be such as to permit the interviewer to extend questioning to a whole range of other issues, including housing conditions, preferences in food and recreational choices.

I have discussed elsewhere (Corner 1991b) a series from this period of development, *Look In On London* (Rediffusion 1955). In one of the programmes in the series, 'Streetcleaners', a streetcleaner is 'encountered' on the streets of Maida Vale and is interviewed about his job and the people he meets. Although other, more conventional reportage is edited in, the programme's main narrative development quickly becomes centred around this single streetcleaner, whose 'significance' as a television accessee is no longer related to his specific job but, more generally, to his social position and housing conditions. Indeed, at mid-point, the reporter takes the programme off on an entirely new course by accompanying the man back to his home to meet his wife and to 'see how they live'. At the conclusion, over a shot of the streetcleaner now returned to his duties, the terms of extended social communication and social knowledge become transformed into the more affective terms of an extended *sociability*. The last words of the reporter include not only the accessee but also the audience in this broadened set of relations, 'This time we shall know who it is we are passing the time of day with'. Not only has access been dramatised, but the programme itself has, in part, turned into an *enactment* of a 'possible' social democratic community.

Such Mayhew-like adventures on the part of the television institution in its discovery of working-class Britain represent a significant stage in the development of the 'televised ordinary'. Though they often seem, by current conventions, to be heavily and clumsily mediated, they represent real moments of uncertainty and expansion in the social relations of the medium. And in the very awkwardness and transparency of their inter-facing activity they establish both new televisual iconographies and forms of talk. The developing impulse towards access has to define its own aims and its own communicative terms in relation to these.

My final example of the access mode within documentary television is much more recent and is therefore concurrent with the modern 'access' movement rather than an element of its pre-history. *A Fair Day's Fiddle?* (BBC 1982) was broadcast in the *Brass Tacks* series of investigative reports. Its topic is the extent of the various 'fiddles' (including undeclared part-time work) engaged in by people on state benefit. In exploring the nature and scope of the 'black economy' in areas of high unemployment, it chose one housing estate in Liverpool upon which to focus selective and personalised attention. Looking at how people manage in circumstances of unemployment, it examines not only 'fiddles' but self-help schemes like locally-organised credit unions, which work to provide low-interest loans. In its opening sequence of commentary-over-film, the programme clearly indicates its access designs: 'In this programme, local people speak for themselves.' The rest of the programme is almost entirely without commentary, working largely through a mix of '*vérité*' sequences of everyday life on the estate and interviews. Perhaps the most important of the interviews is with an unemployed man involved in community organisations. As well as speaking about his own problems as a husband and parent, he sets these in a broader social and political context. Over shots which variously show him alone – leaving his house to buy tobacco, rolling a cigarette, walking on estate paths, moving around his flat, peering out through lifted venetian blinds in his front room, sitting on the couch watching television – his interview speech is placed as reflective, voiced-over commentary and as *argument*. For instance: 'Our fiddles have been forced on us. Our fiddles are not done for gain, or for profits. Our fiddles are done because it is necessary, it's necessary for us to exist'. He also talks of class division, of the political motivation behind the label 'scroungers' and of the manipulative effect of TV advertising.

Research on the reception of the programme (Corner and Richardson 1986) showed that the problem with this sequence as access communication was certainly not that the speaker was unprepared for his interview opportunity. In fact, some viewers considered him to be *too* well-prepared, and also to have exceeded his qualifications to speak by talking of other things than his own experience. The key problem, however, was the mode of his 'objectification' by the visuals, an objectification which placed him in his wider environment and in his home as well as (by sustained close shots) paying attention to his physical personhood. Although there is no evidence of any intention by the programme-makers to 'set him up', many of the viewers in the research sample perceived a mismatch between his claims to poverty and the furnishing and possessions seen in his house (including a video recorder). Even his ability to buy cigarettes (emphasised in a number of close-up shots of him smoking) was seen by some to be evidence of exaggeration in his self-account of deprivation. What *might* have seemed like a visualisation perfectly suited to reinforce his comments, became for many viewers a separate and often conflicting strand of meaning in the sequence. For those who were unsympathetic to him, these objectifying visuals (mediating a 'problem' first personified and then observed) were naturalised as the truth which falsified his talk. For those who judged him more positively, the possibility of a conscious directorial attempt to 'damage' him was often entertained. Certainly, in the interplay between motivation and unconscious practice, between professional requirement and accessee goals, between speech and image, and between overall intention and viewer interpretation, the terms of public representation here are some way from those of *Housing Problems*.

ACCESS FORM AND 1990S TELEVISION.

What implications do these examples carry for 'access' as a communicational enterprise in the nineties? First of all, they show how representation (including self-representation) of the ordinary on television is
always in active relation to the existing professional conventions for
producing immediacy and continuity and for telling a 'human story'.
These conventions are, in part, derived from tested recipes for producing
'watchable' television. But they are not fixed conventions, they are
subject to the social and cultural change which affects the 'social optics'
of the medium as a whole, perhaps extending the range of broadcast
forms which have access functions (if only in part) and requiring that
the modalities of accessed speech and imagery be updated in their
relation to practice elsewhere in the schedules (even if this relation is
finally a consciously oppositional one). The shifts in the history of
'access slot' broadcasting from simple, studio presentations to-camera
through to professionally-assisted documentary productions, contrasting
filmed reports run back-to-back and the range of other formats involving
co-operation between independent production units and various interest
groups are a response to this.

In recent British broadcasting, the tendency has perhaps been for
access to be increasingly 'professionalised' as it has been partly subsumed within the movement towards minority programming, supplied
to the networks by small 'independents' as part of the reorganisation of
the industry away from the established practice of in-house production.
This has gone along with what might be seen as a dispersal of the
access idea across a number of different programme genres, including
children's shows, youth television, national and regional chat shows
and audience participation programmes. Mediations of 'ordinary'
people and of 'ordinary' views have become key ingredients in the
strongly inter-generic developments which have occurred around these
forms.

However, it seems to me that the most significant element of the new
context for access is the emergence of D-i-Y camcorder material as
a source of popular and *cheap* television. With the exception of the
phenomenally successful 'funny clips' shows (e.g. ITV's *You've Been
Framed*; the BBC's *Caught in the Act*), the most important development
to date has been the series *Video Diaries*, shown on BBC2 and produced
by the BBC's Community Programmes Unit (see Fraser 1992 for a
critical appraisal by a Channel 4 access editor). The format of the series
is simple. A member of the public judged to have an interesting idea

for a programme is given the go-ahead to shoot material on a VHS camcorder. The tapes which result (usually a very large number) are sent through to the BBC and edited by a member of the unit in consultation with the 'director'.

Video Diaries was launched in 1991 with 'A Fan's Diary' of the 1990 Football World Cup. With its mix of *vérité* action (including scenes of violence at the British supporters' campsite), its rendering of detailed, personal experience and its highly 'non-official' reportage, it proved very popular with viewers. Subsequent programmes have varied widely in subject matter and degree of seriousness, whilst always keeping a focus on a 'personal' and 'ordinary' perspective and on the projection of an account which both in theme and (necessarily, given the mode of shooting) in form is distinctive from the mainstream. If much recent non-fictional output has inclined towards the more stylistically ambitious, involving a new symbolic density and an overall textual self-consciousness, then *Video Diaries* might be seen as an attractively 'raw' alternative to elaborate varieties of the 'cooked'. But although the method gives accessees a far freer hand in determining how they shall be represented than any previous format was able to do, it nevertheless raises questions both of intent and of viewing relations which may have a bearing on whatever new generic codes emerge in this area. Even within the unit itself some of these questions are being posed. Hugo Irwin, unit researcher and editorial assistant, comments:

> I think that because of *Video Diaries* the Community Programme Unit is smelling of roses. It has been a huge success. I'm not sure that anyone realised that it was going to be quite such a success. It does of course bring up the problem of multi-skilling, doing people out of jobs. It's extraordinary, *Video Diaries*. The secret of it is that it's immediate and it does give you one hundred per cent access to somebody's life and that's what its charm is. Also, it has to be said the diarists are chosen fairly carefully.

Mike Fentiman, no longer involved directly in the work of the unit, and able to reflect on current developments from the standpoint of an access pioneer, goes further:

> I have to say there's an editorial drift towards the sensational, towards those programmes that say 'Hey, you know we've got a man looking for a Loch Ness monster'. Atypical people. Now obviously people don't want to sit down and just watch their neighbour, but I think sometimes the balance goes wrong. . . . So they become very much more personality-based than issue-based. In creating a seeming opportunity for the public

to be on television, which they do, what they are actually doing is separating the idea of broadcasting from being a social tool.

So the emergence of domestic video technology, whilst it radically alters the production potential for access, is still dependent on the institutional system of broadcast television for its public status. The system also regulates the relationship with a potential audience, organising the way in which material is likely to be watched. Fentiman's comments suggest the possibility of a growing tension between the modality of access as social dialogue and that of access as a new, generic commodity. The first model works along the axis 'accessee-public', the second along the axis 'programme-consumers'. This has implications for how access ideas are formulated – for intentions as well as for mode of address and discursive organisation.

As television becomes increasingly open to market-driven channel choice in Britain, the survival of the very public space in which access has always had its difficult, marginalised existence is threatened. Within the new programme formulas, there will inevitably be a tendency for the accessed ordinary to be made *productive* within the terms of market competition. This will undoubtedly mean a move towards the entertaining and towards those modes of objectification (including self-objectification) which are a precondition of social voyeurism. Yet as the layers of professional mediation in public life increase in number and degree of subtlety, as the dynamics by which society is imaged and described grow in scale, intensity and velocity, the particular energies, sheer *awkwardness*, of communication by 'fairly ordinary people' have never been more necessary to political health.

ACKNOWLEDGEMENTS

Interview comment transcribed in this article is from interviews with Mike Fentiman and Hugo Irwin, recorded at the BBC Community Programmes Unit, London, on 19 August 1992. I am grateful for their co-operation.

3

Media and social order in everyday life

ROBERT P. SNOW

This chapter differs from others in the volume in several respects. It is not directly concerned with access to or control of media or audiences. Rather, it focuses on how people use media in a matter-of-fact manner without regard to specific media content or ideological concerns. Instead of suggesting how media may affect audience beliefs, attitudes, or various aspects of social class, this chapter examines how media may be used to establish and maintain social order in a mundane fashion. In addition the author emphasises that claims are based on an American media experience.

There are two aims. One is to further the argument stated most clearly and elegantly by Anthony Giddens (1984) that the 'seeming fixity' of social order and structure resides in the development and maintenance of routine everyday life activity. The other is to demonstrate the significance of media in this process. The perspective that informs this discussion follows, in part, from Simmel (1971), and is based on the assumption that media should be understood and analysed primarily as a social form. As social form, media consist of standardised procedural strategies (formats) for presenting and interpreting cultural content, as well as protocols for interaction among media professionals and between media and audience. The focus here will be on those format characteristics, such as top-forty radio, television entertainment, or newspaper comics that are used as grammatical devices to accompany and aid in ordering the ordinary activity of everyday life.

For nearly two centuries, sociology has offered a Comtean promise for social order – namely that social order results from social structure and normative patterns of authority and power. As outlined in classical works from Spencer through Parsons, it has been held that people are socialised into the norms and values of status and roles in a manner that produces an internalised collective consciousness that insures stability in social affairs.

The role of media in this 'mainstream' sociological approach has always been considered secondary or extraneous to the core institutions of the family, religion, economic structure, government and so on. And yet, media have received significant attention whenever establishment values and norms seem to have broken down. Dramatic examples include the issue of television violence (Eron 1992), the false reality of media (Parenti 1991), the destructive impact of media on taste and high culture (Twitchell 1992), and the trivialisation of intellect (Dorfman 1983). Even when media are accorded some potency, such as in the hegemony thesis, media are cast more as an ideological tool (Gitlin 1987). But for most sociologists, the road to understanding media is through other institutions, namely economics and politics.

An example of the problems that emerge through this secondary analysis approach can be seen in content analysis research. Typically, this methodology tends to decontextualise media content from its format characteristics – more accurately it ignores format – and grounds content in ideological or commercial concerns. This should be considered a classic case of putting the cart before the horse. The problem is compounded when the analysis is placed within a framework of evaluating how media function in support or destruction of the norms and values of the so-called dominant institutions. With few exceptions this has led to a decidedly negative assessment of the media's role in society. Over the years, this view has gained such legitimacy that media are generally thought of as a necessary evil. Clearly this is an underlying tone in Semiotics (Fiske 1987; Carey 1987), and 'agenda-setting' (Shaw and McCombs 1977; Gitlin 1987). The problem in all this is the deterrent toward recognising potentially positive consequences in media use. To overcome that deterrent, consider examining the social form properties of media rather than media content. And, consider examining media as an individual habit or routine that aids in ordering a person's ordinary life. The question is: 'Are media used to establish a sense of social order and control in an ordinary practical consciousness without a requisite concern for value or ideology?'

In defining social order, this essay proceeds from the assumption in chaos theory (Briggs and Peat 1990; Gleick 1987) that stability or order is not the central, inherent, or normal state in physical, biological, or social realms. Rather, each of these realms is in continual movement in and out of order and chaos – neither state constituting a normative condition. Consequently, structure and order in the social world are fragile, and everyone is continually involved in their construction, or as Giddens prefers – 'structuration' (1984). As this view of social life gathers momentum in sociology, its practitioners return to Georg Simmel's question 'How is society possible?' As implied in works by Goffman (1963), a sense of social order results from the repetitive character of episodic encounters, particularly in public places. Giddens (1984), reworks Goffman's highly systematic and rich descriptions into the notion of routinised day-to-day activity that 'binds the fleeting encounter to social reproduction, and thus to the seeming fixity of institutions' (1984, p. 72).

Whereas Goffman's and Giddens' work seems to apply primarily to routine social encounters, it is useful to extend this reasoning to ordinary personal routines that occur in public and private. Reference here is to the daily activity thought of as necessary drudgery and usually of secondary or trivial importance in the structuration of institutional order that Giddens describes. The significance of this so-called drudgery is masked by the often-heard complaint that everyday life routines are the stuff of boredom – that if anything, routine life is too ordered. But, therein lies its importance, particularly for social order and stability. As Giddens states:

> Whatever is done habitually is a basic element of day-to-day social activity. . . . The repetitiveness of activities which are undertaken in like manner day after day is the material grounding of what I call the recursive nature of social life . . . [and this] routinisation is vital to the psychological mechanisms whereby a sense of trust or ontological security is sustained in the daily activities of social life (1984 p. xxiii).

Typically, the daily activity schedule for a working adult in modern urban society consists of waking up, personal grooming, eating, pet care, morning small talk, commuting to work, job routines (including lunch), the homebound commute, meal preparation, the evening meal, clean-up, playing with children, pets or both, evening entertainment, and preparing for bed. Periodic additions include supporting routines for any or all of the previously-mentioned activities, such as stopping to talk with a neighbour while retrieving the morning newspaper, or taking a favourite parking space or seat on mass transit. Other periodic routines include shopping, physical fitness, cleaning and maintenance, hobbies, interpersonal contacts, administration (paying the bills), recreation, waiting, and sleep itself. Although these activities are common to nearly everyone, and of little apparent consequence in the so-called big picture, there is a growing popular interest in the types of mundane activity that people share. Trade books, such as *Inside America*, by pollster Lou Harris (1987), *100% American* by Patrick McDonnell

(1988), and *Do's and Taboos Around the World* (Axtell 1985) are a few good sellers that normalise what may seem to be idiosyncratic routines, and indicate that perhaps urbanites today recognise a mutual bond in this commonality.

Casual observation demonstrates that much daily activity is routinised through repetitive actions, standardised sequence, and a temporal pattern of rhythm and tempo. The few situations of a typical day that are not routinised certainly stand out by contrast. Their unplanned, perhaps spontaneous character may seem fun or serious, fleeting or exhausting, and memorable as hallmarks or even lessons in life. But it is routine life that makes up the majority of social actions that provide a sense of plodding continuity and 'ontological security'. Support for this contention may rest on as trivial an illustration as one's own reaction to the disruption of a morning routine, such as the newspaper that does not arrive 'on time', a lack of hot water for a morning shower, the absence of a cup of coffee or tea, an unexpected detour or wait in the morning commute, or a pet that suddenly does the unexpected. Voluntarily, we are creatures of habit, and those habits instill order and continuity in an otherwise problematic world.

As routinised strategies render daily life durable, life flows in an orderly and stable manner. And, as the psychologist Csikszentmihaly (1990) claims, 'flow' in personal life may be the most important factor in achieving a sense of well-being. In this sense, social order in a broader sense may be abstracted and projected from an ordered personal life. What is essential to this strategy is both continuity or standardisation over time, and the desire to facilitate continuation. How then is continuity achieved? According to Giddens: 'Routinized character of paths along which individuals move in the reversible line of daily life does not just happen. It is made to happen through reflexive monitoring of action which individuals sustain in circumstances of co-presence' (1984, p. 64).

Giddens builds on this to include motivation as a consequence of reflexive activity (an idea based on G. H. Mead's discussion of the philosophy of the act). While reflexivity is central to social action in a Meadian framework, and the reciprocity required in meeting commitments underlies anticipation in social affairs, it has been assumed that these conceptions account for sustained action in the absence of co-presence or in anonymous encounters where interaction appears to be with a 'generalised other'. Without delving into the conceptual problems in 'socialisation' 'internalised norms', 'roles', and so on, it is suggested that 'momentum' as a temporal factor aids in understanding how routine behaviour may be sustained.

To date, sports provides the most acceptable explanation of the nature and utility of momentum. Peter Adler (1981) points out in his ethnography of college basketball that achieving and losing momentum is often the single most important factor in accounting for wins and losses. And, what is critical for momentum is not the rationality of means-ends action. Teams coasting to apparent victory suddenly lose momentum and end up losers. Weaker teams upset Goliaths with a magical momentum that players and coaches can't explain, at least not rationally. In fact, momentum is the antithesis of rationality, as it implies a force that pulls rather than causes. In these terms, it is a temporal phenomenon of rhythm and tempo rather than a spatial pattern or strategy of positioning. How then is momentum established?

One readily available source of rhythm and tempo, and a potential source of momentum, is media. Figure 3.1 represents a fairly typical utilisation of media in everyday routines. Not only are media used extensively throughout the day, they are almost always available to modern urbanites in these situations. In fact, most people would agree that media use in daily routines is essential. Evidence includes the fact that stereo AM/FM receivers are standard equipment in American automobiles, teenagers and young adults are rarely without a headset close at hand, most older mass transit riders carry reading material, the typical American home has a radio or television or both in nearly every room, and recorded music is standard background in shopping situations, waiting areas, bars, and eating establishments. Figure 3.1 covers only the most common routines for typical urbanites in Western society, and most people could add to this list a number of personally unique routines that underscore individuality. Despite the limits of this list, it demonstrates the degree to which daily activity can be routinised, and the likelihood that routines will be accompanied by mass media.

In examining the situations in figure 3.1, a somewhat hidden observation is that most of the routines call for particular media and particular formats. Here format refers to the grammatical (syntax and inflection) rules used to present various kinds of subject matter, such as top–40 format for popular music, TV entertainment (info-tainment) for the newspaper *USA TODAY*, and one-liner stand-up comedy for TV sitcoms. To illustrate, morning wake-up radio is not only set to a particular station, but given the precision of most radio formats (adult contemporary, talk, news, and so on), knowledgeable listeners know how the content (news, weather, type of music), is organised (sequence)

Routines	Media use
Domestic	
wake-up	radio alarm
personal grooming	radio/recorded music/newspaper
exercise regimen	audio headset/print media
pet regimen	audio headset
morning meal	radio/TV/newspaper
evening meal preparation	radio/recorded music/TV
evening meal	specific TV programmes/music
bedtime	radio/specific TV programmes
indoor cleaning	radio/TV/music
outdoor cleaning	audio headset
routine shopping	background music
Work related	
job commute	radio/headset/print
work	background music
homebound commute	radio/headset/print
Routine waiting	
medical	print/background music
traffic	phone and almost anything
telephone hold	programmed music or radio
shopping queues	print
repairs	print/TV
Scheduled media use	
evening entertainment	scheduled TV
Sunday morning	newspaper
children's use	after school TV
	Saturday morning TV cartoons
	weekend TV music
Leisure time	
parties	recorded music
hobby activity	radio/TV
relaxation (beach)	radio/headset/read

Figure 3.1 Typical media use in daily routines

and accented within segments of a broadcast. These listeners can easily use radio format as a clock to monitor as well as 'time' their progress and determine whether they are 'on schedule' in their routines. Morning newspapers must arrive at a specific time, and they are read according to a particular sequence, which in turn may be integrated with particular routines or segments of routines. Anyone who routinely reads a morning newspaper will readily admit to such behaviour. On it goes throughout the day, with particular media and formats becoming routine specific.

A closer look at the association of type of medium, the format, and the type of routine suggests that the format features of the medium may be at least as important, if not more important than the content. The weather report may be obtained from any one of several media, and the choice may initially rest on convenience. However, once the choice is routinised, it becomes an integral part of the routine, and change to another medium for needed information may momentarily destroy the flow of the routine. More to the point, a change in medium, or specifically a change in format, alters the rhythm and tempo of the action, and any momentum may be lost.

Three decades ago, Marshall McLuhan (1964) proposed that fundamental technological differences among the media affected the way in which a message would be interpreted. In other words, 'The medium is the message'. At the time, most students of media thought this idea was absurd. Today, many feel that McLuhan was on the right track. We know that people vary in their familiarity and comfort with various media, and we know that people selectively tune in and out based on these preferences. But, in contrast to McLuhan's position, the variations from one medium to the next are not a direct result of the technological character of the medium. Rather, as David Altheide and I have argued elsewhere (1979; 1991), variation in media selection is due to formats, or how the technology is used to present the content. A vivid example is the application of visual television grammar to rock music in the form or format of music video, and similarly to newspaper journalism in *USA TODAY*. This illustrates the independence of form or format from content, as well as preference among the audience for one format over others. As such, McLuhan's dictum is rephrased to 'The format is the message'. Further evidence of the ability to transfer formats is found in the recent history of commercial radio in America. During the late fifties rock'n'roll music of youth culture found its home on the little used and short broadcast radius of the FM band frequencies. While middle-aged, middle-class parents listened to AM middle-of-the-road radio, the baby boom generation developed highly specialised alternative formats on FM stations. As the 'boomers' grew older many of these FM stations quite naturally attempted to increase their ratings by aiming for broader popular appeal, and tailored the format of the old middle-of-the-road radio to rock music. Currently this can be heard as 'Lite Rock', 'Adult Contemporary', and 'Eclectic'. As might be expected, esoteric alternative formats are now found on the AM band.

While technology is certainly an important factor in explaining the popularity of various media, understanding what people pay attention to rests on the grammatical structure and logic of format. This lesson was learned by the designers of the Reagan and Bush presidential election campaigns, who knew that the primary format for an American audience is prime-time entertainment television. They also knew that as a general format, entertainment television could be used in any medium from billboards and newspapers to network television news. The so-called 'sound bite' is essentially a situation comedy one-liner, and along with simple and dramatic visuals, they were used effectively to help elect Reagan twice and Bush once. The losers, Mondale and Dukakis, followed a traditional campaign strategy of hard news issues combined with long-winded rhetoric which made for boring television. Observation of the 1992 Democratic Party convention indicates that the Democrats may have learned their lesson. Similar success and failure stories are found in advertising campaigns, sports programmes, religion, education, and others. Format won't guarantee success, but there is little success without the right format.

The utilisation of media as an integral feature of everyday life routines is primarily a matter of using formats as organisational features of routines. Among the most important features are the temporal elements of rhythm and tempo. As beat or cadence, rhythm is the accent or inflection achieved through action and pause which marks emphasis as well as progression. To engage oneself rhythmically is to lean into the future through anticipation, and to sustain momentum. As such, rhythm is fundamental rather than extraneous to establishing and maintaining order. At the macro level, Condon (1978), Leonard (1978), Hall (1983) and others, claim that the key to understanding any culture lies in identifying its rhythmic character and sources. For micro-analysis order is synonymous with entrainment, or the sychronisation of self with others in social affairs. By contrast, arrhythmia may occur when core rhythms are lost or rendered monotonous and boring (Brissett and Snow 1993). Nowhere is the threat of this arrhythmia more evident than in everyday life activity, and everyone has strategies designed to meet this threat. When boredom threatens, typical strategies include increasing the tempo and altering the rhythm (the latter being the most successful). Abundant examples are found where the potential for boredom is high, such as travel and captive audience situations. In these and similar situations, media can be a sufficient antidote. Specifically, in the absence of co-presence, media used as a metronome may provide the entrainment necessary to establish momentum, although the more common feeling is simply a wish to sustain a constant rhythm for the situation. One playful example is the practice among youth of constantly changing the car radio station as a strategy for sustaining or changing rhythm.

Every media format has a discernible rhythm, which consists of the inflection or accent features of the format. Those accents or places of emphasis form a cadence of beat and pause that provide progression to an otherwise continuous blur of activity. These rhythms may be identified by reducing the number of cues that are normally used in a particular medium. For example, to capture the rhythm of a particular newspaper begin by looking at a foreign-language paper and glance through the layout. Note the position of photographs to written copy, headlines to copy, long to short paragraphs, column lengths, graphics, colour schemes, and so on. Each type of format from tabloids to finance papers has a distinct rhythmic pattern that may become integrated into particular daily routines, such as headlines, comics and human interest for breakfast, more serious material or the crossword puzzle for the mass transit commute, and the classified section for coffee breaks. With television, the identification of rhythm may be more difficult. As McLuhan (1964) pointed out, television involves all the senses, and has the appearance of a fuzzy mosaic. To reduce the interference, limit the TV experience to either sound or visuals. The most dramatic observations are made with music video, although soap operas, sitcoms, and game shows work well also. Compare different TV formats, such as soaps to sitcoms, and different time periods, such as *circa* 1950s black and white to the 1980s. In the latter comparison it should become apparent that the dominant rhythm today is visual, whereas during the early TV era auditory rhythm tended to lead the visual material. A similar comparison can be made with Hollywood film. In fact today, the dominant rhythmic pattern for most media is visual. Subtle variations in rhythm are found in different film genre, as well as cultural differences, such as the temporal differences between British and American comedy or mystery, and subculture and regional differences in music and talk. Simply reading through academic papers such as this one, illustrates a fairly standard rhythm of 'threes' when an author presents examples. With commercial media, the rhythms can become complex through simultaneously layering two or more sources, such as talk over music, and both over sound effects. To the untrained ear this may be irritating, but to others it demonstrates the degree to which we can be attuned to inflection characteristics in format.

In relating rhythm to a routine activity, it is suggested that maintaining a sequence of routine actions is facilitated by the rhythm or rhythms embedded in media format. Formatted or designed rhythm sustains momentum through the anticipation that occurs in the progression of accent, pause, accent. Restated, activity that might otherwise be experienced as tedious is infused with zest through the subtle ambiguity of anticipating the next act or beat. Given the history of work songs, it seems reasonable to suggest that rhythms in contemporary media formats help us through those unpleasant or potentially boring routines, such as rush-hour traffic, cleaning jobs, grocery shopping, the routine medical visit, and perhaps physical exercise. In more mundane routines the rhythmic accent may be more subtle, but none the less significant as background for the activity. Reading the Sunday newspaper helps establish the routine of 'down time', and classical music may accompany an evening meal.

Whereas rhythm provides the cadence for anticipation and momentum, tempo adds fervour or induces calm. A person can ease into the day or hit the floor running, eat a meal calmly or gobble fast food on the move, race or ease through the rush-hour, and fall into bed exhausted or relaxed. At the extremes, a very slow or very hurried tempo may distort the sense of momentum and result in a feeling of separation from the mundane world. This may be at the root of the hurried or frenzied society, as critiqued by Rifkin (1987) and others. Perhaps most important, tempo enables a person to pace a routine in order to keep it within desired time parameters. To keep a routine manageable, we may admonish ourselves to 'get it in gear, or slow it down a bit'. Although changing tempo can be accomplished without media, in today's urban Western world most people would agree that media are an excellent means of establishing tempo. A common example is the use of radio to keep a driver awake and alert at the wheel, especially at night. At bedtime the procedure is reversed by reading ones self to sleep. In these situations, the tempo in media format becomes a means for controlling the pace of orderly progression. Since we know intuitively that increasing or decreasing tempo too much can destroy rhythm, media may be called upon to check runaway pace or increase the pace when tedium threatens.

Conceptualising rhythm and tempo as temporal ecology may serve to expand our understanding of the importance of temporality in everyday life. A significant step toward defining this concept may be found in Edward Hall's *The Dance of Life* (1983). Hall observes that every culture has well-established temporal rhythms that function as a language for experiencing the everyday world. Following this logic, temporal ecology becomes core culture, and serves to integrate like-minded members in entrained social action, as well as to identify and exclude outsiders. His classification of cultural time rests on a distinction between monochronic (one thing at a time) and polychronic (multiple tasks occurring simultaneously), and his comparisons afford interesting insights into cultural differences, particularly for economic activity. What is needed to further his seminal beginning is identification of the features of culture that directly and indirectly establish a temporal ecology. In today's world media certainly are one, if not the most important element in a temporal ecology, and the power in this element is format.

Whereas format contains what becomes an essential temporal structure for routine activity, continued use of particular formats in specific routines become part of the overall appearance of familiarity and normality. Familiar pictures include a newspaper and morning coffee, cars and their sound systems, television and children after school, Sunday evening and television, Saturday evening and video rentals, waiting-rooms and well-worn magazines, and the list goes on. Each of these situations becomes incomplete and awkward without the appropriate medium or media. A broken car radio makes the morning commute unnerving. A pre-empted television programme at mealtime sends individuals searching for a substitute that will probably be unsatisfactory.

One explanation for these familiar scenes is that the medium is an essential part of the *gestalt* or unity of the event. Side-stepping the gestalt assumption, one could simply say that a missing piece of the picture introduces a degree of ambiguity and corresponding emotional change that at the very least is uncomfortable and at worst intolerable. Extreme cases are those routines which can't be rescheduled and where no alternative media are available. Examples include traffic grid-lock without a phone or radio, meal preparation in the company of guests who can't stand the cook's choice of music or television, or the breakdown in one routine that fouls successive routines so that the media must be abandoned. In such cases we may seek out media that are normally ignored, or we create it internally.

The absence of media may also heighten self-consciousness, particularly when alone in public places and sensitivity to scrutiny from others becomes exaggerated. Waiting at a bus stop, riding the underground, eating alone in a cafeteria, or waiting in an airline terminal are situations of potential discomfort through feeling awkward or vulnerable. In these situations media may be used to divert one's attention from unwanted attention by strangers, to an engagement with a medium as a surrogate other. Here again, the content of the medium is secondary to its use as a form for para-social interaction. Familiar examples include the newspaper, magazines, paperbacks, audio headset, and the infamous 'boombox', which may also serve as a weapon to keep others at a distance. Most important, the medium in these situations enables the individual to avoid or diminish contemplating impressions of 'looking-glass self'. Through the medium the individual is immersed in a safer, albeit vicarious, reality.

Finally, establishing a sense of normality through the use of familiar media formats can be useful for maintaining the proper sequence and temporal order of routines. One of the problems in the video-taping of programmes is with programmes that are normally watched along with particular daily routines. People who go to sleep with a particular programme find it difficult if not impossible to watch that programme in the morning. Doing so may even induce sleep. Similarly, reading the morning newspaper in the evening may feel strange if it is routinely read in the morning. In fact, it may be necessary to replicate the morning routine (coffee or a drink of some kind), in order to read it with comfort. The problem compounds when other routines are expected to follow in sequence. For example, when television programmes are associated with the temporal progression of the work week, shifting a Thursday evening programme to Monday or Tuesday may reduce its enjoyment, as the programme may formerly have been associated with the beginning of the weekend. More dramatic perhaps, is missing a particular evening TV news programme, particularly if that programme is used as a culminating routine for the day.

Just as media routines aid in establishing a feeling of normality for a particular routine, or more accurately the absence of media make some routines awkward and non-normal, a traumatic non-routine situation may be imbued with a sense of normality by using familiar media in the background. Examples include the medical waiting rooms, surgery preparation areas in hospitals, dental offices, airline boarding areas and on-board flight preparation and flight, and even the mildly ambiguous situation of the grocery check-out queue, where we can read outrageous and bizarre tabloid headlines. When standard media sources, such as radio or television are unavailable or become tedious, alternative media, such as billboards, bumper stickers, T-shirts, and business signs may be substituted. In sterile environments, such as temporary confinements, people will go to great lengths to stimulate mental activity. Under such conditions any medium may be better than none at all.

Non-routine situations in which media is often used as supplementary background also deserves brief mention. These include social events, such as parties, and establishing private moods, such as romance or solitary quiet times. Since the primary concern in these situations is to establish an appropriate rhythm and tempo, background media, especially music, can act as a subtle or perhaps dramatic metronome to establishing and maintaining flow. In turn, the most likely potential problem in these situations is the awkward pause that can destroy the flow. Background media can not only fill the pause, it may serve as a topic for a small talk to maintain momentum in the affairs. Moreover, music background is usually an impression management strategy to convey social class and personality characteristics about the host in the situation, which in turn imply certain future possibilities for the encounter. In short, media background may stimulate anticipation among participants in both a temporal fashion and for particular actions and meanings.

The importance of media as background has long been overlooked in staging and enacting social affairs. In fact, the term background is a misnomer to the extent that it implies extraneous status among the factors that comprise a situation. Close observation of any situation in which media seems or are claimed to serve as background usually reveals that its absence leaves a noticeable void and discomfort. Its importance in maintaining momentum or flow, and consequently control (Csikszentmihaly 1990) is obvious to media users. In fact, in some situations such as driving, coming home to an empty place of residence, reading, eating, exercising, and so on, the main activity cannot begin until the media are operating. To ensure immediate media operation, common practices include leaving the car radio power switch left in the 'on' position, connecting the home stereo to a light switch near the front door or to a remote-control device, and making sure reading material is close at hand in dining areas, patios, bedrooms, and bathrooms. In these and similar situations, the medium is integral to the overall activity.

As a means for establishing order and control, the previous discussion has focused on the use of media format as a temporal structure for rhythm and pace in everyday life. These temporal features of media format may also serve as a means for ordering and controlling the space needed to carry out and complete a routine. A familiar example is the newspaper which may be used as a protective barrier against physical and social encroachment while riding mass transit. In a study of subway riders some years ago (Levine *et al.* 1973), the newspaper was also seen as a means for maintaining civility through civil inattention, or as an act of posing no threat to other travellers. Here the physical form of media technology is recognised as a legitimate part of the process of establishing and maintaining social order. Today, stereo headsets, cellular phones, the paperback novel, magazines, and the lap-top computer may serve the same function. While these technologies may also foster an extreme privatisation in public social arenas, the result is still order and control.

Despite the fact that media pervade almost every corner of modern society, people should view the claims made here with some scepticism. Certainly large numbers of people use media sparingly, and these people most likely do not use media to support daily routines. But statistics on the average number of hours a television is turned on each day, average number of radios per household, newspaper circulation, video rental figures, and so on, support the claim that heavy media use is commonplace in Western urban society, and there is no sign of its decline. Indeed, the question of 'why media use is so great?' is seldom heard today.

Media critics, such as Neil Postman (1984), would have us believe that our fascination with media is primarily an ever-increasing demand for entertainment. In the early days of television the fear was that there was something sinister and addictive about 'the tube'. Today we're back to the addiction notion, but this time it's entertainment – we just can't get enough. Clearly almost everything on television, including news and sports, is presented through entertainment formats. As television formats became the preferred media format among audiences throughout America, other media, such as newspapers, magazines, radio, and movies, joined the strategy and reformulated their formats to conform to television. On the surface it appears that every medium presents almost everything through entertainment, which has prompted Postman to suggest that we're 'amusing ourselves to death'. Perhaps. But an alternative explanation is that in many situations, a reason for using a mass medium is to develop and sustain a temporal ecology (a time order) and the appearance of familiarity, particularly in daily affairs.

Today, temporal ecology in Western urban society is established and maintained largely through electronic media formats. While it may appear to the uninvolved observer that media is content-specific, and driven by market strategies, politics, currents in education, sports, and economic realities of daily life, the most common use of media is primarily as support for other activities. In fact, it seems quite plausible that media as form may be one of the more powerful factors in constructing and maintaining social order and control in everyday life. The order and control referred to here is not understood as a consciousness of collectivity, nor is it informed through ideology. Rather, it refers to order in the sense of maintaining individual life as familiar – as usual. It is the orderly arrangement of ordinary activity, task, space, and time. As sociologist Carl Couch claims, 'Temporal structures are an absolute necessity for the production of orderly human action' (1989, p. 29) It is this order that fosters synchronisation or entrainment in those social affairs that are essential to the smooth flow of daily activity. As argued by Csikszentmihaly (1990), this what is well-being is all about.

And yet Jeremy Rifkin argues in *Time Wars* (1987) that we are in the throes of a crisis in temporality. By abandoning the rhythms and tempo of nature and embracing a new temporal order imposed through cybernetics and the computer chip, Western society has developed a temporality based almost entirely on artificial dimensions of time. In the process, Rifkin argues, community and self-assurance are sacrificed for power and control. However, he feels that this control is an illusion, and we must 'seek a new temporal orientation based on an empathetic union with the biological and physical clocks of nature' (p. 194). On the other hand, perhaps we have gained a sense of order and comfort through mass-mediated daily routines. In today's world of apparent complexity, rapid change, and uncertainty, this may constitute the realm where people feel some control over life. That media provide a useful tool in this control ought to be taken seriously.

PART TWO

[4]

The media and the public interest: questions of access and control

RALPH NEGRINE

INTRODUCTION

The title of this chapter is intended to do two things. First, to provide a loose framework which would allow one to pursue common themes: themes such as participation, access, and control. Secondly, to create a space for a fundamental shift in emphasis from a concern with structural issues to a concern with processes. More precisely, this chapter seeks to focus on the theme of access not simply (and more commonly) as it relates to structures, but also as it relates to content – as in access to information. This is one dimension of interest that has been somewhat overlooked in contemporary literature on structural change.

What is this chapter's central organising theme? Briefly, it seeks to argue that the mass media remain core institutions within political and social systems and that what they do, and how they do it, contributes to (or subtracts from) the democratic process. To quote Peter Golding:

> At the heart of political communication research must be enquiry into the contribution of information flows and media institutions to the exercise of democracy. . . . To what degree are people denied access to necessary information and imagery to allow equal and full participation in the social order? (1990, p. 98).

As he goes on to point out, there are barriers – some socio-economic, others mediated – which, when taken together, deny 'resources allowing for full participation in the social and cultural process' and also deny access 'to the full and adequate range of imagery and information assumed by ideal definitions of citizenship'; a term one can interpret to mean something akin to 'full membership of a community' (Golding 1990, pp. 98–9). What is apparent, even from this brief introduction, is that the terms of the debate about 'the media and democracy' already encompass some of the keywords which are central to this chapter: terms such as 'participation' and 'access' which evoke images of a public actively taking part in the running of their own lives and a public attentive to diverse sources of information flowing through the political system; terms such as 'citizenship' and 'community' with their connotations of belongingness, responsibilities and obligations, common interests and the like; and even terms such as democracy and democratic processes with their implicit connotations of a certain type of socio-political arrangement with attendant properties such as political freedoms, and constitutional principles which apply to all and which protect both the strong and the weak.

In this brief description of an idealised political system, the institutions of mass communication have an important part to play: either in enabling individual citizens or groups to 'participate in the social and cultural process', or in making a 'full and adequate range of imagery' or 'access to the realities of the world' (Berrigan 1977, p. 19) a possibility. They are there to uphold and further 'the public interest' and not as a barrier against democratic processes; they should enable those processes. But as John Keane observes,

> . . . there is a structural contradiction between freedom of communication and unlimited freedom of the market . . . the market liberal ideology of freedom of individual choice in the marketplace of opinions is in fact a justification of the privileging of corporate speech and of giving more choices to investors than to citizens (Keane 1991, p. 89).

Keane's 'remedy' lies in recreating the 'public service model' of the means of mass communication. This would ensure that the mass media become less of the market-dominated, audience seeking, competitive media systems so familiar to us all. As he puts it, perhaps rather too grandly:

> A fundamentally revised public service model should aim to facilitate a genuine commonwealth of forms of life, tastes and opinions, to empower a plurality of citizens who are governed neither by despotic states nor by market systems. It should circulate to them a wide variety of opinions . . . (Keane 1991, p. 126).

To his credit, Keane does identify areas where change would have to take place if these objectives are to be achieved. His suggestions include more open government, the re-definition of sovereignty, the establishment of strong democratically-elected parliaments able to support media 'freedoms' (Keane 1991, p. 147), the development of 'publicly-funded, non-profit and legally guaranteed media institutions of civil society' (Keane 1991, p. 158), and so on.

These changes, and in particular the proposals for extensive state support of media, would address, in the main, the structural dimension of the problem of partial, conglomerated media systems. But the attainment of a more 'responsible and representative' media, or the creation of 'a commonwealth of forms of life, tastes and opinions' does not solely depend upon the creation of a sound structure of ownership and regulation. Admittedly, these factors could facilitate the birth of a more diverse and responsive media system, and it might even begin to allow for the diversity Keane seeks to engender, but it would not necessarily help address a somewhat different concern about the ability of the mass media to deliver 'access to the realities of the world'. Mass media content – the stuff designed 'to empower a plurality of citizens' (Keane 1991); the stuff that shows 'systematic deficiencies' when it comes to 'providing an adequate account of social and political processes' (Golding 1990) – is itself a problem area, and not one easily resolved by structural solutions. Why this is so is the main theme of the second part of this chapter.

Briefly, then, the concern with structures of communication is only part of a larger concern about the role of individuals and groups in the political process. In fact, the debate about participation in, and access to, the mass media – a discussion of which follows – operated with a clear, if idealistic, understanding of the significance of public involvement in the political process. Where there were shortcomings was in the pursuit of these ideas as if they were ends in themselves. Participation and access, on their own, are mere tokens. On the other hand, the belief that the mass media can provide a diverse and pluralistic marketplace of ideas is itself open to doubt for reasons of structures and ownership, and weaknesses in the processes of journalism.

These two implicit criticisms of past and recent calls for reforming the systems of communications produce a rather negative attitude towards future change. In fact, one possible conclusion of this chapter would be as follows: in the final analysis, the citizens which Keane seeks to empower may have neither any meaningful access to the means of mass communication, nor any control over them or the information which flows through them.

ACCESS AND CONTROL IN THE AGE OF INTERNATIONAL MEDIA SYSTEMS:
ACCESS FOR WHAT?

The arguments in favour of 'access' to, and 'participation' in, the media were well aired in the 1960s and 1970s in the context of the development of various strains of access programmes on, but also outside of, cable television systems. The main arguments put forward by proponents of these ideas are worth some space for reflection. They are made up of three main strands:

1   that opening up institutions for public participation and involvement is a prerequisite to a more open and active society;
2   that participation in, and access to, the means of communication are not only worthwhile in themselves but could lead on, or contribute, to the creation of a more complete democratic process;
3   that participation in, and access to, the means of communication could not only re-create broadcasting as a two-way form of communication but could also permit non-professionals to communicate.

As Brian Groombridge wrote twenty years ago, 'Participatory programming is, then, a process in which the media are used chiefly as a stimulus to participatory democracy but also in part as themselves are a forum or outlet for participation' (1972, p. 221). Five years later, in a review of the European experience with forms of access television, Frances Berrigan gave the following working definition of access as 'access by the non-professional to media channels, and participation by the non-professional in the planning, management and administration of the media process' (Berrigan 1977, p. 16). In her more detailed description she included such things as access to the policy-making process; access to the power of the media; access to the selection of information; access to a choice of programme material; access to production and media tools, and access to feedback processes (Berrigan 1977, pp. 18–19).

What gave these demands and hopes a degree of currency and relevance was a combination of technological and political change. On the technological side one can point to the development, and availability, of comparatively cheap and portable video equipment in Canada, in the US, in Britain but also elsewhere. There was also the growing interest in cable television systems across Europe and the American continent. On the political side one can easily identify a lively, and sometimes heated, public debate about the control of broadcasting; a debate which implicitly and explicitly questioned the ways in which broadcasting systems were organised and run.

Together, these forces created a desire and an opportunity for change and experimentation. And the embryonic cable systems of the 1970s provided the ideal setting for such attempts at innovation and the creation of alternative structures and processes of communication. They were small and local, and so the locality, the community setting, the neighbourhood became the central focus of attention – they provided a means for each and every individual to get involved at a local level, a level which was meaningful in both a physical and mental sense. To quote from a 1992 cable operator's document: the proposed channels would 'provide a television service which is distinctly different from over-the-air broadcast television services.' They were there to reflect and meet 'the needs , concerns and interests of individuals and groups within [their] communities' and to enable groups and individuals to 'participate actively in Community Programming.' As Kleinsteuber put it, 'the overall impression is that local means something nearby, something cosy – the connotations are positive and supportive' (Kleinsteuber 1992, p. 144).

In addition to these systems being local in a geographical sense, they were also regulated as local systems. In most cases there was also an emphasis on the production and transmission of locally-made content. This would either be made by local individuals and groups or made by them with the technical assistance of a handful of professionals employed by the cable company. Admittedly, not enough programming was ever generated, nor was the material particularly enlightening or popular, but these were not crucial points when considered within the larger picture of the significance of these forms of communication. What was a problem, then as it is today, was finance – and by extension the relationship between these local community channels and the overall cable television organisation.

In Britain, although the local community services were, on the whole, run at arm's length from the cable television operation, they were usually set up, and funded, by the operators. As we shall see, other countries adopted different structures. In the British community television experiments of the 1970s, the community channels were licensed before the cable systems were themselves licensed to carry other services. Operators accepted this as part of a broad strategy to get cable systems off the ground, but their overall commitment to the local community channels was not open-ended. So the existence, and ultimate survival, of community channels was dependent on larger questions and not purely on their success, or otherwise, as community services. Even when they began to carry advertising, it was clear that they could never generate enough revenue to cover their meagre operating costs. In fact, it is doubtful whether they could ever generate enough local revenue given that their appeal is intended to be primarily to a local population.

All this should not be taken to suggest that such channels have no value for cable operators. On the contrary, they are seen as valuable additions to cable systems and likely to entice the potential, if wavering, subscriber. Nevertheless, local channels remain dependent on the whims of the cable operator. They have, therefore, no automatic right of existence. They do not, therefore, exist on all cable systems in Britain though most systems do carry local text services.

In other countries, although the situation was different, the end result may have been exactly the same. According to Porter and Hasselbach, 'open access to radio and television . . . arrived' with the licensing of private media in 1984 (Porter and Hasselbach 1991, p. 96), even though in the German broadcasting system 'the idea of direct access' to the communication media is 'foreign . . . since in theory the system integrates the major social forces into the public communication process by giving them seats on the broadcasting councils' (Porter and Hasselbach 1991, p. 97).

These 'open channels' were open to all on a first-come-first-served basis and, significantly, they were 'offered either through *publicly financed* [my emphasis] access channels on cable networks, mostly for television, and/or on terrestrial radio' (Porter and Hasselbach 1991, p. 99). Porter and Hasselbach quote sums ranging from several under £0.5 million to £2.1 million available from local states for such channels.

Another important difference between the British and German examples was that in the 'open channels' participants themselves 'are legally liable for their programmes' and these programmes did not have to meet content requirements for objectivity and balance (Porter and Hasselbach 1991, p. 100).

But there are some similarities which perhaps outweigh the differences. First, there is today a noticeable absence of the sorts of socio-political arguments which were part and parcel of local community channels. Secondly, there is an implicit belief amongst commentators that these experiments in alternative forms of communication were never taken seriously except by a small number of activists and committed volunteers. In Britain, they were part of a strategy to get cable off the ground, as has already been described above. In Germany, Peter Humphreys believes that the Ludwigshafen experiment, one of the main open channels, was permitted '. . . at least partially, to sweeten the pill for the opponents of cable broadcasting and to legitimise the new media in the eyes of the larger public . . .' (Humphreys 1990, p. 218).

Thirdly, the addition of satellite broadcasting systems has also created a shift towards national and/or pan-European programming. Cable systems have thus been transformed from idealistic local communication systems into a sort of local delivery arm of an international system of communication. The number of levels of communication has thus increased to include a range from local, through regional, national, continent-wide, to international systems. Localism, as an ideal and a practice, has not disappeared although it has been overtaken by a different conception of the audience and its relationship to the technology of choice and more entertainment. There is here a marked convergence between the developments in these two nations.

The fourth, and final, point is the lack of success of the local channels. How could it be otherwise? How can local services survive in an extremely competitive environment? A typical local channel on a British cable system, for example, would have to compete with regional and national commercial television, regional and national non-commercial channels, and a multitude of satellite-delivered services offering a varied menu of content. Will its content of local snippets and tit-bits – locally produced by amateurs with the assistance of professionals – stand up to the competition? Will it catch the viewers? Will it motivate them to participate themselves? Evidence from past research casts doubts on these aspirations, and commentary of the German experience suggests a similar verdict. (See Porter and Hasselbach 1991; Humphreys 1990.)

Yet it does remain the case that it is only on the local (possibly even commercial) communication system, be it cable, radio or UHF, that local community and participatory forms of communication can exist. The more national or international the technology of communication, the less the potential for local, participatory or access communication; similarly, the more commercial the organisation of the medium, and the more competitive the environment, the less the likelihood that forms of local, participatory or access television will play an important part in the schedules. At the same time, it is possible that the more competitive the media environment, the more likely that local services will be offered as loss-leaders to curry favour with both regulators and potential viewers/subscribers. (See McQuail 1992, Ch. 13.)

There is, however, one point of contrast the significance of which is difficult to gauge. One consequence of the regulatory regime imposed on the development of British cable systems in the early years – and also because of their history – was that such systems were either locally-owned and run or were part of national companies operating at a local level. One should not idealise this – EMI and Rediffusion were hardly local, neither were the Canadian companies taking part in the Greenwich cable television system of the 1970s. None the less, in regulatory and operational terms these were local systems or, at best, part of national systems with strong local connections.

But by the late 1980s, the situation had changed dramatically. Now they are part of international systems of communication in an increasingly internationalised setting. It has been estimated that of the '90 cable British franchises awarded by May 1990, more than eighty-nine per cent had gone to American corporations' (Taggart 1992, p. 193); clearly the details of the situation may have changed since then but not in a way that would significantly affect these figures. This is very different from the German and French experiences where the national players such as the Bundespost or France Telecom still play an important role *vis-à-vis* cable systems. Whether this difference in ownership has contributed to the success or failure of local channels is not easy to assess although the evidence points to this factor not making any difference whatsoever.

What emerges most clearly, though, is that the convergence identified above and leading us towards 'television in the year 2000' has squeezed the space available for alternative forms of communication on a significant scale. For example, demands for access and participation have almost disappeared. The internationalisation and commercialisation of television industries have effectively restricted their appearance to discussions at lower levels – technologically and commercially speaking – and to the fringes.

This may not be the only loss experienced by potential viewers/ citizens as a result of convergence; to paraphrase Frances Berrigan (1977), there could also be a loss of a right of 'access to a choice of programmes'. As Jay Blumler has recently written:

> In essence, the West European fear is that the advent of commercial television will shift the emphasis from a principled to a pragmatic pluralism, yielding only that amount and those forms of diversity that are likely to pay. At risk could be poorly placed segments of the population . . . (Blumler 1992, pp. 32–3).

Commercialisation of the media, therefore, also impacts on core values in broadcasting and democratic systems. Not only does it narrow the range of available content but it also restricts the public's access to diverse programming.

A recent wide-ranging *Screen Digest* survey of European satellite-delivered TV channels identified seventy such channels, but the breakdown into categories reveals their restricted range of content. Thus, there were: thirty-four entertainment channels, five general channels, nine movies/entertainment channels, four children's channels, three news channels, seven sport channels, and an assortment of others in ones or twos. (*Screen Digest*, 1991a, pp. 177–83)

None of these services are of the type which are in the business of encouraging access to facilities, to production, or to anything other than the television screen; neither are they 'technologically' suited to do so. Now it could be argued that the public service broadcasters ought to carry out these obligations as part and parcel of their responsibilities as national or regional broadcasters, as some are now doing with respect to people with disabilities, for example. This requirement would seem unjust and over-burdening to already troubled institutions.

The more critical point is that such institutions – even if regionally organised – are not ideally suited for the sorts of access to communication which local communication systems can, at least in theory, provide. This is not only because national/regional broadcasters employ technologies which necessitate reaching a mass audience; also critical is the range of programmes which they transmit and these do not usually offer many vehicles for participation on a regular/continuous basis[1]. If one takes into account the fact that on regional and national television, the public/citizen is most often used as a source of brief snippets, or that the time given over to access-type programmes on regional and national systems of television is very limited, or that many services now depend on such things as imported television programming, then the 'closed' nature of communication becomes transparent.

Where does this leave the *positive and supportive* aspects of locality in broadcasting? We can continue to expect local communication systems – whether radio or cable or even print – to provide the means for alternative processes and relationships. Cable systems may still have a role to play in the communications structures of the future. According to *Screen Digest* 'of the 28 million homes able to receive some of (the European satellite) channels at the end of 1990, over 26 million were on cable and only 1.8 million equipped for DTH satellite reception' (see Table 4.1). The best prospects for DTH were in Britain (seventy per cent of Europe's dishes are found here), Spain and Portugal (*Screen*

Digest 1991a, p. 177); but cable systems were better developed elsewhere so there was some potential for other forms of television.

Table 4.1 Cable in selected countries (mid- to end-1991)

	Cable homes passed 'ooos	Cable homes connected 'ooos	Cable penetration	Cable penetration as % of TVHH	DTH homes 'ooos
France	3,213	647	20.2%	3.2%	40
Germany	16,597	8,953	52.9%	28.6%	1,400
Netherlands	4,800	4,580	95.4%	78%	150
Sweden	1,620	1,482	91.5%	44.6%	120
UK	2,058	461	22.4%	2.2%	1,630

Source: Screen Digest, 1991b

Even so, and as we have seen, local community/alternative systems of communications still find it difficult to survive in a country such as Germany, with its relatively well-developed cable systems and its favourable regulatory climate.

What of radio? De Bens and Petersen provide a brief overview of local radio developments across Europe and conclude that, in general and with the exception of Scandinavia and the Netherlands, commercialism has impacted both on the structures which exist and on the content of the stations; 'as a result of commercialism the programming content of the local stations has drifted away from the original goals' (De Bens and Petersen, 1992, p. 159) – these being defined in ways not very different from the description of local television given above. In those countries which remain wedded to the ideal – Scandinavia and the Netherlands – De Bens and Petersen still see the key difficulty being that of finding a satisfactory 'solution to the financial problems' and fitting it 'into the existing régimes'. They conclude that 'the present half-way position between idealism and commercialism is a political compromise, difficult to police because of its decentralized character, and imperilled by the logic of commercial competition' (De Bens and Petersen 1992, p. 165).

The above discussion points to a sombre future for local channels. Whether because of limited financial and technical resources, or a lack of genuine commitment, such channels are likely to remain peripheral to the mainstream communication enterprises and their mainly commercial objectives. Moreover, local channels are never likely to obtain large audiences, their content is likely to be local and 'unprofessional', and their overall remit parochial. But in terms of the principle which they establish, they are the basis for alternative forms of localised communication in an increasingly national and international commercial system of communication.

What does remain open for debate is the purpose of it all. Why access, and why participation? The sort of idealistic models discussed so far offer a glimpse of what might have been but, even then, it is obvious that such alternative forms of communication are only part of a very complex process. National and regional systems of communications, from television to print, dominate the mass media and continue to be the most important sources of information about national/regional events. Even where local events and issues may be significant, it could be that these are determined by national events and national debates: the more politically and administratively centralised the system, as in Britain, the less room for manoeuvre at the regional or local level.

In that context, forms of communication which provide for participation and access are, therefore, of limited value; they are not of *no* value but their value may lie in specific areas: they may, in other words, provide information about the local community in a way which less local communication systems cannot do for organisational, operational and financial reasons. Where such local communication services are less likely to be of value is those areas in which national broadcasters have been traditionally strong – news and current affairs, entertainment, arts programmes, and so on. The reasons for the restricted range of programming on local systems should be fairly obvious. On the one hand, resources are not plentiful, be they skills or hardware; on the other hand, the amateur is in a different position *vis-à-vis* the audience and the media establishment from that occupied by the media professional.

But there is a more fundamental point which needs to be made here, namely, that in the final analysis it may matter little what structures of communication one establishes if the processes of communication are deficient. If journalism, be it at the national or international level is failing to provide 'the full and adequate range of imagery and information' or access 'to information about the realities of the world' so desired for the purposes of citizenship and in the public interest, what hope is there for amateur journalism at the local or community level?

ACCESS TO INFORMATION AND JOURNALISTIC PRACTICES:
COMMUNICATING THE PUBLIC INTEREST

The concern with structures for example, as in the discussion about the nature and performance of the 'open channels' or the local community television channels, does not focus on a more fundamental problem. How can we ensure that there is a 'marketplace of opinions', alongside a proper analysis of events and their causes and effects.\ Indeed the public interest cannot be assumed to be served simply because opinions and information are available and in the public domain.\ Where these are available, and how they are made public are relevant questions. A 'full and adequate range of imagery and information' must surely mean more than just opinions, whether informed or ill-informed, and the availability of information. The contextualisation of that information is important, as is its availability at points in time which matter. There needs to be a shift of attention, then, from re-designing the structures of communication to re-thinking the nature of information within present-day society, and its processing by mediators. One good illustration of the reasons for this comes from comments made by Porter and Hasselbach in connection with the 'open channels'. Following some statements about the channels' lack of success, they go on to observe that open television cable channels at least could contribute more to political pluralism if they were employed for the live transmission of parliamentary debates by the public stations' (Porter and Hasselbach 1991, p. 104).

Yet what may seem superficially attractive actually offers little of value apart from the opportunity to observe the spectacle of debate. Decision-making processes, in and outside government, are rarely public. On a different level, even if we were made aware of certain events, we might not be fully conversant with their causes or consequences. Thus, *in itself, the availability of a range of opinions and access to information in whatever form is only a small step in the ascent to making sense of events.* The 'public interest' is not upheld simply by making both available, important though that is. As important is when and how that information is made available and the contextualisation of that information.

It is critical to distinguish between the position outlined here, and amplified below, and the more generally accepted one which berates the mass media for providing mainly 'partial and coherently weighted accounts of many areas of social and political life' (Golding 1990, p. 85). Although there are some obvious points of similarity, I wish to go beyond the argument that the media fail to give 'impartial' accounts in order to argue that in many instances there can be no such things as impartial accounts: that the incomplete records of events offered by the media are the end result of both journalistic failures (and sometimes successes) and of the availability of information which is too complex and too contradictory to be easily manipulated to provide coherent accounts of the real world.

The following examples are drawn from a study of press coverage of the takeover of the Rover car group by British Aerospace in 1988[2]. These examples relate not only to the issue of processes highlighted at the beginning of this chapter, but also to the question of access to information generally. The details of the affair are not very important. What is important is that the takeover was surrounded by numerous parliamentary select committee hearings, much press comment and also a good supply of rumour and research.

One, of many, select committee hearings took place in January 1990. In front of the MPs was Lord Young, the Secretary of State for Trade and Industry who had agreed to the takeover in 1988. The session probably lasted some two hours; about one hour of that session was televised live on BBC2's *Westminster Live*, an afternoon programme about parliament and its work. Assuming the viewer stayed to watch all the live coverage, what would he/she have made of it? The question-and-answer format, the bickering over words and phrases, the continual references to different characters, events, and dates would have probably puzzled most viewers. There was no context for the viewer and no easy way to make 'sense' of the evidence in more than a superficial way. Open access on television, although laudable, is therefore of limited value.

The print medium may offer a better alternative because of its different properties and the ability to cross-check endlessly, not only within one document but also across documents. As it happens, the published minutes of evidence of this particular hearing ran to some twenty-four pages, with two columns to the page, excluding appendices. The *Westminster Live* programme carried the equivalent of thirteen pages. The main BBC1 *Nine O'Clock News* used verbatim just nineteen lines drawn from one column. Not surprisingly, the broadsheet newspapers, on the whole, did better than the television news both in the length of their stories and also in the range of issues drawn from this hearing.

Although the performance of the press was marginally better in this instance, and overall, since they provided more, and more continuous, coverage of the affair, the performance of the journalists was less than satisfactory. First, journalists failed to detect that the government had agreed to a deferment of payment for the car group which was worth some £22 million to British Aerospace. They only found out through documents leaked to newspapers – although the information was in the public domain, albeit in fairly 'obscure' Parliamentary documents[3].

Second, the press in 1988 perceived the Rover car group as intrinsically weak and burdened with an historical record of losses and a lack of credibility as a car manufacturer. Few, if any, were able to detect, and therefore comment upon, the fundamental shifts that had been taking place within the car group over the previous two years. Without this background information, it is little wonder that so many were surprised at the prospect of a takeover; after all, who would want to buy a failing company? Had there been a better understanding of the company, such a sombre diagnosis would have been out of place. In fact, no journalist was particularly sure why the deal was taking place, and what BAe would contribute to the Rover group, or vice versa.

From these criticisms of the performance of journalists, it is possible to argue that the press failed to pursue certain lines of enquiry, and to explore certain sources of public information, which would have enabled them to write quite different stories. And a considerable amount of that information, and this is one of the points I wish to stress, was already in the public domain: even the fact that payment had been deferred could have been picked up long before it was 'leaked'. The fact that it did not surface is due to journalistic practices and a dependence on certain types of sources and events.

I noted earlier on that this affair has been punctuated with select committee hearings, and these provide a rich seam of detail both as background and as a source of explanation of actions. The first four such publications in 1988, for example, run to fifty-seven pages, with two-columns of text per page. But by the time each of these emerged in our broadsheet newspapers, they were reduced to a few hundred words. Incidentally, one select committee session seems to have been completely ignored. As one of the *Guardian*'s respected political columnists, Hugo Young, recently wrote,

> ... the media are deplorably bad at using the cornucopia of official information which is already available. ... Newspapers and television often neglect, or never bother to find out about, the tedious details often tediously available in unglamorous government publications (Young 1992, p. 18)[4].

One can argue that there is nothing unusual here. And indeed there is not. Journalists covered 'what was happening' in ways which highlighted what they thought were the key points. And, as always, there can be disagreement about what the key points were. However, I wish to argue that it may be too simplistic to assume that there are such things as key points and that they are transparent. The contextualisation of the story is a much more difficult task than at first appears and sometimes there are no simple structures to make complicated stories meaningful. How are we to judge whether the takeover deal was good or bad, a good decision or a bad one? How are we to judge Lord Young's actions? Did he or did he not save the British car industry? There are no definitive answers. There are too many imponderables and unknowns; too much information to sift through, and too many contradictory opinions. To pretend that there are not, caricatures both political and business life.

Thus the attempt to write a 'good story' may be contrary to writing a piece of investigative and thoughtful journalism. Where the former puts forward seeming certainties, the latter emphasises the complexity of the social world; where the former is after immediate impact, the latter contributes to knowledge.

But there is another point here which merits further consideration. The account of the BAe-Rover deal which appeared in the broadsheets and on television in 1988 and in most of 1989 gave no more than a surface impression of what was 'really going on'. There was little comment about the relationship between the companies and the City of London, and the former's efforts to massage the latter; there was little about the negotiations taking place; or the nature of other suitors. In other words, there is much more to events than can perhaps ever be described in our media: partly because of the nature of the media, but partly because there is much which takes place in private and behind closed doors. It may never be possible to overcome the latter difficulty; its consequences, however, are abundantly clear and suggest that the media will always provide less than they ought to do.

Let me turn, very briefly, to one final example of the difficulties I am describing. In April 1990, HM Customs stopped a shipment of steel tubes from the UK to Iraq. It was eventually decided that these were part of a consignment of tubing which, when assembled, would form the so-called 'supergun'. Following this intervention by HM Customs, a parliamentary select committee sat and looked at the whole question of how this export deal could have been permitted in the first place.

The committee took a considerable amount of evidence – over 500 pages of double column text – in a period of a year or so. Some was reported, some was not. What was and was not reported seems an obvious candidate for analysis, and the keen researcher will soon discover some oddities. One select committee hearing was reported by three broadsheets under the following headlines (16 January 1992): 'Britain and US aware of parts' uses, MPs told' (*The Financial Times*);

'Britain "knew of Mossad supergun killing" ' (*The Times*); 'Mossad accused of murdering Iraqi supergun inventor' (the *Guardian*). A detailed analysis of these three stories would show major differences in the issues covered, yet the correspondents were covering the same event. As worrying as they may seem, these oddities are not as problematic as the more serious question, namely, why had we not been aware of this matter before April 1990? There is circumstantial evidence to show that even in mid–1988 there were concerns about the contract to forge the tubes. Certainly, by 1989 enough evidence was there to signal that something was awry (Norton-Taylor and Pallister 1992).

Why nothing happened cannot easily be explained, partly because the security services were involved in some unknown way. Nevertheless, and this is my general point, the BAe-Rover deal, the 'supergun' affair, the BCCI scandal, and the Maxwell collapse seem to me no more than clear examples of the extent to which business and political life goes on behind closed doors undisturbed by much media interest. It is only when something goes wrong that they surface. My concern is not so much with what happens when they surface, but with the media's inability or unwillingness to go beyond the public face of events. Tom Bower, a well-known journalist, put it like this:

> *The final product [of investigative journalism] is often complicated to read, unentertaining and inconclusive.* No major City slicker has ever been brought down merely by newspaper articles . . . *Financial journalists need the crash before they can detect and report upon real defects* (Bower 1991, p. 23; emphasis supplied).

Bower was writing with reference to the collapse of the Robert Maxwell empire, although the same points could be made in relation to the other examples given above.

The consequences of these journalistic shortcomings are significant because they leave gaps in the capacity of the media to meet their obligations *vis-à-vis* the public interest. The members of the public cannot have been well-served if their pension funds had been turned into someone else's 'Monopoly' money; or if their savings had disappeared; or their husbands imprisoned because they were innocently transporting metal tubes. In these three cases, there was prior information which could have been used to signal danger. And none of these failings or shortcomings can be redressed simply through structural change; a more fundamental change in journalism, and the media, as well as the public's perception of what is in its own interest is needed.

CONCLUSION

The arguments put forward in this chapter are not intended to apportion blame and responsibility for failings in complex communications structures. The intention is to highlight the way structural changes in communications systems have gradually reduced the space for meaningful localised forms of communication: the competitive regime currently being established across many parts of the world will make it increasingly difficult for certain structures of broadcasting and types of broadcasting content to survive. The prognosis for local community services is not good. Stretched for resources, if there are any, dependent on voluntary help, geared to the local and the parochial, it seeks to survive in an unfriendly environment. Can they compete with CNN, MTV, *Sky News*? The fear expressed by many is that those forms which supposedly meet, and are meant to satisfy, the public interest will be purposefully overlooked.

In these circumstances, structural reforms may be of some value. Regulatory arrangements can force broadcasters to undertake that which they would have otherwise left alone; similarly, regulatory arrangements can create spaces for alternative voices, different ownership structures, and new services. What regulatory changes perhaps cannot do is impact on the performance of the journalist, or alter journalistic practice – practices which, as we have seen, do not always satisfy the 'public interest'.

Many of the themes and ideas presented here have been discussed elsewhere in a number of different ways and in different contexts. What I think this chapter shows is how little discussions about the media have progressed over the last twenty years; how far we might have regressed in the face of commercialism; and how the availability of increasing amounts of information in a variety of public settings has not contributed to the 'public interest'. Those who mediate information are themselves caught in a web of competitive media – seeking, in Bower's phrase, 'the crash before they can detect and report upon real defects.'

NOTES

1   It is worth recalling Philip Elliot's work here. In 1972 he set out a typology of mass communication which clearly identified the limited nature of access to regional or national televisions. One of his key points was that the 'access of society as source' was limited to certain forms of television. Control over content rested, in the main, in the hands of the professional communicator (Elliot 1972, p. 155).

2 The study was financed by the Nuffield Foundation. I am grateful for their financial assistance.

3 These were the *Supply Estimates 1988–89, Revised Summer Supplementary Estimate*, Session 1987–88 HC 605, HMSO 1988; *Supply Estimate 1989–90*, Session 1988–89, HC 231 – v, HMSO March 1989.

There is also an interesting parallel here with a recent attempt to re-explore the events of the Watergate scandal. Michael Schudson (1992), reviewing Jay Epstein's work, had pointed out that a considerable number of agencies contributed to uncovering the affair; agencies which, according to Epstein, were 'systematically ignored or minimized by Bernstein and Woodward'. Schudson adds one other point which resonates with mine: 'the journalistic contribution itself was dependent on government officials who risked their jobs or their careers by leaking to the press'.

4 Two researchers from the London Business School have also recently pointed out that 'Parliamentary select committees (and the media) have failed to examine the expenditure white papers and annual reports issued by Whitehall departments' (Likierman and Taylor 1992, quoted in *The Financial Times* 21 August 1992).

5

Understanding 'terrorism': contrasting audience interpretations of the televised conflict in Ireland

DAVID MILLER

It has long been assumed by the powerful that there is a relationship between the media and public belief. Unsurprisingly, this interest has been inextricably bound up with concerns about managing public consciousness. These assumptions are so ingrained that they are often given as evidence for the need for tighter control of broadcasting or other media. Thus British Home Secretary Douglas Hurd prohibited British television and radio stations from broadcasting the direct statements of eleven Irish organisations including Sinn Féin, a legal political party, and the Ulster Defence Association then, but not now, a legal paramilitary group. Hurd claimed that Sinn Fein and the Irish Republican Army gained an 'easy platform' from television appearances which allowed them to 'propagate terrorism' (*Hansard*, 19 October 1988, Col. 893) and that such appearances caused 'offence'. But the broadcasters had received very few complaints about interviews with any of the organisations in the year prior to the ban (Henderson *et al.*, 1990), leading to some speculation that the offence was that taken by civil servants and politicians[1].

It is unsurprising that the conflict in the north eastern six counties of Ireland should trigger the imposition of direct broadcast censorship in Britain. Disputes about the coverage of Northern Ireland have been at the centre of the changing relationship between the British state and the media for the past twenty years (Curtis 1984; Murdock 1991; Schlesinger 1987; Schlesinger 1991; Schlesinger *et al.* 1983). But Northern Ireland is not the only arena for contest between the media and the state. The Home Secretary was echoing Mrs Thatcher's well-known contention that the media supply 'terrorists' with the 'oxygen of publicity', a statement made in reference not to Irish 'terrorists', but to those who hijacked a TWA plane in Beirut in 1985. This followed an intense debate in the USA about the use of the media by the hijackers.

In fact such debates are widespread in liberal democratic states. The media are often attacked for 'irresponsible' or sensational portrayals of a wide variety of social phenomena ranging from accidents, disasters, football hooliganism, sexual violence and other crime, to family and marital breakdown, and even the latest misdemeanours of the royal family. Often debate focuses on the role of the media in creating or exacerbating such 'social problems'. These debates are a touchstone of much political discourse and they fit into a wider concern about the effects of images of violence in encouraging acts of violence, or fear of acceptance of such acts[2]. These, in turn, are all prominent concerns of the debate around the coverage of political violence, where there is a preoccupation with the promotion of 'terrorism' by the media[3]. However, debate is often confused by muddled and contradictory assumptions about the idea of media power.

Amongst the most common of these is that media institutions are powerful in themselves and operate autonomously from, and in opposition to, the powerful – particularly the government. In some variants the media have the power to act irresponsibly in relation to breaches of 'privacy' or in constructing negative images of marginalised sections of society. Alternatively the power of the media is closely identified with the power of the state. In this model 'official sources' supply the themes and issues with which, in turn, the media work. In some cases the media are seen simply as instruments of the state.

In both models there is an additional assumption that the media have a direct and harmful 'effect' on their audiences. This assumption is so heavily embedded in political discourse that it is often not thought necessary to investigate audience responses to see whether the media are as powerful as they are imagined to be.

By contrast the confusion over media power is echoed in some recent reception analysis which has been concerned with demonstrating audience 'activity'. Texts are seen as having no fixed meanings and audiences may (to some extent at least) pick and choose the meanings they take from a given message. Whereas critics of the power of the media tend only to refer to media messages without any examination of reception, so some reception analysts seem to regard the analysis of texts as indicating an attachment to 'naive' notions of media power (Corner 1991c, p. 281).

These contrasting approaches have been one reason for the lack of empirical research that analyses media texts together with their interpretation by audiences[4]. Such an approach is, as Corner notes, 'the most important thing for audience research to focus on' (1991c, p. 275). This chapter examines the relationship between television coverage and understanding and belief. It looks, first, at the range of television representations of the Northern Ireland conflict and then at their interpretation. One added dimension is that it compares the understandings of a single issue as it is mediated by different national media systems (those of the US and Britain). It allows an exploration of the links between texts and audiences and examines the interpretative limits which texts may, in practice, impose on understanding and belief. For, as Corner and his colleagues (1990, p. 108) put it: 'Taking the power of television seriously is as important as recognising the considerable extent to which it falls well short of being omnipotent'.

I will suggest that there are key parallels between the content of US television coverage of the conflict in Ireland and the beliefs of at least some American people. Much research has drawn attention to socio-demographic variations in the way people understand and interpret television; however, my focus here is on differences in *national* interpretations. I will perhaps, therefore, overstate differences between nations and understate the diverse understandings within them[5]. Nevertheless, in my research there were clear national differences of interpretation and understanding to which it seems worth drawing attention.

SAMPLE AND METHOD

This discussion is based, first, on an analysis of US and British network television coverage of the events of March 1988[6] and, secondly, on audience research conducted between 1988 and 1990. The events of March 1988 were extensively covered by both US and British television.

The audience research is based on discussions conducted with pre-existing groups of people who work, live or socialise together, chosen to reflect different socio-demographic factors such as age, region, nationality, class and gender[7]. They were asked to write a news story about Northern Ireland using a set of photographic stills taken from actual news bulletins, representing different aspects of routine coverage of Northern Ireland: pictures of Ian Paisley, Democratic Unionist Party MP; Gerry Adams (then) Sinn Féin MP; British Prime Minister, Margaret Thatcher; Labour Party leader, Neil Kinnock; a British Army spokesperson; an 'Orange (Protestant) Walk'; a crowd scene; a helicopter; a fire; a shot of RUC personnel; a march preceded by British Army personnel carriers; a 'riot scene'; a Republican funeral procession; and a scene of folk music being played in a pub.

Following the writing and presentation of the news bulletins the groups were asked a series of questions about their beliefs about television and about perceptions of violence in Northern Ireland. I conducted discussions with over 200 people who lived in England, Scotland and Northern Ireland as well as with a total of fifty-four American students in three groups. Most of the American students had been in Britain for around a month, while the remainder had arrived within the previous six months. The evidence presented here draws mainly on general perceptions of the conflict.

Television coverage of the conflict in Ireland

Analyses of media coverage of Northern Ireland (whether focusing on British or North American media) have tended to characterise the coverage of Northern Ireland in similar ways. Television news (and the press) concentrates on violence at the expense of background contextualisation, is dominated by official sources, and tends to delegitimate the insurgents and promote official views of the conflict (Elliot 1977; Curtis 1984; Holland 1989; Paletz *et al.* 1982; Knight and Dean 1982). According to some commentators there is increased, though still limited, space to contest official views in non-news actuality coverage on British (Schlesinger *et al.* 1983) and US television (Altheide 1987). However, parallel analysis of the output of one national media system may not be sensitive to some of the divergences observable between media systems.

A cursory glance at European or North American newspapers reveals coverage of the conflict in Northern Ireland which is markedly different from that found in Britain. British mainstream news programmes tend to be relatively closed around the official perspective. 'Terrorism' is the ubiquitous description of the activities of the Irish Republican Army. Outside Britain other, more legitimating, descriptions start to appear. However, as we shall see, this doesn't mean that US coverage tends to favour the 'terrorists'.

Let us consider a few examples from the coverage of the events of March 1988[8]. First, the question of the language used to describe the insurgents. Figure 5.1 compares the language used to describe the IRA or other republican paramilitaries on British and US network news. On US television the IRA more commonly has 'members' or 'leaders' who are occasionally 'activists' and 'guerrillas'. The latter term is highly significant, because it is almost non-existent on British television news (or indeed in the British press)[9].

As we can see from figure 5.1, 'terrorists' is the preferred language on British television. Indeed internal BBC guidelines, published for the first time in 1989, give detailed instructions on the acceptable language for reporting Northern Ireland: 'Members of illegal organisations who bomb and shoot civilians are unquestionably terrorists' (BBC 1989, p. 39.9). US television news coverage of Northern Ireland uses 'terrorist' occasionally – although there is some variation between news organisations.

US TV		British TV	
IRA	26	IRA	41
members	12	terrorists	17
Irish Republican Army	3	bombers	9
guerrillas	3	members	8
activists	2	gang	4
leaders	2	group	4
sniper	2	unit	4
terrorists	2	provo(s)	4
suspected terrorists	2	squad	3
gunman/men	2	what it (the IRA) called/so called	
Fallen Warrior	1	Active service Unit	2
		paramilitary/ies	2
		IRA Commando Unit	1
		Republicans	1
		volunteers	1

Sample: all US evening network news coverage of the events of March 1988 and the reporting of the main evening British network news bulletins (BBC1, *Nine O'Clock News* and *ITN's News at Ten*), as well as ITN's *Channel Four News*, on March 7, 16 and 19.

Figure 5.1 Descriptions of Republicans in US and British TV news March 1988

There was some differentiation too on British television, with the BBC tending to be more restrictive than ITN. BBC guidelines state that journalists should:

Avoid anything which would glamorise the terrorist, or give an impression of legitimacy. In particular, try not to use terms by which terrorist groups try to portray themselves as legitimate – terms like 'execute', 'court-martial', 'brigade', 'active service unit' (BBC 1989, p. 80).

The use of a term like 'Active Service Unit' is allowable on BBC news only if it is attributed. Journalists often make it clear just how legitimate they think such labels are, as in references to a 'so-called Active Service Unit'. For the BBC there is also an issue about using terms such as 'Provos' or IRA 'volunteers'. In the above sample the former was used four times and the latter once, all of which were on ITN. BBC news guidelines explicitly state that journalists should '*never*' (their emphasis) use the term 'Provos' because 'we should not give pet names to terrorists' (BBC 1989 p. 39.4). Similarly BBC journalists are advised not to give the IRA 'spurious respectability' by speaking of IRA 'volunteers' because 'we don't know why they joined' (BBC 1989 p. 39.9). The BBC World Service has a more open editorial policy which, partly because of its different audience, eschews the term 'terrorist'. However, its style guide cautions that only the acronym will do when referring to the IRA. 'The IRA is always the IRA – Irish Republican Army is misleading' (Brown 1988 p. 33). The thought that the IRA might be referred to as an 'army' is beyond the limits of objectivity of even the World Service. As we can see from figure 5.1, this practice is not followed on US television.

The use of less pejorative terms such as 'guerrilla' is only part of the story. In the (British) official perspective the IRA are a criminal conspiracy, without political motivation. Their campaign is simply one of terrorism. While there is some room in British broadcasting to contest this proposition, most notably in documentaries and some fictional output, television news remains relatively closed. However even in the most closed formats of television network news in the US there is a good deal more space to contest key propositions of the official (British) perspective. Nevertheless US television is not an uncomplicated ally of the IRA. Indeed US television reports in March 1988 tended to accept one key official proposition about the conflict in Northern Ireland. While the IRA could be seen as a political actor in the conflict, the (occasionally misguided or mistaken) British government is seen as somehow 'above' it. Characterisations of the conflict in March 1988 tended to leave the role of the British out of the reckoning. Journalists talked of 'the conflict between Catholics and Protestants in Northern Ireland' (NBC, 16 March 1988), or 'a further escalation of violence between the two communities' (NBC, 19 March 1988), or of the IRA's 'war against the Protestants of the North' (ABC, 23 March 1988). As Ward concluded in his analysis of US network television news coverage of Northern Ireland between 1968 and 1979, the major element missing was an examination of the role of the British government. 'The rationale for the British presence had been discussed in 1969 and was never subsequently contradicted or examined in depth' (Ward 1984, p. 210).

NON-NEWS ACTUALITY COVERAGE

In Britain, news coverage of the events of March 1988 was not the only source of television information for viewers. A number of current affairs and documentary programmes covered the killings in Gibraltar and their aftermath. The most critical of these – and the one which caused the most controversy – was an edition of Thames Television's *This Week*, entitled 'Death on the Rock', which investigated the killings in Gibraltar and suggested that government accounts of the shootings had, at best, been misleading. In the US, the killings and their aftermath led to the making of a special documentary for the PBS public television network on the life of Mairead Farrell, one of the IRA members killed in Gibraltar.

It has been suggested that documentaries are amongst the most potentially open of programme formats in both the US and Britain (Schlesinger *et al.* 1983; Altheide 1987). It is instructive to compare these two programmes and the reactions to them, as they illustrate the limits of openness in factual television in Britain and the US. The account given by 'Death on the Rock' directly contradicted the official version, which was based on a statement by British Foreign Secretary Geoffrey Howe, and developed in unattributable briefings to papers such as *The Sunday Times*. Howe claimed that the IRA personnel had been

> . . . challenged by the security forces. When challenged they made movements which led the military personnel . . . to conclude that their own lives and the lives of others were under threat. In the light of this response, they were shot. Those killed were subsequently found not to have been carrying arms (*Hansard*, 7 March 1988, col. 21).

However, eye-witnesses interviewed for 'Death on the Rock' alleged that there had been no challenge and that the IRA members had made no movements, simply putting their hands up as if in surrender. Their testimony raised the possibility that the killings were extra-judicial executions[10]. Essentially the programme challenged the factual accuracy of the official account, *implying* rather than actually *elaborating* an alternative way of understanding the conflict. The latter approach is very difficult in prime time British broadcasting.

The 'Death on the Rock' programme makers themselves were very much aware of the limits of covering Northern Ireland. They were conscious that in order to get their programme on to television they would have to include sequences which showed that they were no supporters of 'terrorism'[11]. Indeed the editor, Roger Bolton, who has a long history of involvement in critical programmes on Ireland, made a special request that the programme slot be extended partly so that this material, which 'underlined the hostile editorial stance of the programme towards the IRA and its methods', could be accommodated (Windlesham and Rampton 1989, pp. 22–4). Bolton, (1990, p. 224) has described this insurance policy as putting the investigation 'in context'. The Chairman of the IBA, Lord Thomson, was to write later that he saw no reason to prevent the broadcast of the programme '*provided* the criminal record of the terrorists and the enormity of the outrage they planned was made clear' (cited in Bolton 1990, p. 232, my emphasis). Such precautions are not required in the US.

In America the networks are able to show documentary programmes which simply could not be shown in Britain. In 1980, for example, ABC broadcast a documentary entitled 'To Die for Ireland' in a peak-time slot. According to press reports British diplomats even complained that it was being shown in America (Glasgow University Media Group 1982, pp. 140–3)[12]. The 1989 PBS film on the life of Mairead Farrell – 'Death of a Terrorist' – (Cran 1989) was structured as an investigation into the reasons why a middle-class Catholic girl from Belfast would join the IRA (at the age of fourteen) and take up arms against the British military. The director, Bill Cran, was keen to show some of the complexities of political violence and organised the film in opposing sections, allowing Farrell and her family and comrades to present her as an ordinary person and determined, but rational, activist. Against this were counter-views which emphasised the official view of the conflict and the suffering caused by IRA actions. The film featured extensive interviews with Farrell, conducted following her release from jail in 1986, as well as with former cell-mates and other members of the republican movement. By comparison 'Death on the Rock' did not feature any interviews with either Sinn Féin or the IRA[13]. In sum, the US programme was able to interrogate critically the official picture of Northern Ireland and to show that it is not universally shared. The programme concluded by emphasising the contested nature of definitions of 'terrorism' and leaving the viewer to decide which version they favoured. 'To some people of the Falls Road she [Mairead Farrell] was a patriot. To the British she was a terrorist. To her family she was a victim of Irish history.' 'Death of a Terrorist' was much more open to alternative discourse than 'Death on the Rock'. The controversy caused by 'Death on the Rock' compared with the lack of controversy over 'Death of a Terrorist' is indicative of just how close to the limits of British broadcasting the former pushed and how different those limits are in the US.

In Britain the broadcast of *This Week's* 'Death on the Rock' was pre-empted by an attempt by the Foreign Secretary to have the programme withdrawn. His request to the Independent Broadcasting Authority (IBA) was rejected and 'Death on the Rock' was broadcast as planned. There followed a concerted government attempt to cast (unattributable) doubt on the credibility of the witnesses interviewed and government ministers, including Prime Minister Margaret Thatcher, publicly attacked the programme (see Miller 1991). Finally, after a long-running campaign by the government supported especially by the Murdoch-owned papers *The Sun* and *The Sunday Times*, Thames Television were pressured into instituting an independent inquiry into the programme (see Windlesham and Rampton 1989). In the US the PBS documentary 'Death of a Terrorist' was not subject to similar pressures.

There are clear differences between US and British actuality coverage of Northern Ireland. There are a greater range of perspectives available and the centre of gravity has shifted so that official nostrums can more easily be routinely questioned. The contrast between the controversy caused by 'Death on the Rock' and the lack of response to 'Death of a Terrorist' seems not to relate to the difference in content of the programmes, but to factors such as the policing of the media and the political closeness of the conflict in Ireland to the British state[14].

The frontline for alternative perspectives on the Gibraltar killings in Britain was the raising of questions about the legitimacy of state actions, measured against the standards of democratic government and the rule of law. In America, television was able to go further and consider the reasons why an Irish woman might take up arms against the British state. In other words, questions could be asked about whether the actions of the Irish Republican Army could be seen as legitimate. It is to the implications of these different limits for audience understandings that we now turn.

Understanding Northern Ireland

Much contemporary audience research emphasises the 'active audience' – the ability of each of us to interpret what we see. For some this has meant stressing the 'creation' of meaning by media audiences. This ability is sometimes seen as an almost unlimited potential to 'read' any meanings at will from a given programme or article. But as Corner has pointed out, such studies have a tendency to work with slippery concepts of meaning:

> The investigation of meaning in reception studies needs to differentiate analytically between 'understanding' and 'response', however interfused these may be in practice. For it is of course entirely possible for viewers to agree as to how to understand an item but to disagree in their responses to it (Corner *et al.*, 1990 p. 50)[15].

Responses are not randomly made. The interpretation of media messages is influenced by what people 'bring to' a given text. Their prior knowledge, commitments, involvement with the topic under discussion, and political culture set the context for understanding and belief. There is now a considerable body of research which demonstrates the links between such factors and interpretations of the media. But we also need to be aware of what people 'take away' from the media[16]. Texts are not infinitely 'open'. What needs to be examined is the way in which the organisation of texts both 'constrains and facilitates audience activity' (Murdock 1989 p. 237).

In the examples which follow I want to look at differences between US and British understandings of the conflict in Ireland and the role of the respective media systems in contributing to such perspectives. I will concentrate mainly on the US groups, with some comparative references to British groups. Finally, I will make some comments about how several of the Americans I interviewed had come to question some of their ideas about the conflict in Ireland since arriving in Britain. This is important because it shows that the ongoing process of judgement is partly related to the perceived quality of empirical evidence available (*cf.* Curran 1990).

The number and range of groups in this study were not sufficient to 'represent' the whole populations of Britain and Northern Ireland, far less the United States of America. Nevertheless, there were some clear differences in political culture and personal experience which seemed to influence how people interpreted the news and how they understood the conflict in Northern Ireland.

WRITING THE NEWS

Although there was a considerable diversity amongst British groups in their understandings of the conflict there were notable differences between news bulletins produced by the British and US groups. The news bulletins produced by the US groups tended to reflect the assumptions of reporting on US television in three ways. First the language and secondly the themes were very similar to US news. Additionally, some of the groups 'mistakenly' interpreted one particular photograph in a way which reflected the logic of US coverage. These three factors indicate a clear familiarity with US television news coverage. In the third case it seems plausible to argue that the mistaken interpretation reflected both their familiarity with US news and their assumptions about the conflict. We ought to be clear however that there is a distinction between beliefs about news programmes and beliefs about the real world.

1. *Language* As with US television, the term 'terrorism' was less common than other ways of describing the IRA. In the bulletins produced by the US students, words like 'leader' or 'member' were used to describe IRA personnel and the IRA itself was referred to as an army. The term 'freedom fighters' was used once, and on some bulletins 'Irish Republican Army' was spelt out in preference to the acronym IRA. As we have seen, even an apparently minor detail like this is the subject of close policing in British broadcasting, but not in the US. This contrasts quite markedly with many of the British groups involved with the research, where there was a distinct lack of alternatives to 'terrorism' in news bulletins.

2. *News themes and structure of understanding* Most of the US groups wrote stories which were dominated by violence. Over ninety per cent of all (US, British and Irish) respondents thought that news coverage showed Northern Ireland as mostly violent, although some of the US respondents believed that US television news showed even more violence than the British news they had seen. The US groups were familiar with foreign news reports about events in Northern Ireland and some reproduced what they saw as routine reports characterising the seemingly endless nature of the conflict. The headline of one 'CNN' report stated 'Four are dead as the violence continues in Northern Ireland'. The report described Northern Ireland as an 'age-old conflict', and concluded that 'No end to the Northern Ireland Conflict is in sight' (Penn. State students, 14 February 1989).

It is relatively easy to find examples of similar newscasts from the actual news. In March 1988 an NBC report on the Israeli-occupied West Bank is followed by this comment from the newscaster: 'Another war without end in Northern Ireland also claimed another life today'. The newscaster then went on to introduce a report from Belfast as follows: 'some people on both sides are horrified by this continuing bloodshed, but nobody expects it to stop' (NBC *Nightly News*, 21 March 1988).

As well as the preoccupation with violence, a number of US groups reproduced news accounts which embodied some of the same assumptions about Northern Ireland as US news reporting. The conflict tended to be seen in political terms rather than as a matter of law and order. Some news accounts emphasised religious aspects of the conflict, leaving the role of the British out of the picture. One bulletin concluded with this characterisation of the conflict: 'There seems to be no easy end to the conflict, between the Protestants and Catholics, plus no end to the highly publicised political warfare' (Penn. State students, 13 February 1990). Similarly, another group had structured their bulletin according to these assumptions seeing the role of the British as peace-keepers:

> Seven people died today when a terrorist bomb exploded in Belfast. The bomb, believed to be set by the IRA, exploded in a local pub, during [an orange] parade. Tensions had been building between the IRA and loyalists for months and climaxed with the explosion today. Troops were sent in by the Royal Airforce to prevent further outbreaks. [An army spokesperson] said that the troops have been doing their best to restore order in the area.

The tensions are seen as arising between the IRA and loyalists and the army intervenes to 'restore order'.

However, in other accounts the IRA and the British army were described as opposing military forces and it was 'innocent civilians', rather than the British army, who were caught in the middle. After describing a British army raid and a retaliatory bombing of a pub by the IRA, the report continued as follows:

> at dawn this morning the townspeople gathered at the ruins to express their sadness. Ethel O'Brien said she was upset with both the IRA and British soldiers because the conflict creates undue chaos in innocent lives. 'We just want our lives to [get back] to normality', O'Brien said . . . (Penn. State students, 1989).

Here the British are active participants in the conflict rather than peace-keepers.

3. *Interpreting photographs* The use of the photographs by the groups illustrated some of the ways in which the US groups were less familiar with various details of Northern Irish politics than their British counterparts. Photographs of Ian Paisley, Democratic Unionist Party MP, and of Gerry Adams (then) Sinn Féin MP, were often not identified. On other occasions groups used terminology inappropriately, as when one group wrote of 'Royal Air Force' troops being sent to deal with a riot. Another group described a bomb exploding in a pub in Northern Ireland known to be frequented by the 'ruling party' – a mistaken assumption about the system of government in Northern Ireland. But while the *details* were occasionally shaky or forgotten, the groups also had quite complex *understandings* of the conflict.

We can illustrate this by looking at one detail which was 'mistaken' consistently in six out of ten groups. This was in their interpretation of the picture of a member of the British army dressed in camouflage uniform and beret (Figure 5.2). These groups of American students used the photograph to represent a member of the IRA and it was held up as they read out passages of news. For example: 'The IRA held a memorial service today for its revolutionary leader, Ian McDougal, and members of his army'. This was a quite unexpected interpretation.

Figure 5.2

It emerged that they had used the photograph in this way because of their conception of the IRA as a sub-state military force. Members of such an organisation, they reasoned, would wear uniforms. Two further groups of Americans were at first unsure of the affiliation of the soldier. After some discussion they decided he was a member of the British army. In this instance it was the badge pinned to the soldier's beret, allied to the fact that one of the group had some specialist knowledge from being in the US army that clinched his identity.

This consistent mistake was very interesting since it showed a level of unfamiliarity with the iconographical detail of the conflict (which seemed to be connected to the lack of time they had spent in Britain) at the same time as indicating a quite different understanding of the conflict to that portrayed on British news. By contrast not a single British group made the same 'error'. Within nationalist or republican groups in Northern Ireland there were quite strong critiques of the official perspective, but none of those groups used the picture of the British soldier to illustrate a member of the IRA even though many of them regarded the IRA as a legitimate expression of resistance to British rule.

The source of this 'mistake' appeared to have been the US media, which most of the US groups gave as their source of information about Northern Ireland prior to arriving in Britain. But this did not mean that they believed everything they saw on television news. People do not inhabit sealed ideological bubbles which prevent them from negotiating with representations of the real world. Apparent contradictions between television and other evidence are routinely evaluated and judgements made on the basis of the credibility of the source or the perceived weight of the empirical evidence. Such judgements allowed some of the US participants to believe that television coverage of the conflict in Northern Ireland was in some respects inadequate.

BELIEF AND OPINION

1. Violence
All respondents said they had seen very little other than violence on television news. As one put it 'TV shows Northern Ireland to be a war zone sort of like Lebanon'. Around twenty per cent of the US students believed, at the time of the discussion group, that this was a true representation[17]. One described his view of Belfast: 'There's secure areas where – except for one or two incidents in the past ten years – nothing's happened. But the rest is just a war zone – you can be shot at any

second'. Of the eighteen respondents who listed the media as their sole source of information, twelve believed that life in Northern Ireland was mostly violent.

But over half of the participants told me that their views about the level of violence in Northern Ireland had changed since coming to Britain (thirty-two out of fifty-four). None of them said that they now thought there was more violence than they had previously, and none had changed their minds as a result of watching British television. Of these thirty-two, six respondents rejected the notion that Northern Ireland was dominated by violence on account of a general critique of television or media sensationalism, or because they had experience of other areas of media reporting which they had found to be inaccurate or exaggerated. One respondent wrote that Northern Ireland is 'mostly peaceful, like anywhere there is fighting. Gang violence in LA, drug wars in DC, religious persecution in Belfast, it's not something you can see looking out your hotel window'. Such critiques were commonly given in addition to another source of information such as having spoken to other students who lived in, or had visited, Ireland (North or South).

This was the most common reason given for questioning the level of violence. This 'personal' evidence seemed to carry more weight than television coverage. As one student put it: 'Before I came here and met students from Northern Ireland, I wouldn't have gone there. Now, I'll probably be visiting in April'.

Evidence from Irish students or from people who had been to the North had made some of them question their ideas about Northern Ireland but they did not necessarily reject those ideas wholeheartedly. Of the thirty-six who said they had used non-media sources of information on the level of violence in Northern Ireland, only three continued to believe that life there was mostly violent. A further twelve were unsure about which evidence to believe, while the remaining twenty-one said they rejected the television account. These latter respondents accepted intellectually that Northern Ireland was not as violent as US television had implied, while at a deeper level they were still uncertain about the prevalence of violence and the personal risk a visit would entail. The credibility of such personal contacts tended to be higher than that of television news but the highest credibility source seemed to be the experience of actually visiting or travelling through Northern Ireland. The 'personal experience' of 'seeing for yourself' has a clear rhetorical power (cf. Kitzinger 1993). A visit to the Falls or Shankill Roads or to Belfast city centre can lend a certainty to a rejection of television accounts which simply speaking with someone who has visited

Belfast may not. For other respondents their critique of a 'violent' Northern Ireland was quite insecure. The clearest reason for this is media coverage of the conflict.

So, while the news bulletins written by these groups were dominated by violence, most of them rejected the news as a factual account of this aspect of the conflict. The experience of living in Britain for a few months, or more precisely the opportunity to meet other students from Northern Ireland, or to visit Northern Ireland themselves had influenced one particularly prevalent perception – although not always decisively so.

2. *Frameworks of understanding*

On the other hand the range of understandings present in US news, which were commonly reproduced in news bulletins were not rejected by most of the groups. For them the conflict *was* either a religious quarrel or a military conflict between the IRA and the British. One of the groups cited above appended their own comment at the end of their news bulletin: 'It is a shame that in this day and age the two groups cannot come together and overcome their differences' (Penn. State students, 14 February 1989). The two groups referred to here do not include the British government. One group of US students, however, did reject the version of events which they outlined in their news bulletin. They had written a bulletin in which soldiers had shot civilians in a riot situation. There is then an interview with a British officer who emphasises the casualties to his own personnel and one with Margaret Thatcher who says that the army 'response was necessary to prevent further violence and to protect the civilian population'. As the bulletin was read out one of the members of the group satirically mimed playing a violin when army casualties were mentioned, in order to indicate that the report was intended to evoke sympathy for the army and the government. This was the picture they saw British news painting of Northern Ireland. For them, news coverage of Northern Ireland was not objective and impartial. As two members of the group put it:

RESPONDENT 1: The news takes a government stance on the issue of Northern Ireland. They never say that it is instigated by British troops or by the British being there or anything like that. It's always the Northern Ireland people.
RESPONDENT 2: [The news makes out that the Army] were forced to fire.
RESPONDENT 1: Yeah, keeping the peace. It's not saying that they wanted to [fire], it's that 'we had no other option'. And it's trying to get sympathy for that.

RESPONDENT 2: It's to reinforce the fact that if the Army wasn't there they [IRA] would have hurt countless civilians and you can let your imagination run wild about what would happen if the British pulled out. (US students at Glasgow University, 12 March 1990).

In their view British news coverage fits in well with the propaganda warfare strategies of the British government. These two students had been in Britain for six months. One of them had been to Belfast and cited this as a reason for questioning the media account, saying that 'they make Northern Ireland out to be this violent cesspool when it's really a beautiful place which is no more dangerous than other places – unless you're in the military'. The other student also cited the experience of speaking to friends from Northern Ireland, but he had another very specific source of information which had influenced his understanding of the conflict before he had come to Britain: he had watched the US documentary 'Death of a Terrorist'. From his memory of the programme (shown nine months previously on the minority PBS channel) he had been able to construct an account of the Gibraltar shootings and had a strong impression of the central character in the documentary, Mairead Farrell. He commented: 'one woman in her 30s, I believe, was given a biography and previous interviews with her before the incident were shown. She was basically asked her views on her stance in N. Ireland. She seemed very reasonable and intelligent' (US students at Glasgow, 12 March 1990).

Much of the film of Farrell in 'Death of a Terrorist' came from unused footage shot for 'Mother Ireland', a documentary made by Derry Film and Video Workshop for Channel Four Television (Crilly 1988)[18]. The director, Anne Crilly, has speculated that the appearance of Mairead Farrell might tend to undermine popular images of irrational 'terrorists' in terms strikingly similar to those given by the US student cited above:

She wouldn't have fitted into the stereotype of the terrorist she was portrayed as in the British media. I think people would have seen an intelligent, articulate, attractive woman on their screens. It might have raised questions about their notions of what is a terrorist. It might have raised more questions about the manner in which she was killed. And it also probably would have made people think, 'What makes someone who looks like the girl next door, take up arms? She looks intelligent. She must have some rational reason for that' (*TV Choice* 1989, p. 7).

The US student's comments showed an interesting affinity with those of Crilly. However, it seems likely that not everyone who saw 'Death of a Terrorist' would have interpreted the film in this way[19].

CONCLUSIONS

The responses of both the US and British groups in this sample give a much more complex picture than that proposed by politicians or by some 'terrorism' theorists. Not even the relative openness of US television coverage tended to favour the 'terrorists'. Nor did the response of the US students to that message appear to be directly favourable to the cause of the IRA. There was little evidence to support the contention that television content or the audience response tended to provide the 'oxygen of publicity' to 'terrorists'. There are many factors which condition belief in addition to the influence of the media. As we saw, almost sixty per cent of the American respondents had altered or become uncertain about their perceptions of violence in Northern Ireland as a result of coming into contact with other sources of information which they preferred over the television account. This was not so obviously the case with their underlying conceptions of the conflict. The range of US coverage of Northern Ireland was quite similar to the range of US audience responses on some key issues. Both were distinguishable from British news coverage and British audience understandings.

Audience interpretations are complex and multi-faceted. It is possible, though, to agree in principle on the intentions of television programme makers and on the orientation of the result of their endeavours. Active ideological/cultural work goes into making television news programmes which, in turn, communicate particular messages. Television news is not unintelligible, nor are the ways in which it is understood a property of the random exercise of audience 'activity'. The option for most viewers is much closer to questions of judgement than it is to the 'creation' of meaning. Amongst the US, British, and Irish groups which took part in my research, there was a very high level of agreement about what television actually said about violence in Northern Ireland. When some people told me that they believed life in Northern Ireland was mostly peaceful, this was not because they believed that television had said this. On the contrary they had consciously rejected the 'meanings' promoted by television as being exaggerated or simply false (cf. Fiske 1989).

However, the research here does indicate that media information can have a strong impact on audience beliefs and can help to structure the way we look at political and social problems. This highlights the continuing importance of debates about access to and control of the media. The information fed into the system and the operation of the system itself do make a difference to public understanding and opinion.

This is clearly understood by Western governments. In their propaganda campaigns on the Gulf War, the state of the economy or the conflict in Northern Ireland, the British government depends to some extent on winning information battles in order to secure its own power as well as its alliances with others. This is why in 1989/90 the British government spent in excess of 20 million on public relations activities in relation to Northern Ireland (Miller 1993).

I am suggesting a move away from the central focus of much recent mass communication research. We ought to be interested in examining the media strategies of the powerful and the methods used by the less powerful to exploit their weaknesses. This needs to be done in combination with research on information processing inside media institutions and the production of accounts of the world by media personnel. Finally, we must indeed look at the understanding and interpretation of the media by audiences and more broadly at the role of the media in the operation of modern societies. But we should not leave debates about access to, and the control of, the media to politicians and the powerful.

NOTES

1 See Moloney (1991). This should serve to remind us that the study of audiences should not just be concerned with the impact of the media on 'public knowledge' and behaviour. Media reporting may also influence institutions and interest groups in ways which they perceive to harmful or helpful. This should also be part of the agenda of audience research (see Ericson 1989).

2 There is an extensive literature which deals with issues around the portrayal of violence (see Gunter 1987; Howitt and Cumberbatch 1989; Schlesinger *et al.* 1992).

3 Much of this debate draws on Laqueur's much-cited dictum that 'the media are of paramount importance in [terrorist] campaigns. . . . The terrorist act by itself is next to nothing, whereas publicity is all' (1978, p. 269). Such notions still suffuse much current work. For example, see some of the contributions to Alali and Eke, (1991); Alexander and Latter (1990); and Alexander and Picard (1991). See also the critiques in Paletz and Schmid (1992) and Crelinsten (1987).

4 McLeod *et al.* cite this as one of the weakness of much audience research (1991, p. 256).

5 Much of my reception research is concerned with variation in interpretation and understanding within a national territory, although the contested nature of the 'United Kingdom' was obviously of particular relevance (Miller, work in progress).

6 These include the shootings in Gibraltar of three members of the Irish Republican Army by the British army's Special Air Service; the loyalist attack on the funeral of the three IRA personnel at Milltown Cemetery in Belfast, which killed three mourners; and finally the killing of two British Army personnel who drove into the funeral cortége of one of those killed at Milltown.

7 See Kitzinger (1990; 1992) for a discussion and an evaluation of focus group methodology, and Hôijer (1990) for a critique of groupwork.

8   What follows is based on an analysis of all US evening network news coverage of the events of March 1988 and the reporting of the main evening British network news bulletins (BBC1's *Nine O'Clock News* and ITN's *News at Ten*). I have also included ITN's *Channel Four News* since, as a variety of commentators have noted (e.g. McNair 1988), it tends to be more open than the news on the other two channels. In the analysis of language used on the British news I have sampled the coverage of three key days during the month of March because of the sheer amount of coverage. The reporting on 7 March – the day after the shootings in Gibraltar; 16 March – the day of the attack at Milltown Cemetery; and 19 March – the day that the two British Army personnel were killed, is I feel representative enough to illustrate general trends in the reporting of Northern Ireland.

9   Taylor (1986) details the views of the editors of the national press and television news. Even liberal papers like the *Guardian* shun the term 'guerrilla'.

10   Such doubts about the official story were not laid to rest following the inquest on the killings in September 1988, which delivered a majority verdict of lawful killing. In the view of human rights and civil liberties organisations the inquest was an inadequate forum for examining whether the killings were extrajudicial executions and the question therefore remained open. See Amnesty International (1989); Bonnech re (1988); Tweedie (1988); Kitchin (1989).

11   *This Week* reporter Julian Manyon, in an interview with the author, 23 February 1989.

12   Such films are quite rare. According to the Vanderbilt Television News Archive at Vanderbilt University, Nashville, Tennessee, there were a total of six documentary reports on Northern Ireland between 1980 and 1989 on the ABC and PBS networks. These included a showing of an edition of the BBC series *Real Lives*. The programme, 'At the Edge of the Union' caused a major controversy in Britain when it was removed from the schedules by the BBC Governors following pressure from the government: see Rudin (1985); Leapman (1987).

13   Interviewing members of the republican movement is difficult on British television. *This Week* did interview Gerry Adams of Sinn Féin for 'Death on the Rock' but decided not to use the interview because it 'would give the IRA a propaganda platform that could not be justified' (Windlesham and Rampton 1989, p. 20). The programme did feature a short audio-taped clip of Mairead Farrell's voice.

14   I am not arguing that US television generally takes a line critical of Western governments on issues of political violence, nor that it is the fourth estate watchdog that some commentators maintain. There is abundant evidence to suggest that the role of the US media in reporting political violence, carried out by governments or sub-state groups opposing US foreign policy imperatives, is in many respects quite similar to the role of British broadcasting in reporting Northern Ireland. See Chomsky (1989); Hallin (1987); Herman and Chomsky (1988); and R. Andersen (1988) for contrasting critical views. Just as British television could, in the 1980s, report relatively dispassionately on El Salvador or Nicaragua, compared to the US media, so the US media can frame the conflict in Northern Ireland in looser terms than in Britain. This relates largely to the political distance of the conflict in Ireland from the immediate exigencies of US foreign policy.

15   It is possible to disagree about the truth of an item of information, or about its importance or relevance. People can have differing 'opinions'. Alternatively, 'disagreement' may be related to matters of 'taste' or 'pleasure'. It has been

suggested that there can be a disjunction between 'Judgement and Jouissance' (Murdock 1989, p. 237), although Corner has argued that this may be more relevant to 'fictional' or 'entertainment' programmes than news or other factual programmes (1991c, pp. 276–7).

16 See, for example, Corner *et al.* (1990); Kitzinger and Miller (1992); Morley (1980); Philo (1990); Schlesinger *et al.* (1992); Seiter *et al.* (1989). See also the chapters by Sonia Livingstone and by Jack McLeod and his colleagues in Curran and Gurevitch (eds) (1991) for discussions of the area.

17 Eleven out of fifty-four said they thought that NI was mostly violent with a further four believing that Belfast was mostly violent, but that the countryside was more peaceful, or that Northern Ireland was much more violent than the rest of the 'UK'.

18 'Mother Ireland' became one of the first casualties of the British broadcasting ban, although Channel 4 had already demanded a number of changes in it prior to the ban (Derry Film and Video 1988; Curtis 1989; Gosling 1991).

19 Of course the audience for a programme like 'Death of a Terrorist' on the minority PBS network is considerably smaller than the number of people who watch the nightly news on any of the three main television networks in the US.

ACKNOWLEDGEMENTS

Thanks to Philip Radcliffe at Manchester University for inviting me to lecture on his course for students of Pennsylvannia State University and to all the Pennsylvannia State and other US students for their tolerance in participating in the research. Thanks also to my colleagues, John Eldridge, Jenny Kitzinger, Greg McLaughlin, Greg Philo, Jacquie Reilly and Paula Skidmore and to participants in the Fulbright Collo-quium in Nottingham for comments on an earlier draft.

PART THREE

6

The (almost) invisible candidate: a case study in news judgement as political censorship

JOSHUA MEYROWITZ

One of the most famous pictures in post-World War II Czechoslovakia was of Czech leader Klement Gottwald standing on a balcony in freezing weather and declaring the birth of the communist state to the crowds below. Next to him stood his close aide, Vladimir Clementis, who, fearing that his leader would take sick from the cold, lent him his hat. A few years later, however, Clementis, the hat-lender, was charged with treason and hanged. And the state propaganda apparatus quickly airbrushed the traitor out of history and out of all state photographs. The new version of the famous picture showed Klement Gottwald standing alone on the balcony. All that remained of his once-trusted aide was Clementis' hat atop Gottwald's head.[1]

It is difficult to imagine such a crude act of censorship taking place in a Western democracy, but airbrushing of a more sophisticated fashion is routinely practised. Consider, for example, the case of Larry Agran.

In September 1991, Agran was one of only two declared US presidential candidates at the Sioux City Democratic Party Unity Dinner. This was to be the first Democratic party event of the presidential campaign season and Agran, the other declared candidate (former Senator Paul Tsongas), and several potential candidates spoke there to an audience of 500 Democrats. A fleeting image appeared on Cable News Network of Agran being greeted by Paul Tsongas, Senator Tom Harkin, and Governor Bill Clinton. But when the same encounter appeared in an AP photo published by the lasting 'newspaper of record', *The New York Times*,[2] Agran was nowhere to be seen. Agran's metaphorical 'hat' in the photo is that the two figures on the left – Paul Tsongas and Tom Harkin – are clearly speaking to some unseen person beyond the right margin of the photograph.

Over the next weeks and months, as other well-known politicians declared their candidacies, the national press spent a considerable amount of time on them as well as speculating at length over whether two prominent non-candidates – the Rev. Jesse Jackson and New York Governor Mario Cuomo – would run. But the national media gave little or no attention to the Agran campaign. In the rare instances when his name did appear, he was described as a 'dark horse', a 'fringe candidate', or 'an obscure contender'. Agran was barred from most of the televised debates on the basis of criteria that shifted as he tried to meet them. When he *was* allowed to participate in forums with the so-called 'major' candidates, he was often left out of news reports of the events or was asked by press photographers to move aside. If he was scheduled to speak last, the press usually left before his talk, and was not there to hear or report on what he said or on the audience reaction. Agran would hold press conferences, and few if any journalists would attend, and still fewer news reports appeared. With paradoxical logic, Agran was told by news media executives that he had not earned the right to media exposure, because, among other things, he had not received enough media exposure.

My purpose in this chapter is to analyse the coverage and non-coverage of the Agran campaign for what it tells us about US presidential campaign coverage in general. After summarising Agran's campaign experiences and the results of some of my interviews with journalists, I will argue that there are at least three competing logics at work in the US for how presidential campaigns should be covered: national journalistic logic, local journalistic logic, and public logic. I will also give a brief sketch of some of the factors that I believe shape the journalistic logics. Finally, I will suggest that by marginalising Agran, the US press transformed his campaign into a form of social deviance and silenced him much more effectively than could have been accomplished by the crude acts of censorship used by totalitarian states.

THE AGRAN CAMPAIGN

Whether one approves or disapproves of the way that the US press handled Agran's campaign, it is not particularly surprising that he was treated the way he was. The press generally ignores more presidential campaigns than it agrees to cover. And Agran clearly did not have the background, experience, position, name recognition, wealth, and power the US press generally looks for in a 'major' candidate. Indeed, in a way, it is surprising that he received as much coverage as he did – a constant smattering, but never enough to enter public consciousness amid the flood of redundant coverage of the other candidates.

Nevertheless Larry Agran's presidential campaign provides an interesting case study to make some of the implicit patterns of coverage visible. Unlike virtually all the other so-called 'fringe candidates', he was not easy to dismiss out of hand. He was a member of one of the two major parties, he had an impressive twelve-year track record as an elected public official, he had some foreign policy experience (indeed, more than Bill Clinton), he was a Harvard Law School graduate and book author, he had the trappings of a serious campaign with a formal announcement speech and position papers, he had the campaign organisation necessary to do the arduous work of getting on most primary and caucus ballots (his failure in getting on the other ballots was usually related to the criterion of 'significant press coverage'), he had measurable showings in some early polls, he was sometimes included in forums with the 'major' candidates, where he often stood out for the strength of his ideas and presentation, he garnered endorsements from a few small newspapers, he outlasted most of the other candidates, he eventually qualified for federal matching funds, and he even received a few delegate votes at the Democratic convention.

Much of the mainstream national press, however, rejected Agran before a single vote was cast or any voter poll was taken. The national press placed him in the same category with any candidate who merely paid $1,000 to be put on the ballot only in New Hampshire and had little else in the way of background, experience, or a campaign.

To be fair to those making such news judgements, thirty-six candidates entered the Democratic primary in New Hampshire. Further, much of Agran's dark horse status derived from his unconventional credentials as a presidential contender. Although at this time he had devoted twenty years to public service, he had never held state-wide or national office. He served for a dozen years as an elected official in Irvine, California, America's largest master-planned city. Most national journalists I spoke with dismissed him, based on his having held only local office, just as they once would have dismissed anyone who was only a Congressmen, or was only a *former* Senator or Governor. As journalist Roger Mudd put it at the start of a rare TV interview with Agran: 'It does stretch credulity to think that a Jewish ex-mayor of a small, suburban California town can make it'.

Agran's supporters, however, pointed out that as Irvine's first directly-elected mayor, Agran initiated a whole series of progressive programmes that received national acclaim (childcare, elderly housing,

mass transportation, one of the nation's first kerbside recycling programmes, hazardous waste regulations, and many others). They noted
that, as Executive Director of the Center for Innovative Diplomacy (a
progressive foreign policy think-tank), Agran played a unique role as a
'global mayor', who pursued issues of international trade, arms
reduction, and human rights, and earned his city a United Nations
award for his pioneering legislation to eliminate ozone-depleting compounds – all from an unlikely base in deeply conservative Orange
County, the county that had given Ronald Reagan and George Bush
huge margins of victory. Agran's supporters pointed out that, regardless
of anything else, since his campaign had done the work to get his name
on about forty primary and caucus ballots, the voting public deserved
to be told something about him in order to be able to make an informed
choice in the voting booth. (No other major party candidate who was
on that many primary ballots was being ignored by the press.) And
they described him as the most articulate presidential contender with
some of the clearest and most systemic plans for solving the country's
problems, including the boldest and most specific blueprint for shifting
cold war military spending to post-cold war domestic needs. Finally,
they argued that the public's reaction to many of his appearances was
so positive that his ideas deserved to be heard – and allowed to influence
the platforms of the 'major' candidates – even if Agran himself had
little chance of winning the nomination.

It is no surprise that Agran's supporters saw more in Agran than did
most national journalists. What is surprising, however, is the extent to
which they received encouragement from the coverage of the *local* New
Hampshire press reporting on the first-in-the-nation primary as well as
from at least two nationally-known columnists, Colman McCarthy and
Sydney Schanberg. In New Hampshire, there were dozens of local
newspaper articles, editorials, columns, and letters to the editor, which
described Agran's exclusion and/or supported his right to be heard in
national debates. Beyond New Hampshire, McCarthy and Schanberg
both wrote columns challenging Agran's designation as a 'minor candidate' and endorsing his right to be heard and seen through debates and
national news coverage.

Agran was also the highest-rated Democratic party candidate in some
progressive publications, including the *Casco Bay Weekly* (20 February
1992) and *Nuclear Times* (Winter 1991–92), the latter calling him 'bright,
earnest, and visionary' and saying he would 'bring the right values to
the White House'. His campaign was followed closely on progressive

computer networks, such as PeaceNet. Yet most national journalists apparently do not keep their ears to progressive grounds.

Agran's anomalous status as a candidate made his campaign a good lens through which to see aspects of campaign coverage that normally remain invisible. To make an analogy to academic tenure procedures, Agran was not simply like the great teacher who does no research and therefore is denied tenure by a ten-to-zero vote. He was like the great teacher who writes only one or two exceptional articles – articles that some argue are of higher quality than the typical book and/or dozen articles that will usually garner someone a permanent position – and then asks for early tenure. When such a person is denied tenure by an eight-to-two vote, the debates and justifications on both sides reveal quite a bit about the unwritten rules of the institution.

To his dismay, Agran found that for him one of the rules of the campaign was: 'To become visible, you must be disruptive'. When he was barred by the Chairman of the State Democratic Party from a televised Health Care Forum with presidential candidates in Nashua, New Hampshire, for example, he stood up in the audience and demanded to know by what criteria he was being excluded. Responding to a signal from a state party official, security police began to remove Agran from the hall, but the crowd's shouts of 'Freedom of speech!' and 'Let us vote!' embarrassed the men at the dais into inviting him to join them. This confrontation was Agran's first widely reported 'campaign event' – but little mention was made of his innovative proposals for health care reform.

To prevent this sort of public call for inclusion from happening again (the state party chair called it 'intimidation'), the state Democratic party moved its next debate to a high-security TV studio with no audience. Agran stood outside the studio, among a crowd of four hundred people who braved zero-degree temperatures to protest the exclusion of candidates from the debates. (Most of the protesters were supporters of New Alliance Party candidate Lenora Fulani, who ran as a Democrat in New Hampshire). As reported in the *local* press, the protest offered many dramatic moments, with the 'major' candidates forced to pass 'picket lines for democracy' as protestors shouted 'Scab! Scab! Scab!' Yet perhaps because there was no violence and the closed debate was not disrupted, the protest went unreported in *The New York Times*, *Washington Post*, and in all but Agran's home-county edition of the *Los Angeles Times*. (CNN Headline News made brief mention of a protest, without pictures, as a tag line about every fourth time it presented its well-illustrated report on the debate.)

The odd contrast between the local New Hampshire media and the national media on what was going on in the campaign was one of the things that drew my attention to this topic. Even though New Hampshire was flooded with national reporters, the local coverage of Agran had no impact on national coverage. When I asked an editor at a major link to the national media – the Associated Press in Concord, New Hampshire – about the lack of mention of these local articles, letters, and editorials, I was told bluntly: 'We don't report on editorials'. I was also told that the instructions about which candidates should receive 'blanket coverage' on the part of the local AP came from the national AP in Washington.

Agran and his staff believed that at some point local press attention would build into national exposure. But several reporters and editors at national newspapers and magazines whom I spoke with admitted that the longer one has not covered a candidate, the harder it becomes to do so. 'The obvious question in such situations', said Alvin Sanoff, a senior editor at *U.S. News and World Report*, 'is "Where have you been that you just discovered this person?" ' He also noted that 'it's always safer to stay with the pack and be wrong, than to risk going out on a limb and covering someone who then turns out to not be that important'.

When local press coverage and protests had no impact on his national media profile, Agran's campaign staff became convinced that his status as a 'fringe' candidate could be erased if he tied or passed one or more of the 'major' candidates in the polls. They were wrong.

When Agran made his first measurable showing in a University of New Hampshire/WMUR-TV (Channel 9) poll taken from 6 January to 11 January 1992, the AP story on the poll grouped Agran's score into a total score for 'minor candidates' without mentioning his name. (There was also no mention of the irony that a 'fringe candidate' who was receiving almost no national press coverage had tied 'major' candidate Virginia Governor Douglas Wilder, who had received a great deal of national press but little public enthusiasm, and who abandoned his campaign four days into the six-day polling period). When a 22 January poll, conducted by the American Research Group (ARG), showed Agran tied with former California Governor Jerry Brown and Iowa Senator Tom Harkin, the polling group's press release had three suggested headlines: 'Bush Rebounds in Republican Race', 'Democratic Debate Had Little Impact on Preference', and 'Agran Appears in Democratic Race'. But the Associated Press buried Agran's result in a single sentence two-thirds of the way through a story. When a follow-up ARG poll showed Agran doubling his support and moving ahead of Brown, the AP incorrectly referred to it as Agran's 'first measurable showing'. When the next ARG poll showed Agran still ahead of Brown, ABC's *World News Sunday* – perhaps to avoid the complexity of explaining the identity of a candidate they had not been covering – reported on the poll by simply skipping all mention of Agran, and moving directly from Harkin to Brown. Other news organisations solved the 'problem' by reporting only on the top three names.

ARG pollster Dick Bennett told me that had Agran's surprise strength in the polls been played up by news organisations it might well have led to a further rise in the polls. But instead, he said, 'the press completely ignored the story, and he began to sink'.

Agran's unusual appearance with four of the so-called 'major' candidates at the US Conference of Mayors in Washington DC led to the first significant mention of his campaign in *The New York Times*, which in effect declared him the winner of the debate. A 24 January article by Richard L. Berke, 'Mayors Unmoved by Major Candidates', began by saying that, after listening to the candidates, 'dozens of mayors . . . seemed to agree on one thing: the single candidate who truly understands urban needs is Larry Agran'. Agran was mentioned in passing in several other newspaper reports on the conference. Yet none of the TV news reports I saw on the forum even mentioned Agran's presence. The AP release on the event also made no mention of Agran's participation. (A viewing of the C-SPAN video coverage of the forum confirms the positive reaction to Agran. It also reveals that at the pre-event 'photo-op' at least one photographer gestured for Agran to move to the end of the row of candidates, presumably so he could be cut from the picture. Agran refused to move, and none of the scores of shots taken by the bank of photographers is known by Agran's staff or the conference organisers to have appeared anywhere.)

Similarly, when Agran participated with the 'major' candidates in the Global Warming Leadership Forum in February, the audience, according to conference organiser Carole Florman 'was very enthusiastic about Larry Agran and less than enthusiastic about Bill Clinton and Bob Kerrey'. But the major national news organisations covering the event – ABC News, CBS News (through a local affiliate), and the AP – omitted all mention of Agran from their reports.

Most of the national journalists I spoke with at the *Los Angeles Times*, *Washington Post*, *Time*, *Newsweek*, *U.S. News and World Report*, *NBC News*, *Nightline*, *The Boston Globe*, and other places expressed little surprise over the press treatment that Agran received, and they offered similar explanations for it. Tom Rosenstiel, for example, who is based in Washington and writes on media and politics for the *Los Angeles Times*, suggests there are several reasons. For one thing, said Rosenstiel, political reporters tend to cover those candidates that their sources – the party professionals – tell them are the major candidates. Reporters ask them: 'What are you hearing? Who is lining up endorsements? Who is doing fundraisers for whom?' 'This year, especially', said Rosenstiel, 'the last thing the Democratic leaders want is to have attention paid to someone like Larry Agran, which would reinforce the impression that they are putting forward a "field of unknowns" '.

Journalists also look to each other to see who is being taken as a 'serious' candidate. Bill Wheatley of *NBC News*, which excluded Agran from its televised debate, told me that press coverage was 'certainly one of the factors'. He continued: 'A number of independent news organisations had made that judgement to exclude Agran. It's not a conspiracy. One needs to pay attention to one's colleagues' decisions'. Yet while Wheatley saw press decisions as 'independent', he admitted that 'journalistic consensus in part reflects consensus of party professionals who have some experience knowing who is electable'.

Similarly, Alvin Sanoff, Senior Editor at *U.S. News and World Report*, told me: 'Journalists all talk to the same people, the same readers of tea leaves. We have similar kinds of input from similar sources. It takes a leap of faith to say, "we're missing the story". . . . We all read and talk to each other. We speak to similar experts and gurus and poll takers. We're influenced by the same influences'.

Once Agran was excluded from 'the consensus', there seemed to be nothing that he could do to register with the national media. Press language even excluded evidence of 'minor' candidates' existence. CNN would report something such as: 'Four out of the five Democratic presidential candidates were in Manchester, New Hampshire today', as if there were no other candidates. Or a report would say: 'Bill Clinton spoke in Nashua, New Hampshire today. The other candidates were in other states' – while Agran was very much *in* New Hampshire and actively campaigning. National media would offer routine coverage of whatever the 'major' candidates were doing, such as Senator Bob Kerrey speaking uncomfortably to uncomfortable patrons at a local restaurant. But few journalists would attend Larry Agran's press conferences. To the best of my knowledge, Agran's name did not appear even once during the campaign in the pages of the major news magazines, *Time*, *Newsweek*, and *U.S. News and World Report*.

By the end of March 1992, Tom Harkin, Bob Kerrey, and Paul Tsongas had all joined Douglas Wilder in suspending their campaigns, but the narrowed Democratic field did not generate any increased attention to Agran. Indeed, the media's near silence with regard to Larry Agran set the stage for the criminalisation of his attempts to be included in campaign forums. Even when Agran garnered more voter signatures to be placed on the New York ballot than Jerry Brown, only Jerry Brown was allowed to participate in New York City debates with Bill Clinton. At the start of one debate on urban problems (Agran's specialty) at Lehman College in the Bronx, one of the five boroughs of New York City, Agran stood up and said 'I respectfully ask to be included in this forum'. For this crime, he was quickly tackled to the floor by plain-clothes police, dragged down a flight of stairs head-first, handcuffed, thrown into a police paddy-wagon until the debate was over, and then kept in custody at a Bronx jail for four hours on charges of disorderly conduct, trespassing, and resisting arrest. (Agran notes that his only crime was to speak, that he had a ticket to the event, and that he offered no resistance to the men who tackled him, who neither identified themselves nor told him he was under arrest.) Agran's New York campaign manager, who was merely sitting next to Agran was also arrested. The arrest received some coverage in New York, including a brief mention in *The New York Times*. Agran's home state paper, the *Los Angeles Times*, condemned the arrest in an editorial. But beyond that, there was largely silence. The *New York Post* (1 April 1992) covered it in a fashion, reporting: 'Two men were arrested inside the Lehman College auditorium when they started heckling the candidates, according to police'.

One criterion for coverage that journalists cited when I spoke to them early in the campaign was federal matching funds. (A candidate qualifies by collecting $5000 in twenty states, with maximum individual contributions of $250.) Agran, they told me, was unlikely to qualify. But when Agran, without any significant press coverage, did eventually qualify for federal matching funds in mid-May, there was virtually no press mention of this, and no change in the attention level he received.

As you might have guessed, Agran did not win his party's nomination. But he did receive a few delegate votes at the convention. They were listed on the TV screens as votes for 'Other'.

PRESS LOGIC VERSUS PUBLIC LOGIC

The media's handling of the Agran campaign reveals a gap between the public's and the press' view of campaigns. Although almost all the citizens I spoke with on this topic accepted that some candidates do and should receive more coverage than others, many of them were also shocked to learn that a candidate articulating serious positions would be censored from reports of events that he participated in, especially when he was received very well by those at the event. In contrast, almost all the national journalists I spoke with were shocked that anyone would be shocked by this (and a few of them even started yelling at me for being so naive and stupid as to ask about such a thing).

In following the coverage and non-coverage of Agran's campaign and in interviewing journalists and in speaking to voters, I believe I discerned three distinct and competing logics for campaign coverage. Although the boundaries for these are not as neat as the following labels imply, I call them:

1   national journalistic logic;
2   local journalistic logic; and
3   public logic.

On some issues, two of these operated in tandem in contrast to the third. For example, both national and local journalists were very concerned with their limited resources and were eager to narrow the coverage down to a limited number of candidates as soon as possible, even as polls showed the public disenchanted with all the 'major' candidates and in search of alternatives.

In other cases, however, local and national journalistic logics were in competition with each other and with public logic. For example, when Agran participated in the Global Warming Leadership Forum in Tallahassee, Florida, the audience was much more enthusiastic about him than about a few of the 'major' candidates. The 'public logic' I encountered in speaking about this event with average citizens was that this fact should have been reported. The public had a 'let the best person win' philosophy and was hungry for 'good ideas' regardless of the source. Yet all the national news organisations covering the event omitted all mention of Agran's presence (and several journalists who did not cover it told me they would have omitted mentioning him had they covered it, regardless of his performance relative to the others). The national journalists saw all such events as symbolic of the national campaign, and regardless of what happened in that particular forum in that particular place, Agran was not viewed by them as a contender in the national arena. Their concern was not with ideas or with the public's reaction to ideas or with the winning of a local debate, but with 'who can win the presidency'.

Local journalistic logic seemed to fall between the other two: reporters described the event partly as a symbolic 'national' event, but also as one that happened 'in our town' in real space and time. (The logic seemed to be: 'Had you gone downtown to place X, this is what you would have seen'.) Local newspaper accounts therefore generally mentioned when Agran was at an event and summarised his views, but they usually focused primarily on the 'major' candidates. Much of the local excitement, after all, was over the local presence of nationally-recognised figures. Unlike the national media, however, the local media also had many stories that were just on Agran, based on the logic, 'He was *here*'.

The greatest contrasts were between national journalistic logic and public logic. Even when the two logics defined a problem in similar ways, the solutions were quite different. When, for example, *The New York Times* (2 February 1992) wrote that George Bush has no 'blueprints for the future' of the US, and that he has little competition among the major presidential contenders or in Congress, this reflected fairly accurately the scepticism of the public. But public logic dictated that one solution should be that the mainstream media look beyond the typical political spotlight for new ideas. National journalistic logic suggested otherwise. The national journalists I spoke with seemed to see this sad state of affairs as a reason to protect the 'insiders' even more. One journalist told me: 'One of the problems that people in DC see in the presidential primary season is that anyone can run. There's a body of thought among insiders, including the media, that this is not necessarily a good thing'. He pointed to former President Jimmy Carter as an example of someone who was too much of an outsider to know how to govern the country effectively. He noted that there is a 'divisiveness' that comes from candidates attacking and running against 'the institutions that run the country'. So while the public was clearly demanding change, national journalists seem closely aligned, perhaps more fiercely than ever, with the *status quo*. Within national journalistic logic, the public's anti-mainstream mood was even more of a reason not to give 'undue' coverage to 'fringe' candidates. (While the journalists I interviewed seemed very sensitive to the possibility that giving Agran coverage might unduly boost his campaign, they were hesitant to admit that not covering him might unduly hurt his campaign.)

When Governor Wilder dropped out early in the race, many ordinary citizens I spoke with felt that there was now 'an empty chair' for another candidate. But national journalists had the opposite reaction: 'We can't wait to winnow the race down even further', said Tom Rosenstiel of the

Los Angeles Times. He explained that it is difficult and expensive and confusing for the media to have to contend with a lot of candidates. 'Journalists don't sit around in newsrooms asking "Whom else should we cover?" The big question is "Whom can we *stop* covering?" ' Ultimately, Rosenstiel notes, 'if we think someone is not likely to win, then we do not think of them as someone to devote much time to'. Another journalist for a major newspaper echoed the desire to narrow the field as quickly as possible and noted that for his publication 'every extra candidate means another reporter and another $150 a day hotel bill'.

Similarly, rather than seeing Larry Agran's passing of Jerry Brown in some polls as a possible indication of the legitimacy of the Agran campaign, journalists I spoke with saw it as further proof of Brown's fringe status. 'It's just one marginal candidate passing another marginal candidate', said one reporter. (This was before Brown's surprise strength in a number of primary votes.)

Most of the voters I spoke with were hungry for a candidate with new ideas, and they saw a presidential campaign as fostering a national dialogue on key issues. But the national journalists I spoke with mostly saw the campaign as a horse race. According to Tom Rosenthiel: 'An election is not a matter of who is the smartest, the most articulate, or who has the best ideas. It's much more complicated than that. What it really comes down to is who can win the most votes'.

Similarly, Jonathan Alter, a senior editor at *Newsweek* described the 'fairly simple rules of the press pack: if we don't think that you have at least some chance of being elected, you just don't get any coverage. Perhaps it's not the way it should be, but that's the way it is.'

Regardless of which logic, if any, is correct, there is clearly a gap that needs to be addressed. The public does not seem to know or understand the national journalistic logic, and the national journalists do not seem to know, or perhaps simply do not care, that their own logic is at odds with the public's.

THE ORIGINS OF NATIONAL JOURNALISTIC LOGIC

In examining why the 1992 coverage/non-coverage followed the pattern that it did, I have been drawing partly on what journalists told me. But because many of their claims did not bear up under scrutiny (there was not a single criterion told to me that journalists would apply evenly to every candidate) I have also been relying on my own observations and interpretations, which have been informed by the excellent and rapidly growing literature on news practices.

Since the logic I encountered among national journalists was more at odds with public logic than was local journalistic logic, I have been focusing thus far primarily on the factors that interact to shape national journalistic logic. To keep this brief, I will merely outline some of the key variables I believe worked together to shape the logic used by the national media:

1 *Limited resources for gathering news within each organisation* (made worse in 1992 by a bad economy) and limited news space/time (made worse during this campaign by the decline in advertising revenues) led to a logical attempt to narrow the field of candidates.

2 National journalists' *reliance on 'official sources'* for definitions of what and who are 'news', for a general 'informed perspective', for 'objective reporting', and for feedback on their reporting, led the national media to define 'major' candidates in relation to what party officials believed – and wanted the press to report – rather than in relation to the potential response to candidates on the part of the public.

3 The significant *influence of centralised news organisations*, such as the Associated Press and the three major TV networks, and the *influence of the élite political press* (the *Washington Post*, *The New York Times*, and *Los Angeles Times*) allowed a relatively small number of decision-makers to shape the general patterns of coverage for over 200 million citizens.

4 National journalists' *herd instincts* led journalists to move into synchrony with each other in terms of who they were and were not covering, as well as the general style of coverage. Since this synchrony was not the result of an explicit conspiracy, it was viewed as the result of the independent judgement of many different journalists.

5 Journalists' *desire to hide the arbitrariness of news judgements* and the impact of such judgements on the outcome of campaigns led them to stick with their initial decisions not to give much coverage to Agran, regardless of what happened later. (To my mind, this also explains why journalists felt they had to cover no-party candidate Ross Perot as soon as he even hinted that he might enter the race. Since billionaire Perot had the money to buy direct access to the public through the media, *not* covering him would make the public aware of the media as 'censors'. In contrast, true third-party candidates, such as Lenora Fulani of the New Alliance Party and Libertarian André Marrou, were virtually ignored by the news media and were excluded from the nationally-televised debates.)

6 Journalists' *patronising attitudes about the public's intelligence and attention span* made them concerned about keeping the 'campaign story' and possible outcomes as simple as possible.

7 Journalists' *desire for 'prestige assignments'* led them to focus on 'the stars'.

(From the very beginning, the Clinton campaign was seen as the premiere assignment, which led to both more positive and more negative coverage of Clinton as the campaign proceeded.)

8 The *primacy of television in the campaign* lent weight to criteria that made sense to commercial TV network executives, such as keeping the debates short in order not to lose too much commercial time, and limiting the debates to celebrity candidates and celebrity journalists in order to maximise ratings (and flow through to subsequent commercial programmes).

9 *Non-campaign-season news conventions* limited the range of voices that were viewed as legitimate during the campaign. (The highly selective range of typical news narratives fostered the perception that only candidates who discussed domestic and foreign policy within those narrative frames were 'reasonable' and 'serious' and 'moderate' enough to be elected. One typical narrative within the US press with regard to foreign aid, for example, has involved the debate over 'how much the US should spend to promote democracy in other countries'. There has been little questioning of whether that is indeed what the money has been intended to do. Thus, Agran's plan to end all foreign *military* aid because it has typically gone to support dictators, and his suggestion to offer foreign '*people* aid', did not fit easily into a familiar mainstream press narrative and made him seem radical, non-serious, and 'fringy'.)

All these variables tended to foster a relatively closed system that was only slightly sensitive to high degrees of public dissatisfaction with so-called 'major' candidates.

CONCLUSION

The 1992 US presidential election stood out as one where opinion polls suggested an unprecedented level of voter dissatisfaction with politics-as-usual. Polls showed disenchantment with both parties and with all the so-called 'major' candidates. Voters expressed the wish that other candidates had entered the race. The press dutifully reported on these polls. But a truly responsive democratic press would go further. It would widen the spotlight beyond the centre-stage that is the subject of public discontent. The 1992 election was also the first to follow the revolutions in Eastern Europe that swept traditional leadership aside and brought to power those who had once inhabited the political margins, even jail cells. The US press generally applauded these changes and saw them as movements toward 'our way of life'. Yet there is little indication that the US press is willing to expand US democracy by widening its coverage, even now that the claimed threat that drove much US foreign policy and pervaded the image of the world presented by much US journalism has vanished.

I do not mean to suggest that there is a conscious conspiracy or that there are no exceptions to the general trends I describe. No conspiracy is necessary to reach general consistency of thought and action if journalists come to the situation with similar training, follow similar routines, interact with the same sources and with each other, and monitor each other's judgements. Through typical national press routines, incestuous and intersubjective judgements among a cluster of élite decision-makers (party officials, news executives, and debate organisers) take on the aura of objective reality.

In conclusion, I suggest that news judgements serve as a form of political censorship, but they comprise a system based on an internal logic that – unlike the clumsy deeds of Czech censors who manipulated a famous photo – makes journalistic practices seem reasonable and safe for democracy. Yet this case study points to the possibility that current national journalistic practice in the US is nevertheless at odds with public logic and with public good.

A presidential candidate who was shot or tortured by another country's secret police, would become a *cause célèbre*. But Agran, though physically unharmed, was much more effectively silenced. He was dubbed 'not newsworthy'. As a result, his sober quest for office was framed as an act of deviance, and his attempts to enter the arena of legitimacy were criminalised. With the non-reporting of a judge's ruling on the eve of the Democratic Convention in July to delay his trial, first until September and then twice more to later dates, Agran – though still under a threat of imprisonment for requesting inclusion in a debate – was pushed further and further into the black hole of non-news. There he and his plans for the country join many other throwaway candidates and many other throwaway ideas.

NOTES

1 This incident is recounted in Kundera (1980, p. 3). I thank John Shotter for making me aware of it.
2 *The New York Times*, whose motto is 'All the news that's fit to print', is generally considered to be the US's most comprehensive newspaper. Many US libraries keep a complete set of the newspaper on microfilm as an official record of daily events.

7

An institutional perspective on news media access and control

RICHARD V. ERICSON

In this chapter I use research on news media to address five basic questions about broadcast media access. What is access? Why is access desirable? Who obtains access? How is access obtained? What remedies are available when access is not obtained?

In answering these questions I analyse institutional structures and process that control, and are controlled by, news media. The news media form a complex institution comprising diverse organisations, technologies and people. The news media institution not only has a complex life of its own: it is also constituted by other institutions through the access it grants to them; and it in turn constitutes other institutions through the access they grant to it. While analysts must respect the integrity of the news media institution, they also need to take into account its relatedness as a social institution. 'The study of media in Western capitalist democracies is inextricably bound up with central social institutions that seek to manage the flow of information' (Schlesinger 1989, p. 293).

WHAT IS ACCESS?

Access is intentional participation in other institutions and their communications media. Access includes the desire to participate in the communications of other institutions and to have some influence over the terms of participation. The participant must be knowledgeable that she or he is participating in the communications of other institutions. She or he must also be knowledgeable about appropriate tactics for participation and influence.

Seen in these terms, access to the news media excludes audience members who do not also participate as news sources or journalists.

While broadcast news is available almost universally, and is comprehensible even to very young children, not everyone is in a position to participate in the institutions that comprise it. As Curran (1990) and Seaman (1992) have observed recently, while an 'active' audience member can imaginatively interpret a broadcast item any way she or he likes, the interpretation counts for nought unless there is more direct participation in the structures and processes by which news is produced and distributed. One must investigate who cares to participate in news communications, their motivations in participating, and their capacity for participation.

The definition tendered also excludes those who become news sources unintentionally. Access is not achieved, for example, by the criminally accused person who is shamed by news depictions of her or his alleged crime and flawed moral character, or by the corporation that unilaterally experiences the sting of negative publicity about its unsafe products.

Intentionality in communications is always framed and circumscribed within institutions. An institution is the relations, processes and patterns associated with particular interests. It includes material/physical/spatial components (e.g. buildings, mechanical technologies), cultural aspects (e.g. traditions, rituals, scientific and legal technologies), political processes (e.g. it must be legitimated) and social dimensions (e.g. all of the above are produced through social knowledge and activity). The main activity of institutions is the social production and distribution of knowledge for risk management, problem solving and routine decisions.

People do not participate in news communications except as they are defined within roles, identities and positions for speaking and acting constituted by institutions. Access only exists as it is warranted by institutions. Warrants are issued by both the news media institution and by the diverse source institutions with which the news media join in making news. The news media and source institutions are best conceived as *part* of each other, mutually influencing their respective ways of classifying, organising, thinking, and acting. Thus the journalist on a regular news-beat becomes part of the communication network of the source organisation, a participant in the process of giving meaning to texts, and of having those texts enter back into the source organisation to affect social relations and practices there. She or he is interdependent with others in the source organisation regarding both knowledge production and its various uses inside and outside the organisation. The reality of news is embedded in the nature and type of social and cultural relations that develop between journalists and their sources, and in the politics of knowledge that emerges on each specific newsbeat. Access must always fit the format of the communication medium, and therefore is always dependent upon format considerations.

> Any medium's first commitment is to itself as a legitimate format for the definition, recognition and communication of meaning. . . . Whatever defines a particular medium, e.g. sound for radio and visuals for TV, will essentially define and shape how the event's temporal and spatial features will be translated into those of the listener or viewer. Furthermore, whatever content is produced, e.g. people, places, things, will be subservient to and largely a result of these format considerations (Altheide 1985, pp. 40, 56).

Sources vary in their preferred formats for news – e.g. personal interview, news conferences, other staged events, print or video releases or packages, regular hearings, published documents – and therefore in the particular news organisation and medium they prefer. For example, the courts format news within their public hearings and the print medium, the police emphasise news releases tailored to radio, and politicians give primacy to television formats (Ericson, Baranek and Chan 1989). News organisations also vary substantially in their preferred communication formats, depending on whether they are using television, radio or print media, and on the particular sources and audiences they see themselves as serving and influencing (Ericson, Baranek and Chan 1987; 1991).

WHY IS ACCESS DESIRABLE?

Access is desirable because news is the most widely-available and immediate means by which institutions can achieve meanings that articulate with their particular interests. While news is all words and images, it constructs bridges for activities that span institutional spheres and serve specific interests. As Macdonnel (1986, p. 51) observes regarding all discourses defined as institutionally produced meanings, 'what is at stake is ultimately quite a lot more than words or discourses.'

What is at stake for a given organisation in the news is control of the organisational environment both internally and externally. News is an agency for the policing of organisational life. As a discourse of deviance, control, law and justice, news is important for organisations that want to suggest the impropriety of others and control their activities, while at the same time displaying their own propriety and legitimacy. As expressed pithily by a police official involved in news management, 'the more we disclose, the more we control' (Ericson, Baranek and Chan 1989, p. 309) indicating that publicity can be as much a control device as is secrecy.

It is the way in which news directly participates in selecting and classifying deviance and effecting control on behalf of other institutions that explains why so much news is about deviance, control, law and justice. Indeed news has many parallels with the legal institution itself as a society-wide vehicle for discovering deviance, effecting control and achieving justice (Ericson 1991a; 1991b; Ericson, Baranek and Chan 1991). Both law and news serve as agencies of policing regarding the allocation of resources, the regulation of conflict and keeping the peace. They are both instruments of organisation: they define symbolic boundaries, rules, and the legitimacy of hierarchical roles and relations. They both pursue justice, the primary building block of social institutions, through an obsession with rule-governed behaviour, in particular the procedural propriety of decisions by authorities.

What is important in this regard is not whether news is true or false, but how it enters into power relations and serves to legitimate or undermine those relations. Major institutions take news seriously regardless of its veracity, biases or value as knowledge. Asking pragmatic questions about access, sources are far more concerned about news that is influential and helpful than about news that is impartial, accurate and balanced. Objectivity is less an issue than political objectives. The quality of knowledge in news is less significant than its qualities for giving sources greater control over their external and internal environments. The news media provide state institutions with a daily barometer of private corporate and interest-group values, rights claims and activities that is essential to the capacity to govern. At the same time, the news focus on policing government institutions is an important source of intelligence for the business community. Schiller (1986, p. 26) argues that 'business corporations today compose *the* vital audience for authentic news and information'. News access is also important for the organisational need to appear vital. Less established or organised groups in particular benefit from news that shows that they are indeed organised, and in that respect at least, recognised. More established organisations benefit from news that shows them to be in control, or at least dramatises the appearance that they are in control even if actual control remains elusive. All organisations require news access to demonstrate their legitimacy. It is crucial that both state agencies such as police (Ericson 1989), and private corporations (Fisse and Braithwaite 1983;

Braithwaite and Fisse, 1987) maintain their reputations as moral actors, and the news system is the most significant vehicle for doing so.

Intelligent, in control, and legitimate, organisations can use news access as a powerful resource that in turn enhances other resources. While access to the news depends on the possession of other resources of social, political, cultural and economic power, the news resource itself is used to regulate the distribution of these other resources. Unions, especially civil service unions limited in their capacity to strike, successfully use the news media to pressure management into enhancing their members' resources (Ericson, Baranek and Chan 1989, Chs 3, 4). Business enterprise not only relies on news intelligence to police state institutions, but uses news access to enhance its own resources (Ericson, Baranek and Chan 1989, Ch. 5; Blyskal and Blyskal 1985; Schiller 1989). Past governments were active in buying and subsidising newspapers, and journalists were also 'bought' (Burns 1979, pp. 48–9). Governmental purchases of media access have continued, including such practices as keeping journalists on retainer (Royal Commission on Newspapers 1981a, p. 61), buying advertising space (governments in Canada are the biggest advertisers in terms of expenditure – Singer 1986), and most importantly, establishing national broadcasting corporations (e.g. the British Broadcasting Corporation; the Canadian Broadcasting Corporation). While direct purchases are giving way to apparently more distant and benign public relations machines, behind this veil of administrative decency contemporary public relations perpetuates the same purpose of being part of the news media in order to participate in their communications.

WHO OBTAINS ACCESS: INTER-INSTITUTIONAL COMPARISONS

In this section I draw upon a systematic survey of news media in Toronto to illustrate that access always involves the imprint of institutions, and that certain institutions predominate (see Tables 7.1–7.4, pages 113–15).[1] Table 7.1 enumerates the proportion of news sources of different types that appeared in quality (Q) and popular (P) outlets in each of newspaper, television and radio media. Table 7.2 indicates the proportion of such appearances in which government, private corporate, community and individual sources were shown to be subject to control and therefore did not achieve access. Table 7.3 indicates the proportion of such appearances in which government, private corporate, community and individual sources were control agents – taking control actions over others – and in that respect achieved access.

Table 7.1 News-source types

Type	Newspaper		Television		Radio		Sig. diff.
	Q	P	Q	P	Q	P	
Journalist of organisation	146 13.9%	141 18.9%	459 38.7%	297 41.4%	365 43.1%	285 45.3%	M
Other journalist	127 12.1%	84 11.3%	54 4.6%	33 4.6%	6 0.7%	18 2.9%	M
Criminal justice	31 3.0%	79 10.6%	64 5.4%	40 5.6%	71 8.4%	44 7.0%	N
Public administration	60 5.7%	30 4.0%	60 5.1%	30 4.2%	42 5.0%	43 6.8%	
Other government sources	332 31.6%	148 19.8%	191 16.1%	76 10.6%	151 17.8%	115 18.3%	M/N
Private corporation	82 7.8%	60 8.0%	95 8.0%	63 8.8%	76 9.0%	34 5.4%	
Occupational association	43 4.1%	21 2.8%	32 2.7%	11 1.5%	35 4.1%	11 1.7%	
Political organisation	38 3.6%	12 1.6%	26 2.2%	9 1.3%	4 0.5%	7 1.1%	
Community organisation	47 4.5%	25 3.4%	85 7.2%	41 5.7%	41 4.8%	22 3.5%	
Individuals	78 7.4%	119 16.0%	73 6.2%	96 13.4%	37 4.4%	38 6.0%	N/T
Unspecified	56 5.3%	25 3.4%	20 1.7%	18 2.5%	14 1.7%	11 1.7%	
Don't know	10 1.0%	2 0.3%	26 2.2%	4 0.6%	5 0.6%	1 0.2%	
Total sources	1,050	746	1,185	718	847	629	5,175

Percentages are by column. Tests of significance based on tables with news-source types dichotomised into 'yes/no' for each of the categories. The last column indicates comparisons that show significant differences: chi-square statistics significant at the 0.05 level with Cramer's V or PHI $\geq$ 0.10, when N is large. Significant differences may occur between the newspapers (N); television stations (T); radio stations (R); or among the three types of media (M). The last column also indicates the presence of significant interactions with the variables being analysed and the coders (C) in a separate log-linear analysis.

Source: Ericson, Baranek and Chan 1991, p. 187.

Table 7.2 Targets of control – not access

Institutional field	Newspaper		Television		Radio		Sig. diff.
	Q	P	Q	P	Q	P	
Government	307	137	275	123	163	161	M/N/T
	53.7%	32.3%	39.7%	26.6%	29.1%	37.4%	C
Private corporate	84	75	144	91	144	76	R
	14.7%	17.7%	20.8%	19.7%	25.7%	17.7%	
Community	87	58	112	81	100	145	R
	15.2%	13.7%	16.2%	17.5%	17.9%	10.5%	C
Individual	75	147	150	163	131	144	N/T/R
	13.1%	34.7%	21.6%	35.3%	23.4%	33.5%	C
Total actions	572	424	693	462	560	430	3,141

Percentages are by column. Missing cases = 68. Tests of significance based on tables with institutional context targeted in control action dichotomised into 'yes/no' for each of the categories. The last column indicates comparisons that show significant differences: chi-square statistics significant at the 0.05 level with Cramer's V or PHI $\geq$ 0.10, when N is large. Significant differences may occur between the newspapers (N); television stations (T); radio stations (R); or among the three types of media (M). The last column also indicates the presence of significant interactions with the variables being analysed and the coders (C) in a separate log-linear analysis.

Source: Ericson, Baranek and Chan 1991, p. 318.

Table 7.3 Control agents – access

Institutional context	Newspaper		Television		Radio		Sig. diff.
	Q	P	Q	P	Q	P	
Government	385	265	410	269	352	311	R
	67.3%	62.5%	59.2%	58.2%	62.9%	72.3%	C
Private corporate	55	47	73	53	68	30	
	9.6%	11.1%	10.5%	11.5%	12.1%	7.0%	
Community	88	59	134	73	92	50	C
	15.4%	13.9%	19.3%	15.8%	16.4%	11.6%	
Individual	33	45	55	47	30	23	
	5.8%	10.6%	7.9%	10.2%	5.4%	5.3%	
Total actions	572	424	693	462	560	430	3,141

Percentages are by column. Missing cases = 94. Tests of significance based on tables with institutional context of control agents dichotomised into 'yes/no' for each of the categories. The last column indicates comparisons that show significant differences: chi-square statistics significant at the 0.05 level with Cramer's V or PHI $\geq$ 0.10, when N is large. Significant differences may occur between the newspapers (N); television stations (T); radio stations (R); or among the three types of media (M). The last column also indicates the presence of significant interactions with the variables being analysed and the coders (C) in a separate log-linear analysis.

Source: Ericson, Baranek and Chan 1991, p. 304.

Table 7.4 Control agents mobilised by others – access

Institutional context	Newspaper		Television		Radio		Sig. diff.
	Q	P	Q	P	Q	P	
Government	403	307	462	329	427	359	
	70.5%	72.4%	66.7%	71.2%	76.3%	76.5	
Private corporate	77	57	95	45	64	46	
	13.5%	13.4%	13.7%	9.7%	11.4%	10.7%	
Community	58	34	67	61	37	25	
	10.1%	8.0%	9.7%	13.2%	6.6%	5.8%	
Individual	2	7	8	6	1	2	
	0.3%	1.7%	1.2%	1.3%	0.2%	0.5%	
Total actions	572	424	693	462	560	430	3,141

Percentages are by column. Missing cases = 192. Tests of significance based on tables with institutional context mobilised in control dichotomized into 'yes/no' for each of the categories. The last column indicates comparisons that show significant differences: chi-square statistics significant at the 0.05 level with Cramer's V or PHI $\geq$ 0.10, when N is large. Significant differences may occur between the newspapers (N); television stations (T); radio stations (R); or among the three types of media (M). The last column also indicates the presence of significant interactions with the variables being analysed and the coders (C) in a separate log-linear analysis.

Source: Ericson, Baranek and Chan 1991, p. 311.

Table 7.4 indicates the proportion of such appearances in which government, private corporate, community and individual sources were control agents mobilised by others – taking control actions over others on behalf of a third party – and in that respect achieved access.

In order to underscore the institutional dominance of news, I will focus on how individuals without institutional affiliation are presented in the news. This analysis is followed by some brief observations comparing the access granted to government officials, private corporate officials, and members of community groups.

A: INDIVIDUALS

The relative frequency with which individuals appear as news sources is indicated in Table 7.1. Regardless of the medium or market orientation of the news outlet, individuals appear as news sources relatively infrequently. Bridson (1971; cited by Crissell 1986, p. 181) observes that in the case of British broadcasting, the idea that a 'man in the street should have anything vital to contribute to broadcasting was an idea slow to gain acceptance. That he should actually use broadcasting to express his own opinions in his own unvarnished words, was regarded as almost the end of all good social order.'

This view has changed somewhat, especially with the advent of non-news formats such as phone-in shows on radio and television. However, the data in Table 7.1 indicate that in the news, individuals are still cited infrequently relative to the institutional voices of authorised knowers.

Tables 7.2, 7.3 and 7.4 indicate that when individuals appear in the news, it is most often with respect to being targets of control actions taken by others and therefore not access. Comparing Tables 7.2 and 7.3, it is clear that regardless of medium or market orientation, news focuses much more on control actions taken against individuals (not access) than by individuals (access). The citation of control action against individuals as compared to control actions taken by individuals was two times greater in the quality newspaper; three times greater in each of the popular newspapers, quality television newscast and popular television newscast; four times greater in the quality radio newscast; and five times greater in the popular radio newscast. The relative powerlessness of individuals without institutional affiliation is underscored in comparing Tables 7.2 and 7.4. While all news outlets depicted individuals being subject to control action (Table 7.2), they almost never depicted individuals being mobilised by another party to effect his or her control purpose (Table 7.4). Power for control resides in institutions. In the news, institutions take a lot of their control actions in relation to individuals to make them fit their institutional criteria, but almost never mobilise the individual citizen as a resource in control actions. When individuals appear in the news as control agents, it is often in the vox pop format of the little person fighting bureaucracy. The individual imputes the deviance of a government bureaucracy or business enterprise, and the journalist joins the individual as a control agent mobilised in seeking justice. This is accomplished both through regular features, such as action line and consumer complaint slots, and in ordinary news stories. In some instances the journalist makes a judgement in favour of the bureaucracy and against the aggrieved citizen. For example, a man complained that he was not receiving enough money from welfare sources and therefore was unable to look after his two children. A television crew visited the man's apartment and visualised *his* deviance by showing beer cases stacked beside a colour television set. The reporter used these visuals with a voice-over to indicate in no uncertain terms that the fault rested with the father's spending practices rather than with the welfare system. In another case, a prisoner brought a law suit against prison authorities who had refused to grant him direct access to the news media, arguing that this was a denial of his basic constitutional rights. In reporting this story, the journalist gave prominence to an affidavit from a psychiatrist which said that the inmate suffered from a personality disorder, one aspect of which involved attempts to discuss his crime with the news media!

Another use of individuals in the news is to have them offer 'public' reaction to events or states of affairs already framed by institutional sources. The construct of 'the public' in effect means all those without a direct institutional role or stake in determining the matter, even if they may be affected by it. The individual does not appear in the news as a representative of an organisation, nor even as representative of 'the public' in a statistical sense. Rather, the individual is typically used to make a representation on behalf of 'the public', to express what are visualised to be public sentiments about government policies, industrial strikes, calamitous events, etc. As such, the individual presents the fiction of 'the public' that is central to mass democracy.

In constituting 'public' reaction, news organisations seek to advance the story in terms of their own interests. This is illustrated in a story regarding proposed new legislation, approved by all political parties at the legislature, banning the use of lie-detector tests in various employment contexts (Ericson, Baranek and Chan 1991, Ch. 5). The day after it reported on the announcement of the legislation, a newspaper published an item in its regular vox pop column, 'You Said It,' in which five individuals interviewed 'on the street' all expressed approval of the legislation. As with *vox pop* interviews generally (see Voumvakis and Ericson 1984, pp. 53–5; Ericson, Baranek and Chan 1987), these accounts from the people were not based on a representative sample in scientific terms, but on representations the newspaper wanted to make to advance the story. The 'public' was used to express popular consensus, the after-clap of accord, in support of the legislature's wisdom in developing the new law. The day after this item, the newspaper published an editorial headlined 'Right to Snoop' in which its own purposes were revealed. This editorial denounced the legislation as an infringement on the liberty of employers to investigate employees as they see fit. Through the editorial, the newspaper turned the story into a tale of itself as minority voice in conflict with political opinion at the legislature and popular opinion on the streets. It converted the story into an opportunity for the expression of its own ideology supporting 'free enterprise' defined as freedom from government interference.

Vox pop formats in newspapers, as well as 'streeter' or on-the-street interviews in television, are also used to have people simply fantasise

power. For example, in the context of continuing stories about political controversies or significant legislative proposals, the 'public' is asked what they would do if they were a Member of Parliament or in some other position of influence. Of course, fantasising power in this way underscores the fact that the individuals concerned have no power over the matter at issue.

The place of individuals in the news is also revealed by who gets published in letters to the editor columns. In a study of 366 letters written to the editor of a quality newspaper over a one week period, we found that letters were much more likely to be accepted if they indicated the organisational affiliation and status of the writer than if they were authored by individuals without such indication. As in regular news columns, it is the authorised knower rather than the individual without an identified institutional status and stake in the matter who is given preference in the letters columns. Furthermore, letter writers who in turn cite other authoritative sources in their letters are much more likely to have their letters accepted than those who cite no sources. Just as the reporter has to find a source or two to say it so, so the letter writer is better off functioning as a 'reporter' by citing other authorities in support of his or her view. Letter writers are better off not only if they can represent their own authority through organisational status and affiliation, but also if they can in turn cite other authorities to make their case.

Many letters are rejected because they are categorised by the editor as being written by 'cranks' and by untrustworthy people; and/or because they are not properly tailored to the news format (e.g. they are too long, too 'emotional', too inflammatory, based on unsubstantiated claims, and/or possibly libellous). The letters editor involved in our study emphasised that it is almost exclusively the individual citizen, rather than regular sources representing established organisations, who sends in letters within these categories for 'automatic' rejection. Authorised knowers, as *organised* representatives of their bureaucracies, know precisely what will be acceptable within the letters format, whereas most individuals are less attuned to the basic requirements for consideration. In the words of the editor in this case:

> The majority of the letters that are not even read . . . come from private individuals with no affiliation given (approaching a hundred per cent); the acceptability – in terms of legally-usable letters, not counting their expressed opinions – from corporate sources ('élite authorised knowers') is vast (approaching a hundred per cent). If we show a bias toward these

'elite authorised knowers', it's simply because we begin with a far larger proportion of their letters.

Access by individuals is also qualitatively different because their involvement is personalised, individualised, and based on the expression of emotions. While individuals are often used to express their emotions, those acting in official institutional capacities usually appear emotionless, even stoic. The visualisation of emotional individuals helps journalists to represent the 'public' impact of calamitous events that government officials are responsible for controlling, and of laws and official decisions. Thus, crime victims, and their neighbours and relatives, are often used to express grief, revenge, and yearnings for security. This is part of the more pervasive 'What is it like to be involved?' question designed to add human interest to stories. While such questions are also put to institutional sources, especially police and other emergency service operatives shown in cathected scenarios of heroic achievement, they are used most often to capture individual and 'public' sensibilities.

The news also uses various visual and sound devices to visualise individuals in terms that differ from institutional sources. For example, newspaper photographs, television talking heads and radio voice clips are used with greater proportionate frequency for individual and other non-government sources compared to official government sources. Photographs, visuals, and actuality clips provide a reading of the individual's character and status, which blends with other functions, including personalisation, a sense of realism, and a sense of factuality regarding the previously unknown person and the events he or she is involved in. In contrast, officials are often already known, and in any case are made credible and authentic by their institution. Their familiarity in these respects can be used to have them make a statement without the additional readings available in a photograph, visual or actuality clip.

B: GOVERNMENT INSTITUTIONS

As documented in Table 7.1, government sources (criminal-justice, public administration, other) were cited more than private sector sources and individual citizens. On a proportionate basis, government sources were cited in the newspapers and on radio about twice as often as private sector-organisation sources. In television, however, government sources were cited only marginally more than were private-sector sources.

While government sources have the greatest access to the news (Tables 7.3 and 7.4), they are also the most likely to be shown as the targets of control action (Table 7.2). The focus on controlling government institutions was especially strong in the quality television station compared to its popular counterpart, which focused more on controlling the individual. Although the quality television station was itself part of the Canadian Broadcasting Corporation, an agency of the government, it nevertheless gave particular emphasis to control actions taken against other governmental institutions. There was an even stronger emphasis on control actions against government institutions in the quality newspaper, compared to its popular counterpart, which focused more on control actions against individuals. While the quality newspaper had a major business section and had a self-proclaimed focus on business interests, it was the least likely of the six news outlets surveyed to depict control actions taken in relation to private corporations. This fact underscores the point that this newspaper policed governmental operations on behalf of the private sector, providing a form of intelligence about governmental activity, useful to business. The news media, and especially quality newspapers, provide knowledge about, and police, the information-production activities and procedures of government on behalf of private corporate interests.

C: INSTITUTIONS OUTSIDE GOVERNMENT

Herman (1986 p. 172) observes that 'second only to the government as a news source is the business community, which also showers the media with a vast array of press releases for both individual firms and associated trade and public relations offshoots'. However, the data in Table 7.1 indicate that private corporate sources are not represented frequently in news. While there is some variation by type of news outlet, they appear with about the same proportionate frequency as individuals, and sources representing non-state groups. These data lend credence to the view that private corporations have the power to stay out of news (Tuchman 1978; Ericson, Baranek and Chan 1989, Ch. 5).

Private corporate institutions are depicted as the targets of control actions with some frequency (Table 7.2). Like individual 'criminals', private corporations and other institutions outside government are typically 'framed' in the news by legal categories of government. Reporters approach many private sector activities in terms of the regulatory and compliance-enforcement processes of government. On the other hand, private corporate sources do not receive much news access as control agents (Tables 7.3 and 7.4). They are more likely to be depicted as subject to the compliance law enforcement actions of government agencies than as taking control actions against others, or being mobilised as control agents on behalf of others.

Community interest organisations, in contrast, achieve proportionately more news access in the role of control agents (Table 7.3). However, as is the case with news access given to individuals, community organisations that appear in the news bear the strong imprint of both news media and government-legalistic formats and frameworks. The news media and government regularly select and define various 'insider' and 'outsider' interest groups, alternatively granting them access which makes them part of 'majority' circles, or denying them access which confirms their 'minority' status. For example, the news media and government embrace aspects of women's rights, especially as these relate to consensual issues such as violent criminal victimisation, much more than they embrace, say, gay rights (Rock 1986). Another example is provided in the case of community organisations that try to participate in the control of crime. In Canada, organisations that have failed, such as the Guardian Angels citizens' patrol organisation, have been unable to accord with police and media hegemony regarding what is in the public interest. In contrast, the Crime Stoppers organisation has joined forces with the police and media in the process of crime detection and control. In collaboration with the media, Crime Stoppers serves as an additional means by which the normal crime discourse of the police is legitimated (Carriere and Ericson 1989).

Individuals, small businesses, and most community organisations simply lack the resources to cultivate reporters, establish trust, and sustain ties in ways that allow them regular membership in the deviance-defining élite of authorised knowers. Major government institutions and private corporations are able to combine the authority of their offices with extensive knowledge resources and sophistication in packaging news to obtain better coverage. In particular, access to the news media is often dependent upon access to other institutions and their forms of knowledge. Resource-rich institutions can afford expertise that is inaccessible to others, and this expertise gives them an upper hand in influencing news communications. For example, Stone (1975) reports that a major utility company hired a prominent scientist to address environmental concerns in the public culture, and had this expert report directly to its Vice-President for Pubic Relations (see generally Blyskal and Blyskal 1985; Ericson, Baranek and Chan 1989).

The ability of powerful institutions to obtain routine access is best revealed by comparing them to the situation of community organisations representing minority interests. In general, a reporter can portray a minority interest negatively without risking an ongoing relationship based on trust and reciprocity. Indeed, the reporter can often enhance her relationship with powerful official sources through negative portraits of marginal organisations and individuals. A representative of an organisation concerned with minority rights articulated how his group faced this situation constantly:

> Usually what happens, of course, there is *the* side, which is usually an official one of some sort. We're always the other side. . . . *The* side, by what it's doing or saying, defines what the other side is and that's finally how, journalistically, it gets represented. . . . There's an order in these sides, a prioritisation. Usually what we get to do is react to something that has already happened (Ericson, Baranek and Chan 1989, pp. 295–6).

Major institutions have established the factuality of their discourses. Their texts are treated as if they are unmediated, as if they capture what really happened or is at issue. This is overlaid by the power of the news medium itself, especially television, which provides a recognised format that leads people to accept what it presents as what really happened (Altheide 1985). Against this double template of factuality, non-institutional sources are doubly disadvantaged. This structured inequality in news access is articulated by the same minority group member quoted above.

> About the only way we can ever get into the news is when in fact there is a conflict between us and one of these more reputable sources of information or of action. . . . [But] what we print and send out in press releases is not regarded automatically as information, whereas the output of the police forces is regarded as information. That's because we are perceived as an outside group, outside of society, and therefore our information is not likely to be information but propaganda. Whereas what the police print is merely the truth, or a series of facts at the very least. Obviously this gives the police a special access to the process of forming public opinion. As long as there are these great institutions in our society which can churn out reams and reams of stuff that's called information or news, we're competing with this huge machine (Ericson, Baranek and Chan 1989, p. 295).

WHO GETS ACCESS: INTRA-INSTITUTIONAL COMPARISONS

The analyses presented to this point document substantial variation in news access and control *across* different institutions. However, it is also important to emphasise that even *within* a given institution there is variation in access and control related to particular needs for news and the ability to alternatively gain access or stay out of the news. This intra-institutional variation is exemplified in the case of criminal justice, one of the institutions that appears most frequently in the news. A comparison of prison, court, police and legislature (criminal law-making) news access reveals substantial variation in the need for news, and in the spatial, social and cultural arrangements for controlling access.

Prisons are relatively closed institutions for the purposes of news. It is rare to find a regular 'prison beat' reporter, the exceptions being communities where prisons are dominant (as with the *Whig-Standard* in Kingston, Ontario) or where there are special ties between the prison administration and a particular news outlet (as occurred in Chicago over a twenty-five year period – see Jacobs 1977). Prisons are run in terms more of administrative discretion than of external review and accountability, and this veil of administrative decency has effectively kept out the news media. This observation is borne out by content studies that indicate that stories emanating from prisons, or about prisons, are rare statistically compared to court coverage and especially police coverage (Dussuyer 1979; Graber 1980; Garofalo 1981; Jacobs and Brooks 1983; Ericson, Baranek and Chan, 1991; Doyle, 1992).

Courts are relatively less closed. Reporters are given an office and develop ongoing relations with reporters from other news organisations, and with sources, in a distinctive beat culture. However, they are very restricted to particular spaces (e.g. the courtroom, but not the Crown Attorney's office during plea-bargaining sessions), and to particular organisational documents. This restriction emanates from a combination of formal source control (including the law), work expediency, and norms of propriety that evolve among journalists and their sources (Epstein 1975; Fishman 1980; Dreschel 1983). Key actors in the court are reluctant to divulge knowledge because they are legally restricted from doing so, or have been socialised into being reticent about talking to the news media about a particular case. For example in Britain and Canada judges will not 'second-guess' their decisions to a reporter and are even reluctant to talk about issues on a regular basis for fear of tainting the image of their office as independent. The reporter is left to convey what the court has pre-established as public information, knowable through its presentation in public display settings such as the courtroom.

The police are relatively more open. Unlike the courts, they have full-time public relations specialists and news-media officers who are proactive in disseminating knowledge and arranging for 'media events'. While this aspect of openness is a sign that efforts are being made to exact more control over the news media, it is also a sign that the police recognise the need to be more open and to accommodate perpetual demands for news-media coverage. In the face of being used at the forefront of public debates about the relation between the individual and the government, and as a sign of government accountability, the police recognise the importance of allowing reasonable access to the news media and the accountability allowed by its discourse. An additional consideration is that the police are unable to contain knowledge about their operations. The large urban police organisation is open to myriad communication channels because of its size (often several thousand members), and internal divisions, which make control guidelines and official contexts (news releases, the press room) only partially effective in controlling news (Chibnall 1977; Ericson 1989).

Legislatures, as law-making bodies, are most open. They must show public accountability routinely, and the news media are the most significant vehicle for displaying it. Legislature news-beats are characterised by myriad full-time media-relations personnel and consultants whose job is to represent political interests through gaining news access. Politicians and senior civil servants recognise the importance of the news media not only to the authority of their office, but also to their ability to stay in office (Sigal 1973; Cockerell *et al.* 1985; Golding *et al.* 1986). In the interest of maximising their news access while relegating their opponents to less access or marginal coverage, sources at the legislature expend enormous resources through a variety of proactive media strategies, and allow considerable access to selected back-region settings. On the other beats, reporters must pester sources and remain dependent upon them. On the legislature beat, sources must pester reporters and it is reporters who are in control.

HOW IS ACCESS OBTAINED?

There is little overlap in coverage among news outlets in a local market. In our survey of popular and quality outlets in radio, television and newspapers in Toronto (Ericson, Baranek and Chan 1991, pp. 242–3) we found that, with one exception, there was concurrence in coverage in only a minority of instances. In a separate analysis of popular and quality newspapers, we found that there was overlap in only about one-quarter of the items. These findings of low concurrence are consistent with studies that analyse concurrence in crime news (e.g. Hauge 1965; Davis 1973; Ditton and Duffy 1982) as well as those considering concurrence in all types of news items (e.g. Epstein 1974, p. 367).

These findings suggest that what yields news access is not embedded in the event itself, nor in the commonalities of the craft of journalism, but in what can be visualised by the journalist and his or her sources within the medium and market constraints of the particular news outlet: 'What is newsworthy . . . is not the particular act or deed itself so much as what can be done with it, how it corresponds to the criteria of accessibility, visual quality, drama, action, audience relevance, and ease with which it can be encapsulated and given a thematic unity' (Altheide 1985, p. 20).

Medium and market format constraints determine what journalists and sources are able to categorise, choose, organise and represent as news. Some aspects of format, in particular those pertaining to medium characteristics, are essentially invariant and autonomous features of news communications and therefore of the very ability to communicate.

The influence of medium format constraints on access can be illustrated in the case of television news. Television is the exemplar of 'drama in a dramatised society' (Williams 1989). Television news, like the advertising system that supports it, has moved in the direction of non-discursive, entertaining formats of presentation. All sources wishing to appear in television must dramatise their appearances. A television producer stated to me in an interview that news must be packaged in a glittering way so that viewers who have just finished watching Carol Burnett will stay tuned for the news. In noting that the show's rating had gone up to twenty-four per cent of the audience in the previous eighteen months, this producer observed that Kellogg's is widely assumed to spend more on their boxes than their cornflakes (Ericson, Baranek and Chan 1987, p. 86).

Some sources benefit from his development more than others. Within the criminal justice sphere, for example, the British and Canadian courts remain largely print- oriented, and have actively resisted television in the courtroom because of the assumed effects of its dramatised formats. In contrast, the police have embraced the dramatised formats of television because they fit with the views of crime, law, and order the police generally wish to espouse. A remarkable North American development in this regard is police and rescue shows – e.g. *America's Most Wanted, Top Cops, Cops, American Detective, Rescue 911* and *Code 3* – that re-enact criminal cases or provide actualities of the police and rescue teams at work on cases. In this new genre, news becomes an entertainment police serial, and an entertainment police serial becomes news. These shows have high ratings because they are about 'real' events. They do what television news cannot do in its ninety-second items: they show the process of police work; offer sympathetic 'what is it like to be a police officer fighting serious crime?' understanding; and provide detail. The same type of blurring occurs in the other direction in films such as *JFK*, which are presented as entertainment but with news footage and related formatting suggesting that the drama accounts for what really happened.

The dramatised format of television news gives it expressive power. As such it is more accessible to, and benefits, sources who are able to appear authoritative and knowledgeable regardless of their knowledge-ability. As Meyrowitz (1985, pp. 103, 108) observes, it is therefore acceptable for a politician to appear on television reading a speech everyone knows was prepared by someone else, but it would not be acceptable for that someone else to appear on television reading a speech everyone knows was prepared by the politician. Moreover, television allows certain charismatic characters to become powerful communicators through their expressive rather than their discursive capacities. Thus President Bush chose Arnold Schwarzenegger as one of the 'personalities' in support of his 1992 election campaign.

Television also has special validation powers because of its visual capacity. The visual capacity of television allows it to bind its messages to the context in which they were produced. The greater the capacity to bind messages to context, the greater the validation powers of the medium. As politicians who preen themselves for television interviews know best, television can capture not only the offices and assembly rooms where important decisions are made, but also the source's dress, demeanour, and direct reaction to questions, from which readings of character are made. Television's capacity to bind messages to context and thereby validate its messages accounts for the fact that survey research in Britain, Canada and the United States consistently shows that readers find television news more believable, fair, and influential than radio news or newspapers (Glasgow University Media Group 1976; Royal Commission on Newspapers 1981b; Robinson and Levy 1986; Fiske 1987).

The dramatisation, expressive and validation powers of television news are especially valuable to sources who do not have validated knowledge to present. What appears on television news is not usually some visual evidence of an event actually occurring, but simply talking-heads or voiced-over-head shots of people talking. For example, less than two per cent of the news sources in a television programme we surveyed were shown as actually involved in the event reported on, in spite of advertised claims that it was 'everywhere' with its 'live eye' cameras to bring events to people spontaneously and instantaneously. This news programme was not different from other news media we studied in mainly presenting sources as normative witnesses to events occurring elsewhere and previously. Moreover, in over ninety per cent of instances sources provided no additional sources of evidence to back up their claims. It is their statements alone that stand for the reality of the matter, statements that are dramatic and expressive yet validated by the television medium (Ericson, Baranek and Chan 1991).

Newspapers have not escaped the imprint of television's dramatised formats. Popular newspapers in particular have been described as the closest thing in print to television (Royal Commission on Newspapers 1981c). Yet newspapers have distinct capacities which provide for different kinds of access. They cite a greater number and range of sources within a given news item than either television or radio, thereby providing a more discursive presentation (Ericson, Baranek and Chan 1991, p. 184). As part of their discursivity, newspapers provide a range of explicit opinion formats, while television and radio news offer virtually none (Ericson, Baranek and Chan 1991, p. 151). Whether in features or in complex continuing stories, newspapers are more capable of introducing experts and their specialist knowledge than is television or radio news. While television news can use its visual capacity to establish context and to present written materials on the screen, this is of little help when it comes to detail and expert knowledge being conveyed because the television news audience member, unlike the newspaper reader, has no chance for retrieval, for introducing his or her own redundancy, unless he or she goes to the trouble and expense of recording the material and playing it over. While specialist knowledge is conveyed in other formats on television, it is revealing that 'ideas' programmes provide follow-up printed transcripts of what was said so that the reader can introduce his or her own redundancy at leisure. It is also revealing that in televised distance-education programmes, such as those offered by the Open University and the BBC in Britain, the written textual materials are paramount and the broadcast materials are secondary (Paulu 1981, p. 270).

Medium formats are entwined with market considerations in influencing the distinctive nature of access offered by a given news organisation. The market orientation a news outlet tries to find for itself combines with its medium-format constraints to yield a distinct process of access, of knowledge-flow, system of knowledge, and type of knowledge. The popular format is characteristic of all television news because of medium considerations, and is chosen by particular radio and newspaper outlets for marketing purposes. It features particular knowledge: factual updating (largely bureaucratic constructs); and evaluation and tertiary understanding (largely from the people as *vox pop*, and from low-level government operatives such as the police), both of which are personalised and dramatised. Enclosed in these terms, the popular format is preferred by particular sources, especially the police, politicians, and others whose personal and institutional careers are crucially dependent on helpful news and positive images. The quality format suits particular newspaper and radio outlets, but is available to television in a more limited way because of medium constraints. The quality news outlet features a more discursive presentation of knowledge: multiple institutional sources who offer greater depth in the form of explanation of events as well as evaluations and recommendations pertaining to legal change and political reform. Relatively more accessible in these terms, the quality format is preferred by particular sources, especially those who can benefit from specific instances of adversarial-style journalism to bring about the legal changes and political reforms they desire.

WHAT REMEDIES ARE AVAILABLE WHEN ACCESS IS NOT OBTAINED?

As much as a source institution tries to routinise participation in the news media, there are many occasions when it fails to achieve the access it desires, loses influence over news communications, and suffers negative publicity. When these problems occur the source institution can take various initiatives to remedy the negative publicity and improve access. However, with the exception of law suits, the formal mechanisms for redressing access problems are fundamentally within the control of the news media institution. News media formats and practices still control the terms in which access is given to deal with a previous problem of access.

One formal mechanism for remedying access problems is to ask the offending news outlet to publish a correction or retraction of offensive material. However, sources see published corrections and retractions as limited and problematic. They can perpetuate publicity about matters sources would prefer to see disappear quietly. They often re-state the original problem publicised and therefore fail to undo the damage. They are subject to news editing, so that for example they are delayed, copy-edited, and given less prominent play than the original item. If the journalist intended all along to control or hurt the source, complaining can give a clear indication that he or she is having the desired effect. Remedies that keep the matter alive through more publicity carry the threat of further damage to the source. Knowledgeable in this regard, most sources believe that it is better to be silent than sorry. Furthermore, to negotiate a factual correction is to accede to the news institution's parameters of factuality, range of opinion, and interpretive framework. It therefore contributes to the power of the news institution and its preferred readings of the matter, rather than being a challenge to it. Moreover, a news outlet can benefit from publishing the occasional correction or retraction because it indicates that such errors are indeed only occasional, thereby giving greater factual legitimacy to everything else.

A second formal mechanism for remedying access problems is letters-to-the-editor. As addressed earlier, while letters columns may appear as the most accessible of all news formats, they are actually closed in terms of the same criteria of selection and use as all other news copy. In the letters format, letters must fit prevailing newsworthiness criteria; preference is given to regular sources who appear elsewhere in the news; and letters are not published if they complain about competing news outlets or advertisements in the newspaper. Letters are conceptualised as idiosyncratic personal opinion, and as self-serving, and therefore not as factual as the original items they address and might complain about. They also have all of the problems of published corrections and retractions enumerated above.

A third mechanism for remedying access problems is to seek access through a different news outlet. However, this alternative is limited because one cannot count on the different news outlet to directly criticise the offending news outlet. Competition among news outlets in a local market does not go to the extent of direct criticism of one another because they would quickly regress into doing nothing but – and because it would erode the credibility of the news-media institution and therefore affect the commercial interests of everyone. The best the aggrieved source can do is offer an account to other news outlets in the hope they will provide more reasonable coverage than the offending outlet.

A fourth mechanism for remedying access problems is to buy access in advertising space. The fact that institutions spend so much on advertisements to correct the record on matters of importance to them is a clear sign that journalists do not always give them the access they desire (Singer 1986, Part III). At the same time advertising is less attractive than news space because it is more clearly contextualised as self-interested in comparison to the greater neutrality implied by a 'third party' news account.

A fifth mechanism for remedying access problems is the use of regulatory agencies such as press councils or broadcasting commissions. While these agencies are in some sense external mechanisms for redressing access problems, they are seen by most regular news sources as operating squarely within the criteria and interests of the news media institution. These mechanisms involve delays of several months, and therefore have no immediate relevance for remedying access problems. These bodies are also seen as having no real sanctioning power against offending news organisations. They are there to cool out complainants and to secure the autonomy of members more than as a mechanism of accountability and control (Kingsburg 1981; Royal Commission on Newspapers 1981a; Ericson, Baranek and Chan 1989). One of the few news sources we interviewed who had bothered to complain to a press council said his organisation was 'not expecting anything to happen, but it just makes you feel better, I guess, just writing the letter.'

Libel and defamation suits, seen by the news sources we interviewed as the only truly external remedy for access problems, were also seen as the least effective. Interviewees reasoned that these law suits are too expensive, involve wrongs that are especially difficult to establish or prove legally, perpetuate negative publicity, affect the source's ability to obtain any type of more favourable access in the future, and involve settlements that are minimal and that sometimes include the requirement to remain silent about the settlement. Faced with these perceived limitations of formal mechanisms for remedying problems of access after the fact, most sources recommend informal mechanisms of cultivating positive relations with journalists. In our survey of news sources, one-third said there is simply *no* effective remedy for past access problems other than trying to improve relations directly with the journalists concerned. Their central message was that if you have not taken precautions to meet the requirements of access in the news-media institution's terms, then you are left to take your lumps.

CONCLUSIONS

The news media institution is entwined with all other major institutions in society, and what it publishes or broadcasts is a product of its involvement in the everyday life of these other institutions. While the communications must be within the terms of news discourse, the news media template is not the only one evident in the news nor is it autonomous. There are also the templates of the institutions being reported on. News presents the ways of knowing of both the news media institution and source institutions. The news is open and plural in this respect: myriad voices are represented across and within sources institutions, and across and within news outlets whose formats vary substantially by medium and market criteria.

It is 'a lived hegemony' as a process, not as a 'finished article' that appears in the news. Through a focus on conflict and opposition in and between major social institutions, the news provides 'indicative features of what the hegemonic process has in practice had to work to control' (Williams 1977, pp. 112–13). Daily news about procedural propriety, rights claims, value conflicts, official versus unofficial versions of events, and expert renditions of events testify to hegemonic processes at work. Since there is a high level of conflict and contradiction in the discursive struggles of news production in these terms, conflict and contradiction are also evident in daily news.

News must remain accessible to a considerable degree in order to accommodate the plurality of institutional participants in the process of news communication. The social relatedness and intertextuality of the news media institution mean that news is necessarily diverse, equivocal, transitory and contradictory: news outlets are compelled to produce much more than can be policed (Schlesinger *et al.* 1983; Fiske 1987). Moreover, the influences of news texts have similar qualities of diversity, equivocality, transitoriness and contradiction. Influence, too, is a function not only of news media organisation, content, and mode of presentation, but also of the broader social networks of which the news media and their sources are a part.

Access is not as neat as others have argued. In answering five basic questions about media access and control I have presented a view that differs from other sociological approaches to the subject. The *dominant ideology* approach, exemplified by the work of Hall *et al.* (1978), views the news media as an ideological apparatus that maintains class formations. The news media are treated *ab initio* as a mechanism for reproducing ideology and maintaining hegemony. Dominant meanings are seen as an *a priori* effect of pre-ordained privileged access to particular sources rather than the outcome of strategies and struggles in the social contexts of news media production and reception. The *organisational ideology* approach, exemplified by the work of Fishman (1980), views the news media as an ideological tool of source institutions and bureaucracies. News content is pre-ordained by the formats and practices of sources, whose bureaucratic propaganda is transmitted with little struggle or even thought; and by the routines of journalists, which articulate with these source formats and practices. The *media ideology* approach, exemplified by the work of Altheide (1985) and Altheide and Snow (1991), views the news as pre-ordained by media formats. The power of the medium not only dictates what appears in the news, but unidirectionally affects how people in other major institutions format their own activities.

All of these views of access are unidirectional and overly-deterministic. It is patently wrong to say dominant meanings are always a given because of pre-ordained privileged news access to the powerful (Hall *et al.* 1978), or because journalists 'expose themselves *only* to settings in which formally organised transactions of official business occur' (Fishman 1980), or because news formats always dictate what sources do in various social arenas (Altheide 1985; Altheide and Snow 1991). News is more open and plural than any of these approaches allow.

Access stops at the doors of institutions. Individuals without institutional credentials are shut out. People who are not bilingual – who are not able to speak simultaneously in the terms of their own institutional discourse as well as the discourse of the news media institution – are shut up. There are many options among source institutions and news outlets, but once a choice is made there must be conformity to the terms of the discourses involved. Thus access is not free. It bears the imprint of institutional templates and the positive and negative freedoms these templates entail.

NOTES

1 For more detail on how these data were derived, see Ericson, Baranek and Chan (1991, Ch.3). We sampled news items over a thirty-three day period in six Toronto news outlets, including a quality newspaper, a popular newspaper, a quality television station, a popular television station, a quality radio statio, and a popular radio station.

2 The design, sample and analysis of data for this study are described in Ericson, Baranek and Chan (1989, Ch. 6).

3 See Ericson, Baranek and Chan (1989, pp. 346–9). Where an organisational affiliation was indicated 57.5 per cent (46/80) of the letters were accepted, compared with only 27 per cent (76/282) where the organisational affiliation was not indicated. These findings are statistically significant (where $X^2 = 20.80; df = 1; p < 0.01$ corrected for continuity in 2x2 table).

4 See Ericson, Baranek and Chan (1989, p. 349).
Only 15.7 per cent of those who did not cite other sources had their letters accepted, compared to 38.4 per cent of those who cited one source, 41.3 per cent of those who cited two sources, and 54.5 per cent of those who cited three or more

sources. Where at least one source was cited 40.9 per cent (108/264) of the letters were accepted, compared with only 15.7 per cent (16/102) where no sources were cited. These findings are statistically significant (where $X^2 = 19.78$; $df = 1$; $p > 0.01$ corrected for continuity in 2x2 table).

5 The subtleties of newspaper and radio medium format constraints cannot be considered here, but are elaborated in Ericson, Baranek and Chan (1991), especially Chapter 2 and Table 2:1, 'A comparison of newspapers, television and radio news formats', in that chapter.

6 The observations in this section are based on interviews with ninety-three persons who were regular news sources. For greater detail, see Ericson, Baranek and Chan (1989, Ch. 6).

7 Preparation of this paper was funded by a research grant from the Social Sciences and Humanities Research Council of Canada, and by the Contributions Programme of the Solicitor General of Canada to the Centre of Criminology, University of Toronto.

8

Postjournalism: journalism is dead, long live journalism! The Gulf War in perspective

DAVID L. ALTHEIDE

Access was not really the issue . . . greater openness would not necessarily have produced better coverage

(Michael Massing)

INTRODUCTION

The nature of access and control has changed in our time.

A French television journalist described his experience in covering the 1991 Persian Gulf War:

> 'I started to work on 2 August. We wanted to go to Kuwait . . . Of course, nobody went to Kuwait. I reached Dubai on the third of August. . . . I stopped my coverage just before the ground attack, around 15 February. I spent around three months in the area. The most important thing I remember . . . is that in Saudi Arabia, we saw absolutely nothing . . . that was one of the reasons I came back, I got fed up' (Field notes).

This sentiment was frequently expressed by journalists we talked with in the US, UK, France and Italy. Ironically, even though journalists were generally unable to do 'their work', the Gulf War nevertheless received the most intensive news coverage of any single event in our history! My attempt to explain how this occurred will include an overview of how **media logic** has altered the relationship between news organisations and sources; how military officials learned to better orchestrate information from coverage of prior wars; and how a new kind of **war programming** has emerged.

This chapter takes a somewhat different approach to the issues of access and control in the news media. It is important to stress how access to the media takes on a different meaning today. Access, while still relevant, is not the problem it once was, especially as channels and outlets have expanded. We are in a situation beyond access; the bigger problem is not access but rather what is necessary to gain it, and what happens to your material? Answers include the potentially disquieting contention that the Gulf War was perfect television, and that treating the government sources in the usual post-mortem of such events as cunning propagandists and manipulators may obscure some other developments in journalism.

Historically, access has been part of the ecology of communications and control. The *ecology of communication refers to the structure, organisation and accessibility of various forums, media and channels of information.* One way views and interests could be controlled in a media-technological age was to control access to media channels. This was basic throughout history, including controlling and regulating who had knowledge-access via technologies and skills for using various media, including language, speech, writing, etc. These were all features of control and order, and their codes and logics defined the hierarchy of order and legitimacy in a society. Social power, communication, discourse and control have historically been joined. Yet, throughout history, the relevance of various forms of control changes. As availability and access to various dimensions of life increases, then its relevance diminishes (Couch 1990). The intellectual challenge is to recognise new moments in the *reflexive process* of the ecology of communication in order to develop more comprehensive paradigms and perspectives for adequately interpreting events. This means being sensitive to finding even other barriers and limitations, impediments which interfere with **the capacity to contribute to meaning and dialogue**. This is essential for defining the situation; to share in the definition of situations, and to explore the consequences. It is the nature of 'access', then, that must be articulated within an understanding about the ecology of communication.

AN APPROACH

I will proceed as follows. My guiding premise is that how an event is communicatively organised is very important for what is communicated. First, I will give an overview of the logic of TV news and suggest how this played a key role in setting the stage for the production of the Gulf War as a programme. Second, an overview of the nature (rather than only the content) of news coverage of two events, Grenada and Panama, will be presented in order to establish a kind of baseline for comparing the production of the Gulf War. Previous work on other Middle East conflicts, e.g. the Iranian hostage crisis, and several related analyses of news coverage of terrorism also informs my approach (cf. Altheide 1985). As I discuss in more detail below, the news coverage of the Gulf War has been exhaustively investigated, and I will not duplicate that effort here, but instead will present materials from the Gulf War coverage to illustrate the **production logic**, including what was special about this war as a kind of television programme (cf. Morrison 1992; Taylor 1992). I will also address this analysis to clarify this new genre of coverage that has been nurtured by information technology, global communications, and an increasingly convergent set of perspectives among world leaders and news organisations about the nature, relevance and role of the mass media in our time.

In order to further draw out some of the theoretical implications of previous work, I will not repeat what was obvious from this coverage, and what numerous other critics noted, namely that 'all the truth was not reported', and that this was due to various pressures and influences on the news media, e.g. corporate control, overly compliant news sources and officials, and journalistic dislocation. Rather, my approach is to 'reverse angle', so to speak, and focus on the news media perspectives and orientation because my studies of the mass media's impact on culture suggest that media logic and communication formats dominate the ordering of events. My approach is to view the Gulf War in terms of news media work, perspectives, logic and formats.

MEDIA LOGIC AND POSTJOURNALISM

What most Americans – and most of the world – knows about the Gulf War and the 'combatants' is related to the dominant information sources they use. This suggests that the sources and the media which carry them are major players in any information game. We now know unequivocally that these media are not passive, neutral, and inconsequential for shaping the messages. While this understanding does not negate the importance of some 'event' – in all its ambiguity and uncertainty – for news content, it does strongly suggest that news messages are not merely reflections of some event, but rather, that some complex relationships are at work.

In general, *media logic consists of a form of communication, the process through which media present and transmit information.* These elements work together within the confines of what we have termed 'media logic', or the general guiding assumptions and principles which govern the interaction between **audience members – a medium (technology) – a subject or topic**. Since media 'answer' or 'solve' this relationship in various ways, each medium has its own format. Indeed, research indicates that within a particular medium, e.g. television, there are also distinctive genres which can be identified by format differences. Elements of this form include the various media and the formats used by these media. Format consists of how material is organised, the style in which it is presented, the focus or emphasis on particular characteristic of behaviour, and the grammar of media communication. **Format becomes a framework or a perspective that is used to present as well as interpret phenomena**. A key element of this perspective is *format control*, or how the content is defined, selected, organised and presented. Material is continually selected in the modern (and postmodern) age on the basis of **what can be done with it**, does it have the necessary requirements for the medium, and its purpose, e.g. commercialism, entertainment, and so on? These are key questions, and are central to issues about access now, but especially in the future as more countries communicatively converge around similar formats and modes of information processing.

This relevance of format in modern newswork for all news, and in the perspective and activities of 'news sources' that have learned the news formats as a key to news access, is considerable. It is the rise of format-driven planning and orchestration that has helped produce our **postjournalism era**. As we stated elsewhere (Altheide and Snow 1991, p. x ff.):

> In a media world, organised journalism is dead; we are postjournalists for two general reasons. First, journalistic practices, techniques and approaches are now geared to media formats rather than merely directing their craft at topics; second, the topics, organisations, and issues that journalists report about are themselves products of media – journalistic formats and criteria. In a sense, it is as though journalists, and especially TV journalists, are reporting on another entity down the hall from the newsroom. Public life subscribes to the media logics and formats that have been spawned in our age of electronic information; the politicians and others who are covered use the same criteria the journalists do, and often more skilfully!

A key element which has helped create the postjournalism era is also central to any discussion about access to media outlets. I refer to

sources and the way in which their position has changed with respect to news organisations. As a plethora of work on the perspective, tasks and interaction of sources and news agents has shown, sources have learned the discourse, formats and logic of newswork, and have incorporated them into their own planning and construction of events (cf. Ericson *et al.*, 1989; Schlesinger *et al.* 1983; Paletz and Schmid 1992).

The formats for the selection, organisation, and presentation of mass mediated information are ever expanding and becoming more sophisticated. *A key feature of this format for TV news reports is the nature and extent of visual information that is required, and increasingly provided by prospective news sources.* Television 'tells time', or allocates time according to the news item's capacity to generate and be presented with visuals, particularly entertaining video tape representing action, drama, emotion and conflict. Our work, along with others, has shown the power of this perspective in accounting for the expanded use of TV and other news channels by law enforcement, criminal courts, undercover police procedures, the process for defining a range of 'social problems' ranging from 'missing children' to domestic violence, to child abuse and molestation, to drug wars, 'gonzo justice', and many others. It is no longer the case that the state is the sole agent as a 'source' for managing information and seeking to influence information; rather, the format knowledge, skills, discourse and techniques for 'getting our story out' is widespread and embracing. Social issues, events, and their sub-texts of morality, punishment, and control can no longer be separated from the frameworks employed by journalists and others who work on them. More than ideology, postjournalism cuts to the core of the very appearance of information and knowledge. It is for these reasons that my work for more than a decade has focused on how communication is organised, and especially, what must 'information' look like in order to be sanctioned as 'newsworthy'. This approach, while still mindful of the content of information, shifts considerably toward the more generic form and shape of information. I find coverage of recent wars a useful place to continue the investigation about the form or information.

A plethora of work on the logic and perspective of the work of TV news production indicates that a significant element of any prospective news item is its visual representation and potential. Visuals are a key element of TV formats, which refer to the way in which communication and information is organised, presented and recognised. Formats are meta-communication features of any information or message. One example is the shape and size of a television screen; a related one is the volume and channel controls on electronic media. Regardless of what one wants to see or hear, these devices and their accompanying logic must be encountered. It turns out that the **technological** features of a medium can spill over into other constraints and requirements of a particular medium, including **production-logical** and **purpose-logical** formats. For example, the cultural context in which TV news is organised and used – including its commercial features – is an important part of the 'news code' or the news formula. Similarly, the related concerns of 'how to attract an audience' in order to gain more advertising revenue has implications for entertainment, dramatic visuals, emotional resonance with an audience. I am examining here some core elements of entertainment and 'good programming'. Of course, there are others, but these are among the most important.

These considerations are central to understanding the nature of recent news coverage about peace as well as conflict since such topics are interpreted within the organisational world of newswork in different ways. What is selected for coverage and how it will be presented is largely contingent on 'what can be done with it' in terms of the prevailing format and logic. In a sense, then, news events are not 'selected' so much as they are 'recognised' as a likely news item. Conflict, drama, action, and especially war is newsworthy for a number of reasons, but it has special relevance to TV news because of its potential for dramatic visuals, e.g. explosions, bombs, people running, and a range of emotional reactions of people.

From the perspective I am offering, TV content is a production through and through; it begins with and is guided by certain news codes and format criteria. Those occurrences or 'happenings' which are most compatible with TV news formats, then, are most likely to be sought out for inclusion. Quite often, since newsworkers also solicit certain news sources which can provide 'the kind of events we need', the sources themselves are highly selective (cf. Ericson *et al.* 1989; 1991).

THE DISAPPEARING EVENT

Examining some of the news coverage of the recent Gulf War, and contrasting it with coverage of other conflicts and events, illustrates some of the points about temporality, control and formats, and how sources and journalists share perspectives. The Gulf War was a television war, but it was done through accepted formats of news, sports, and press conferences. And just as a plethora of research has demonstrated how the nature of this coverage has altered events, e.g. politics and sports, so too has it changed 'wars as news events' (cf. Altheide and Snow 1991). It was reported on 28 March 1991 (*The Arizona Republic*, p. A2) that National Football League (NFL) Films 'is putting together highlights of the Persian Gulf War for a documentary co-produced by the Pentagon'. A spokesman for NFL Films stated: 'I don't want to say that war is the same as football, but our talent as film makers can very easily be transferred to this sort of venture.' After the article noted that the production 'will include footage of bombing missions and ground assaults on the Iraqi army', and that viewers 'should expect booming narration and orchestral music with the declassified military footage', the NFL Film spokesman added 'Football is obviously the military's sport of choice . . . President Bush even called it his "Super Bowl" '.

Information was put together in ways required by TV formats in particular, and news information in general. More was involved than simply being a 'media event' discussed by Dayan and Katz (1992); this was not a mere broadcasting of history as they suggest, but rather, from a different perspective, history was being constructed through media logic. Citizens throughout the world became TV-war-viewers, and incorporated their viewing activities into what Robert Snow has referred to as the routine order or 'temporal ecology' of everyday life. Not only did it interfere with other activities, but people called television stations wanting even more information. CNN's ratings soared by several hundred per cent, and newspapers became a secondary source of information for many people. Some print and radio journalists were quite critical of the coverage. The Director of Information for France's most popular TV station TF1 explained:

> The same problem with pictures of the war existed for the other channels. There was not enough pictures, but people were very interested. People watched, and the press was very jealous. "We had experts each day . . . military experts." That's not enough for the press. Everything we could do was . . . wrong' (Field notes).

The Gulf War and the major conflict-managed events that preceded it, poses major problems for journalists, but especially scholars and other critics. **The Gulf War news coverage, and especially that of television, was a production in its own right. The Gulf War may be the first 'news PROGRAMME' rather than a conventional NEWS programme**. It was not regular news reporting, or regular special reporting; rather, the coverage was planned months in advance of the actual 'start' in order to have 'up to the minute', if not 'live' coverage, but it would be different from anything that had ever been telecast. The nature of the news coverage about the Gulf War was not simply due to journalists' being duped or misled; most realised that they were part of a massive propaganda and 'disinformation' campaign, even prior to the bombing of Baghdad. Still, the war was covered, usually on the 'sources" terms because they supplied the visually dominated reports on which TV news formats thrive. News organisations covered the war even when they knew they were being misled systematically; putting on the newscast and grabbing the audience was more important than 'getting it right', because there were other considerations than 'getting it right'. As Meyrowitz (1991) noted, 'TV's hyper-selectivity of stories tends to present events without the context and perspective needed to make rational sense of them'. And, 'In the recent coverage of the Gulf War . . . we heard more about the siren-interrupted sleep of the correspondents than about the history and context of the conflict'. The main idea was to 'get it', to be 'part of it'. The journalists were even smaller components of this production than regular newscasts. The same French journalist noted above, explained:

> 'When you work in Lebanon, you know what you do. If you are on the West side you work with the Syrians. It is clear. If you work with the Christians [you work with someone else]. It was just a small piece of truth. During this war, nobody knows what the truth [is], nobody knows what we saw . . . we have so many things, so many pictures, we don't have the possibility to check, to be sure, of anything'.

Our work to date makes it clear that the French journalist was not alone. Networks, in the USA, the UK, Italy – and likely, others as well – knew they were part of a massive propaganda effort, a practised 'disinformation' campaign, at the beginning of the coverage. For example, during a conference I attended of the Royal Television Society in Manchester in November, 1991 – some two months before the Gulf War began – a top British correspondent, Nik Gowing, made the following comments as part of a videotape presentation to the audience:

> Since the airlift of American forces to Saudi Arabia began within hours of Saddam Hussein's invasion of Kuwait, military and political planners seized on the television image as a vital tool in their strategy . . . [notes that the early images were of military preparedness, putting massive forces into Saudi Arabia]; television images that were beamed into Saddam Hussein's bunker had achieved their aim of halting any planned military advance but the military reality was different. There was less hardware in the desert than claimed and fewer troops and personnel. We now know there was less of a military capability than these images suggested [notes the overworked transport systems, loss of spare parts, and no reliable

inventory] but despite this confusion sources say that television images have achieved what President Bush and his strategists wanted – the impression that the anti-Hussein allies would sacrifice no effort or resources to stop Iraq's aggression. For Iraq, too, Western media coverage has clearly been a vital tool as Hussein weighs his options . . . it's known that foreign news reports are a major source of his intelligence; television is therefore a medium and transmission, not just of images of hostages, and of statements, ultimatums and information, but also for disinformation. In other words the potential for both sides to manipulate facts and intentions in order to deceive the potential enemy . . . [people are then quoted; conflicting messages noted]; as the world sleepwalks into war, broadcasters are having to decide how far they compromise and succumb to the news management of war; do they report without question or do they expose the inconsistency and thereby possibly undermine allied strategy?'

Still it was covered, night after explosive night. And like many other events, the TV coverage informed newspaper and news magazine accounts as well. The distortions, propaganda and manipulations have been widely noted by others. One piece which summarises much of this criticism and adds its own analytical critique is Kellner (1991, p. 2):

In this article, I shall analyse some of the ways that the mainstream media served as a mouthpiece and amplifier for U.S. foreign policy in the crisis in the Gulf. I will argue that the range of policy discussion in the mainstream media during the pre-war crisis period was woefully restricted and that the media thus failed to serve their public interest requirements of providing a diverse range of opinion on issues of public importance. In particular, they failed to inform the public concerning what was at stake in the Gulf crisis, what the consequences of war would be, and who would primarily benefit from a Gulf War. In retrospect, I would argue that the uncritical coverage of Bush administration and Pentagon policy worked to make war practically inevitable and helped to promote and legitimate the eventual military attempt at solving the crisis.

I concur with the thrust of these other studies and criticisms. Indeed, my extensive data from TV news reports in several countries take the critique a step further, to explore how it was possible that such essentially single-minded coverage could have occurred. What was the 'it' that was covered, then? What was it that a world-wide audience watched in 'real time' and in video-tape replays? What does this kind of coverage tell us about the nature of TV in the face of peace and conflict, and the nature of journalism more generally?

THE LOOK OF WAR

A general thesis of this work is that war looks like good television. That is, if it is done 'right', meaning what is right for television. As stressed above, the key is what is visual, and what qualifies – and seems more likely – to be capable of, and selected for, visual news coverage. No wonder that 'social conflict' is a staple of TV news (cf. Cohen *et al.* 1990). In a sense, conflict is potentially better 'television' than 'peace' which might also be very newsworthy, e.g. the reconciliation of East and West Germany. Indeed, the reaction by TV journalists to the 'Fall of the Berlin Wall' was much less involved than the coverage of the Gulf War. The Director of Information for France's TF1 explained: '[We] had a crisis cabinet – working twenty-four hours a day; people [journalists] liked it. People did not want to take time off. People were proud to be with the channel'.

I asked if they did anything different in covering the Berlin Wall and related events and the response was, in paraphrase: 'The Berlin Wall was very important for us, more so than it was for the American people, but the war was very spectacular; the implication is that nothing like a crisis cabinet was formed; it did not have the same meaning, even as the war' (Field notes).

But some wars are also more interesting than others if they are more relevant to TV coverage, including the all-important visuals. On our road to clarifying whether there is something about 'peace' that runs counter to TV formats, and therefore is likely to not qualify for rather extensive coverage, the remainder of this chapter will look at how some recent wars and conflicts involving the United States were covered by television in particular. I will examine briefly some relevant aspects of the Grenada and Panama invasions as television events, followed by the most recent Persian Gulf War.

The Gulf War coverage grew out of a television tradition, including the Vietnam War, and the more recent military conflicts including the Iranian hostage crisis, the Falkland Islands, Grenada, and Panama. Some very raw numbers for Grenada and Panama provide a shadowy overview of the relative amount of time given to these events by one American network, compared to the Gulf War.

Grenada: for the two-week period 24 October to 7 November 1983, ABC news devoted approximately 115 minutes (less than two hours) of its regular newscast to Grenada.

Panama: for the two-week period 20 December 1989 to 4 January 1990, ABC news devoted approximately 111 minutes of its regular newscast to the invasion of Panama. Several of these newscasts were pre-empted by NFL football games!

Persian Gulf War: for the two-week period 16 January 16 to 1 February 1991, ABC virtually revamped its regular evening newscast around the Gulf War, and devoted 406 minutes – nearly seven hours – to its coverage. As the Vanderbilt University Television News Archive Index noted:

> The Persian Gulf War, which virtually began on 16 January during the evening news time period, often altered the half-hour format of the week-day news broadcasts. A few times the evening news programme was pre-empted by, or simply extended into, special reporting on the war. At other times, the evening news was expanded into one hour coverage, sometimes with the second half hour pre-empted by the local affiliates.

Indeed, ABC presented its regular one half-hour newscast on only two days (30 and 31 January) during the two-week period!

The Gulf War coverage differed from the two most recent American invasions, the Grenada excursion in 25 October 1983, and the invasion of Panama on 20 December 1989. These two came on rather suddenly. The Gulf War differed because the major TV news networks had advance warning to plan better, had more lead-time and preparation, and did not have to rely on the 'press pools' exclusively for coverage, since they had months to prepare. But there were also some other major differences between these conflicts. These included ideology, planning and preparation, duration, destruction, and media antagonism/adversarial and partnership relationships.

Very salient for Grenada and Panama TV coverage was the network's lack of access to preparation and 'combat' zones. Indeed, there was a clear hostility toward the press in general, and an explicit attempt to keep them uninformed. After all, these were 'surprise' attacks, albeit the word was out days, if not weeks, in advance. Moreover, the news coverage was avoided and forbidden with Grenada and Panama, as journalists were prevented from having initial access to the general 'theatre', and in a few instances with Grenada, US armed forces directly prevented craft bearing journalists from proceeding to the island, threatening to destroy them! At the other extreme, the Persian Gulf War, journalists and TV cameras were welcomed and deployed in controlled and regulated 'press pools', but the important point is that they were a major part of the staging of the operation. Indeed, the military/government(s) involved in operations 'Desert Shield' and 'Desert Storm' went to some lengths to assist the major networks in obtaining 'appropriate' video materials.

Grenada was the worst defeat for the US press, especially TV news, because they were not allowed to accompany the invasion, and had a tough time landing visuals. Still, they presented visual reports, but they were just not of the fighting, but ranged from simulations of forces, graphics of maps (with voice-over), radio reports in which the words were put on the screen, and a few interviews.

On 25 October 1983; CBS news allocated 7 minutes 50 secondss to the coverage of the Grenada invasion itself, with another 4 minutes 40 seconds focusing on Reagan's rationale and the State Department activities. The first report is what concerns us. The report was separated into eight segments, or parts, in which there was a clear division in attention, e.g. shift to locale, different reporters, etc. The thematic emphasis of the initial reports were informed by the recent bombing several days earlier of a Marine barracks in Lebanon.

Americans are dying again in military actions in foreign countries. Some died in Beirut and some were killed today in a military operation that began today in Grenada after events in island last week led to a US invasion.

US now has strong military and used it, but hopefully will not have to stay long in Grenada.

There are reinforcements if necessary.

We need to have some justification in being there, and have some not only in American civilians being there, but also due to the build-up of Cuban and Soviet interests there.

US officials promise that we won't be there longer than necessary but still, lives may be lost.

There was some negative reaction globally.

These points were illustrated with graphics (e.g. slides); radio transcripts; words on the screen from film provided by a student on Grenada; Defense Department (DOD) file film of various weapon systems; DOD film of military aircraft on the island of Barbados, ships; file tape of Grenada's beaches.

Since journalists were not given direct access to the very brief encounter, which was over in a matter of days, a good deal of press attention was given to visual topics that were more accessible, including critics comments, which included many from the Soviet Union as well as allies led by the vociferous Margaret Thatcher. It was not until 27 October that the US military permitted fifteen journalists and their escorts to enter Grenada (Mungham 1987, p. 301). But it was the unloading of bodies at Dover Air Force Base which provided some of the most memorable video footage.

The following is from our data about the coverage from 29 October and 1 November. The importance of actuals, or tape of a recent event is noted.

29 October:

a. At Dover AFB, ceremony for men killed in Beirut bombing – the mood was very different there: flag draped coffins resting on floor of hanger, fourteen marines and one sailor killed at Beirut bombing and one captain killed in Grenada.

A few of families travelled here for brief service – the chiefs of the services most affected led the mourning: 'come home to our beloved US' (the Navy). After twenty-minute ceremony, chiefs offered condolences to each of the families; father spoke and said they were proud to have their son be a marine – the son wrote many times and said 'we needed to be there'. There will be many more ceremonies here as this base becomes way station for those who fell in Lebanon and Grenada . . .

c. 'Mood was very different' – 'caskets rested on the floor' – 'services most affected' – 'I salute you dear brothers in uniform' – 'as I wept inside I asked, Lord, where do we get such men?'-'the way station for those who fell in Grenada and Lebanon'.

e. ACTUALS: *anchor with graphic flag and heart shaped locket; flag-draped caskets on floor of hanger labelled Dover AFB; to zoom-out showing caskets and soldiers standing at attention; families sitting in chairs, couple being escorted to seat by uniformed man; close-up of hanging flag with zoom-out showing caskets and soldiers at attention; couple, man has arm around woman, looks sad; family; caskets; chiefs giving speeches at podium; band playing 'Halls of Montezuma'; service chiefs shaking hands, saluting crowd lined up; father speaking at podium with marine behind him; marines in dress uniform walking in single file with rifles raised; anchor solo.*

8. Some joy, some sorrow follows war. Dangerous mission for Rangers. Parents of son killed in Beirut think he should have been there. More sombre ceremonies will follow for Beirut dead.

9. More ACTUALS *– less file.*

1 November – Segment 1 – 2 minutes 30 seconds:

a. Twenty-three killed in Grenada and Lebanon honoured at Dover AFB in Delaware at largest service yet for men killed in service of their country. Army spokesman: 'they join a long line of compatriots'. One of compatriots (note use of one dead to exemplify others) buried in Ohio, first 'of at least four Ohio sons to come home this way' (shows casket being carried by pall bearers) – nineteen, been in marines one year.

Mother says: he 'was American all the way, we talked about what Communism is, and he didn't want that in America'.

Mark Cole was good at football, average academically, knew everybody.
Principal says: he'll be remembered as boy 'with quick smile, pleasant personality'
(audio bad, hard to hear) . . . brotherhood of marines . . . Mark liked . . . (audio
hard to hear) . . . last photos he sent parents days before he and others were killed . . .
Father: 'he knew he had to be there, those people could not survive without it'.
Helped parents build their modest home; put his name and 'mom' in cement ceremony
in Baptist church; eulogised as a Christian first; family has 'rationalised' as God's
will, not military or political miscalculation.
Mother says: 'people should be proud of country and stand behind president'.
b. Family's dealing with death of young son in military action.
c. Army spokesman; US military; father and mother of son killed in bombing; high
school principal.
e. Anchor with graphic of flag/locket.
ACTUALS: *dress-uniformed marines carrying casket into church, labelled 'W. Milton,*
Ohio'; close-up of photo of Mark Cole in dress uniform; close-up of interview with
mother; W. Milton high school; pictures of football team, showing Mark; interview
with high school principal; photos sent home by Mark, of marines in group, marine
looking through binoculars on stand, marine near building, close-up of marine in
uniform with helmet. ACTUAL *of interview with father.*
ACTUALS *of family's home, close-up of where Mark carved his name and the word*
Mom in wet cement.
ACTUAL *of parents walking; church; inside of church; close-up of woman crying;*
pastor eulogising; marines carrying flag-draped casket at burial; marines raising
rifles; Delaware labelled; 'voice of Sandy Cole'; soldier playing Taps; photos son
had sent home.

Panama was different: despite the lack of complete access, there were
a lot of visuals available. This was mainly because the networks had
more extensive visual files about Panama and Noriega, and also because
they had more time to prepare them. Compared to all other conflict
events we have studied, the coverage of the Panama invasion used more
graphics (including photos, logos and maps) per news report.

PANAMA

The entire newscast on 20 December 1989 was devoted to the invasion
of Panama. A key reason for this was that press pools had been established, there had been speculations for weeks that an invasion would
take place, and alleged attacks of Americans living in Panama had
been widely publicised during the weeks preceding the invasion. More
importantly, there was a coherently orchestrated effort to depict Panama's leader, Manuel Noriega, as the drug-devil incarnate, complete
with pre- and post-invasion raves about his heterosexual and homo-

sexual activity, voodoo, scarred complexion – 'pineapple face' – and about his drug-running and dealing that was claimed to be affecting the United States. In short, few informed people were surprised when George Bush ordered the invasion of Panama to arrest and 'bring to justice' his former CIA colleague. When 'Operation Just Cause' was planned and then launched, the electronic and print press was primed, had been working on press pool arrangements for some time with the Pentagon, and were ready to work.

The invasion of Panama occurred in a context of other major events in Eastern Europe, especially Rumania. My findings concur with Morrison (1992, p. 73 ff.) that news reports often featured comparatively more tape of actual fighting in several of the Eastern European countries, because the reporters were less restricted. I present only those materials from ABC's coverage pertaining to Panama here. Summaries of some five segments follow of actual footage of the attack, fire and smoke, soldiers. The early segments dealt with the invasion itself.

> *The general message is that the invasion of Panama has been completed, but news people have been kept away from action.*
> *Bush thinks he had good reasons for invasion; Noriega may be a bad guy but U.S. went along with him before.*
> *Rumanian demonstration shows increasing tension where soldiers demonstrated along with crowd. In Lithuania there was rare split in Communist Party. To say the least, a very strong message of world unrest, told by a calm Jennings who appears to have the world at his fingertips, yet uses 'we' terms as if he is sitting right in viewer's living room.*
> *The main focus was on Manuel Noriega, who had been demonised by extensive press prior to the invasion. Some of this tape was provided by the Defense Department.*

Also included in my summated presentations are comments about numerous graphics, maps, and visuals of President Bush, other White House officials, and some congressmen who challenge the decision, and some discussion of who might follow Noriega into office e.g. Endara. (Note: as we collected some of these data I wrote in my notes 'CBS basically completed in one newscast for Panama, what they did for several months with Iraq!')

In sum, the entire broadcast essentially dealt with Panama, with the largest amount of the coverage focusing on 'The Attack'. ABC anchor Jennings carefully articulates words when he talks about casualties (as if to show concern); beginning with actual videotape of helicopters instead of the usual anchor shot suggests the importance and action of what is to follow. This initial coverage of Panama used far more actual videotape of fighting than the Grenada invasion, although the coverage of both supplemented their 'actuals' with graphics and file materials. My research team got the distinct impression that this invasion was not questioned as much by news people, and others, compared to the Grenada invasion. One change that did occur was the coverage of death; in the Gulf War we saw little even though there was a lot; in Panama, as with Grenada, despite the low number of American casualties, they seemingly received a good deal of coverage partly because the 'wars' were short, but partly because the visual opportunities at Dover were too good to not emphasise. A portion of the CBS news transcript on Christmas Day (25 December 1989) gives the tone of this coverage during the invasion of Panama.

DAN RATHER: *'The bodies of two more US soldiers killed in Panama were returned today to Dover Air Force Base in Delaware. The Pentagon says officially twenty-three US servicemen have been killed in action and 303 wounded in the invasion. Correspondent Bruce Morton looks at this Christmas Day as it was observed by some Americans who fought in Panama, and by the American families who cherish them. (Church service; congregation singing 'Joy to the World'.)*
BRUCE MORTON: *All over the country today Americans prayed for their soldiers in Panama.*

Before proceeding to a discussion of the Gulf War coverage, it may be helpful to reflect on a few key comparisons in coverage of Grenada and Panama. There are some other troubling points to be considered in trying to assess the nature of the news coverage across these conflicts. In a manner that was consistent with some of the practices carried out by the British government during the Falklands War, journalists' access was severely limited. Also, like the Falklands experience, the press was increasingly aware of how its access was being limited to certain events, yet it was still able to cover the events; indeed, they became more determined than ever to present even censored materials, on their regular newscasts and numerous specials. We will see that this was particularly true during the Gulf War. Another consideration is that despite the limits on video tape – the most important visual tool for the networks – they relied rather heavily on graphics, still photos, and simulations, seemingly in inverse relationship to the availability of video tape: that is, *the less tape there was available the more graphics and simulations would be used.* With Grenada, compared to the Gulf, the networks were a bit caught off-guard, since it happened so quickly. With the former, the networks really had to freelance – sometimes literally using freelance 'ham radio operators' on Grenada or Barbados. We shall see that in the case of the Gulf War, they had ample warning and preparation that the events were being planned, beginning in August, until the actual attack on 16 January 1991. It should also be noted that there were 'reflective' and critical pieces broadcast about both ventures within a year or less of the completion.

There is another curious feature of the coverage of these conflicts. Conflict is quite normal to news operations, and indeed, many would argue that news- worthiness or news values are implied by the notions of conflict, deviance, and even war. What is also important is the co-presence of network criticism of an event, particularly governmental action, and the extent to which the access opportunities are open or closed. Stated differently, if news access is limited, if news agencies are not part of the action, so to speak, it appears that they are more likely to be somewhat critical of the overall operation. No causal connection is made here since even if networks gain access it does not guarantee that they will engage in favourable, promotive reports of the government pursuing those aims. Indeed, analyses of news coverage of the Falklands War (cf. Glasgow Media Group 1985; Morrison and Tumber 1988; Mercer *et al.* 1987), Grenada (cf. Mungham 1987), as well as other conflicts suggest that the political context in which journalists find themselves often treated as administration adversaries should not be overlooked. However, to not let something 'be public', and 'secretive' does clearly imply control, so there must be some sharing or openness, at least of a strategic nature, to partly offset the negative features of coverage.

Another element of this rather crude equation is that the work of the networks changes if visuals, and particularly the all-important videotape is not available. Recall, that a central feature of the TV news format – especially the regularly scheduled evening news report – is that time and importance are 'marked' with videotape, especially dramatic, action tape. Thus, the interest in combat footage (or Superbowl highlights), arose. From this perspective, what the journalist needs is exciting video-tape for the evening newscast; their work entails access to the tape, the visuals. That defines 'air time', 'importance', and to a remarkable degree, 'good work'. If the access and the tape is not forthcoming, as was the case in Grenada, then we have a peculiar situation. On the one hand, some coverage must follow since, after all, one's country is involved, and viewers are interested in this sort of thing – in part because of the constant hype of conflict and violence that pervades news and entertainment programming. Also, the other news organisations are likely to cover the war. There is the archival file and graphic materials to use, as was done with Grenada and Panama in particular.

Following the invasion of Kuwait by Saddam Hussein's forces in August, complex negotiations, military posturing, planning, and extensive media work took place before UN (primarily US) directed fire which descended upon Baghdad on 16 January 1991. Thus nearly five months of preparation was put to good use by the networks, particularly in view of what they had learned about Pentagon and Defense Department distaste for their presence during Grenada and Panama. They knew that the notion of 'press pools' would be invoked for the Gulf War coverage, and it was, despite the journalists' protests. During a congressional hearing on the control of the press by the Pentagon, the dean of American journalism, Walter Cronkite, stated:

> With an arrogance foreign to the democratic system, the U.S. military in Saudi Arabia is trampling on the American people's right to know. . . . Because of these onerous and unnecessary rules, the American people are not being permitted to see and hear the full story of what their military forces are doing in an action that will reverberate long into the nation's future.'

Cronkite took aim at the Pentagon's pool system, which dispatches limited numbers of reporters accompanied by military 'escorts' to units chosen by the military: 'The press should be free to go where it wants, when it wants. . . . We have a pre-censorship now with the military deciding what will be reported and when. . . . I'd rather have a post-censorship.'

Cronkite said such a system of free reporting with censorship before publication worked well during World War II and could be equally workable in the Persian Gulf despite advances in television technology that enable live coverage: 'It doesn't really matter whether we report it this minute or this hour or this day even . . . as long as we can report it in due time'.

The American networks took several steps to provide entertaining coverage for their viewers, including special news programmes for children! First, they developed additional simulations, beefing up their computer graphics. Being uncertain of what they would get in terms of 'hot visuals', they developed extensive graphics which, with the sophistication of computer software programmes, went over very well indeed. Recall, that there had also been the bombing of Libya in 1986 in retaliation for that government's suspected complicity in aiding those who bombed a disco in Athens, resulting in injury to some American troops stationed there. This was shown with computer, cartoon-like caricatures of planes on bombing runs, and it was all edited to Kenny Loggins' *Highway to the Danger Zone*, the theme song for the hit movie, *Top Gun*. (Note: Air Force pilots were reported to 'psyche up' for combat by listening to rock music through their own 'earphones' in the cockpit of their jets.)

Second, the networks lined up military experts to discuss tactics and weapons. These people became quasi-co-anchors, since they were on the air so much between August and the end of the Gulf War in March. While we will return to this point a bit later, it is critical to stress the significance this had for coverage; anchor sets were constructed as space was made for the military experts who were given equal – if not greater – voice and credibility than the journalists! One post-war observer, Danny Schechter (1992, p. 30) noted how the use of these 'experts' further joined source and journalist:

> The Pentagon's chief in-house briefer, General Thomas Kelly, would later joke with Johnny Carson about how easy it was to control the press conferences. He drew laughs when describing how the briefers met before-hand to strategise and plan who to call and who to ignore. The 'trouble-makers' were put in the back, out of camera range. When Kelly retired after the war he was promptly hired by NBC News. ABC's military consultant Anthony Cordesman previously worked at a conservative think-tank and for Arizona Senator McCain, an ultra-right-wing Vietnam PoW . . . Now Cordesman is back in McCain's office – jumping back from the centre of media power into politics.

Moreover, the network anchors learned the military discourse and lingo from these men, while the military experts became ever more skilled at speaking to video of weapons, and the timing and rhythm of exchanges with the anchors as well as other reporters. Similar adjustments occurred in other countries including France and Italy.

Another thing the networks did in preparing for their Gulf War coverage was dig into their extensive visual files. Now computerised in sophisticated filing systems, these materials could be retrieved, copied, edited and updated by being inserted into 'historical' reports and 'situation' reports, which were being laid out in advance of the actual conflict.

Our presentation of the TV coverage of the Gulf War can be described in several stages:

1   the invasion of Kuwait, negotiations and planning;
2   the air war;
3   ground war;
4   settlement; and
5   post-war.

1: Invasion of Kuwait, negotiations and planning
The emphasis of most of this coverage was on the history, common features of Arab unity – especially problems with Israel, accounting for the US' previous support of Saddam Hussein's government – the demonisation of Hussein, including accounts of his untrustworthiness, the close ties of the US to the Emir of Kuwait. In addition, considerable attention was focused on the nature and extent of military support to Saudi Arabia, diplomatic excursions to line up the United Nations coalition, and the massive movement of troops, particularly from the United States. Television was the star as leaders challenged each other via satellite hookups, and even aired videos of their adversaries on television! We noted elsewhere (Altheide and Snow 1991, p. 253):

> During these tense times, several US network news anchor persons raced for 'on the scene' reports, including CBS Dan Rather's 'scoop' interview with Iraq's leader Saddam Hussein. Ted Koppel was there for *Nightline* reports, and thousands of video-cameras were sent to GIs so that they could record their experiences. Bush complained that he did not have the same access to the Arab people as Hussein did to US news-watchers, although Bush would accept Hussein's invitation to give an eight-minute taped statement to the Iraqi people; Hussein would request equal time; and comedian Jay Leno would opine during the 1990 Emmy Awards (for television) that the war was being fought through television! Indeed! Organised journalism covered it all.

Domestically, while there was considerable public discussion about various options to the situation, the news media – and especially TV – as documented by analyses by FAIR (*Community Data Processing*: Mid-east media, 16 January 1991) a 'media watchdog', gave little attention to alternate views:

> A new FAIR survey shows that nightly network news programmes largely ignored public efforts to oppose the Bush administration's military policies in the Persian Gulf. FAIR examined five months of TV coverage of the Gulf crisis, from the first commitment of US troops on 8 August 1990,

until 3 January 1991. Of a total 2855 minutes devoted to the Gulf crisis – nearly two full days of coverage – only twenty-nine minutes, roughly one per cent, dealt with popular opposition to the US military build-up in the Gulf.

FAIR executive director, Jeff Cohen, commented (16 January):

> Now that a war is actually starting, the networks are finally noticing the anti-war movement, but the coverage is often no more than a blur of street action – from mass marches to the flag-burnings of the fringe. Missing from the news are coherent statements from national peace leaders explaining their positions.

The relevance of TV news formats for ideology has been established in previous work and will not be repeated here, except to note that despite the intent of various interest groups to 'propagandise' and promote their positions, a key feature of the message is the way it is packaged. In a style reminiscent of the way Manuel Noriega was 'demonised' to help justify the invasion of Panama, known as 'Operation Just Cause', the Iraqi situation was given the video persona of wicked Saddam Hussein, compared to Hitler, outlaws, terrorists, with the most lasting nickname, 'The Butcher of Baghdad'. Such imagery appears to have contributed to the discourse and vocabularies of motive which helped frame the impending war. The media dimension was considerable.

In our media age, public relations (PR) firms have adopted the TV news formats' penchant for visuals and dramatic 'sound bites' and have shaped them to their interests. Public relations firms have become partners with interest groups on topics ranging from Mothers Against Drunk Driving (MADD), various children's and domestic violence groups, a host of medical interest groups including Muscular Dystrophy and, more recently, the phenomenally successful public relations campaign of AIDS advocates. A related approach to access is for sources to provide 'video news releases' (VNRs) of packaged messages that meet the temporal and visual requirements of news formats. This was done by 'Citizens for a Free Kuwait', to enlist American – and Congressional – support for intervening against Iraq. With primary funding from this committee, for some $11.5 million, which included the Royal Family of Kuwait, a major PR firm, Hill and Knowlton, distributed a series of atrocity stories about Hussein and the Iraqi army. A crowning point of their effort involved the use of a 15-year-old Kuwaiti girl, Nayirah al-Sabah, to give testimony in a public hearing to the United States Congress's Human Rights Caucus, on 10 October 1990 (*Columbia*

Journalism Review, Sept/Oct 1992, p. 27 ff.). She testified that she saw babies removed from incubators and killed by Iraqi soldiers. Numerous print and TV reporters presented this testimony, and subsequent accounts of terror to the UN Security Council, which were also directed by Hill and Knowlton. Her comments were referred to by President Bush in a public statement, as well as those by several senators during the US Senate debate about whether to give President Bush authority to declare war – a debate which passed by five votes. By the time the House Committee on Foreign Affairs held a hearing on the Kuwait situation, the number of alleged incubator deaths had jumped to 312, a figure that was also supported by Amnesty International, which later retracted it. Military action was officially approved four days after this hearing, and Baghdad was bombed four days later.

It was not until about a year later, January 1992, that it was revealed that Nayirah was not merely a hospital worker, but was the daughter of Kuwait's ambassador to the US, and related to the royal family. Subsequent efforts by journalists and others to confirm the alleged baby killings have consistently claimed that they did not take place. A transcript from the ABC News show *20/20*, on 17 January 1992, illustrates the journalists' 'surprise' at what had occurred. The segment 'The Plan to Sell the War' included the following comments:

DOWNS: *Do you remember, when Iraq invaded Kuwait, a report that Iraqi soldiers had yanked babies from incubators? President Bush used that story to help marshal public opinion. But is there proof that it really happened, and did a PR firm hype that story to help sell the war to the American people? Tonight, a 20/20 investigation.*

WALTERS: *No-one disputes that Kuwait's citizens were victims of Iraqi atrocities and, given what we now know about Iraq's plans to make nuclear weapons, few question that Saddam Hussein was a menace who had to be stopped. But our focus tonight is how the idea of going to war was sold to the American people. Was it sold with slick marketing and exaggerated claims? And if it happened then, could it happen again? ABC News correspondent John Martin has been following this story for nearly a year, and has this remarkable account.*

After the rather lengthy report was presented showing the testimony, the way politicians used it in promoting their definition of Hussein and Iraq, and comments by detractors who could not substantiate the slaughter, Barbara Walters and Hugh Downs had this closing exchange:

WALTERS: *Well, what does this do to the credibility of Kuwait? After all, they're going to have relations with us, they may need us in the future.*

MARTIN: *It threatens the credibility, and the government is very concerned, the ambassador is very concerned. He told me that they are scouring the country, more or less, for*

witnesses to all these atrocities, and will try to make a complete case for it in the coming weeks.
WALTERS: *As they said, absolutely fascinating, and in the emotionalism of war, the kinds of things we may never know.*

For students of the media, culture and social change, this was more than merely 'absolutely fascinating'. It was the continuation of a trend to incorporate news values, technology and formats into the process for defining a situation in a credible manner. Similar to the way in which network reporters, anchorpersons, politicians, and even Pentagon brie-fers are selected, the PR firm used focus groups, did coaching for delivery on camera, studied tapes, and emphasised key slogans and expressions for the final products that would be delivered to con-gressional committees, but more importantly, millions of viewers throughout the world.

Moreover, many informed journalists, commentators – national and local – either realised the distortions at the outset, or were quickly convinced by reading the plethora of press criticism which quickly appeared (cf. FAIR, 16 January 1991; 26 February 1991). The thrust of many of the well-documented comments is that the news coverage was strongly oriented to the views of military and governmental sources; that virtually no attention was given to non-military options until just weeks before the first missiles were fired; that the nationalistic, jingoistic and ultra-patriotic coverage was not only reflective of the military, and especially the 'hardware' and 'state of the art' weapon orientation, but that the military 'experts' (often retired) graced national news desks to provide additional 'background'.

As President Bush's deadline approached, more attention was given to the now infamous meeting between April Glaspie and Hussein before Iraq invaded Kuwait. This meeting came to symbolise the ambivalent US position toward Saddam, and the way in which he was permitted to do his own bidding without official censure, largely because he was our ally against Iran. The culminating lack of attention was when the major American TV networks did not broadcast live the Senate debate about a Declaration of War. (It should be noted that these same net-works gave extensive coverage to nomination proceedings for Supreme Court Justice Clarence Thomas, particularly following the exciting charges by Anita Hill: that he had talked dirty to her on several occasions.) The tone of most of the coverage was on strategy, and general impact of such a war, with little hard-hitting TV reportage about the likely ravages of war until around November, which then subsided until a few weeks before US Cruise missiles found their Baghdad targets on 16 January.

2: *The air war*

The visual emphasis took over during the most destructive part of the war. Featured as a kind of surreal music video, the day and night reports of 'sorties', missiles, high-tech accuracy, and focus on military targets alone surrounded the subtext, about Western industrial dominance, with humanity. Live video tape mingled with file tape, photos, computer simulations of last week's, today's, tonight's, earlier, and scenarios for future attacks. Some accounts of damage and destruction to civilians were carried partly due to compelling tape provided by Iraq and others. Speed and antiseptic 'neutralising' without blood was the point; there was little tape available for this, especially since the movement of many journalists was restricted. We became accustomed to military experts serving as co-anchors on the news sets, as war coverage became divested of political discourse in favour of tactics, weapon-lingo, and the military frame. Battle elaboration to the nth level complemented and interspersed the terrific videos of victory, as viewers became accustomed to three-dimensional maps, videos, instant replays with commentary, and forecasts for the impending action (second half?). Network anchors, here and abroad, quickly became accustomed to this format and integrated it within their vocabulary and language.

But the coverage of the earliest hours of the war were via radio by Cable Network News correspondents who gave eye-witness accounts of the bombing of Baghdad. For CNN this would be the key for worldwide planning and execution of coverage. It was the first complete satellite war which permitted the beaming of military signals and television transmissions throughout the world. CNN became a primary source of information for the militaries in the conflict, the politicians, and world-wide audiences. It came with instant replays, commentaries by retired generals who stressed the tactics, and correspondents who gushed with amazement and chagrin that they could not keep up with the pictures being received by audiences thousands of miles away from the battle scene. Even the CIA tuned in.

William Webster, newly retired head of the CIA, said . . . that he used to tell the White House to turn on Cable News Network for updates on Iraqi Scud missile shots. 'I used to get the call when the sensors detected a Scud going up in the air with its probable destination', Webster said. 'And I would push the button to [national-security adviser] Brent Scowcroft, and I'd say: "A Scud has just been launched from southern Iraq

headed in the general direction of Dharan or Riyadh . . . Turn on CNN" '
(*The Arizona Republic*, 27 August 1991, p. A18).

CNN became the standard, and the seemingly instantaneous flow of images led the way as journalists used the film they were given and permitted to obtain by military censors; the TV-valued visuals were owned and operated by the military sources and they had immediate access to around-the-clock coverage. The networks could not get enough of dramatic visuals from 'gun sight' cameras as missiles and 'smart bombs' were tracked on to the targets and into a word-wide audience connected with TV receivers. It was largely the availability of such visuals, which the networks knew would be forthcoming well in advance of the initial attacks, that led to the adjustment of formats for presenting the information. Countries around the world adjusted their news presentation to the dramatic visuals; it did not matter that months later the 'obvious' success of these numerous 'hits' would be challenged as 'misses'. What we saw is what we got. Consider some detailed notes about CNN's role in the organisation of 'war news' in Italy and France. First, France.

TF1, French TV, Tape 1, 17 January 1991:

Opens with anchor describing situation, nearly one minute. Compared to US and Italian TV with more flashy openings, including logos, graphics, there is none of this; just start with anchor.

Segment 1: *The following segment took approximately 2 minutes 50 seconds; approximately eighteen cuts are used.*

ACTUALS: *plane landing at night, on the runway, then graphic, map of Arabie Saoudite (Saudi Arabia) with cities, aircraft indicated, and flags of US, Great Britain and France. The idea seems to be to show that their forces are there, perhaps to interest viewers; the presence and actions of one's own forces are what makes the war interesting.*

Tape of aircraft flying at night; then a few seconds of a camouflaged fighter; real versus graphic? After looking at additional coverage in this report in which similar visuals are used, I realise that it is a computer simulation; this too had to be taken from CNN or elsewhere.

The French reporter talks over a graphic of CNN, a map/graphic Baghdad, with the US Embassy marked, Iraqi TV, a few other places; the face of Gary Shepard, and it says so at the bottom. This lasts for about ten seconds; the cuts are very quick, some as brief as five seconds; it is a collage of visuals, many of which are taken from CNN.

Next ACTUAL is from the USS Wisconsin; CNN credit is given; it shows a missile leaving the ship, then a quick cut to a computer graphic showing a missile leaving a ship and heading for Baghdad, about five seconds; then cut to Marlin Fitzwater speaking before a podium, then a ten-second simulation of a fighter flying, with a tank shooting at it on the ground; then an immediate cut to ACTUAL *film of a bomb going off through bomb sights, after a plane passes over; then a battery of tape of bomber runs; the terrain looks like Vietnam, with trees; more file tape of Apache helicopters; Iraqi troops, with missile launch vehicles, Iraqi TV is given credit; Scuds,* CNN *credit is given; cut to graphic/map from* CNN*; John Hollimann reporting from Baghdad, describing the missile attack: that lasts ten seconds; then computer graphic of missile striking a target in Baghdad, with flashes of flames; then cut to troops at airport, pilots walking:* CNN *credit: US Pool tape: aircraft taking off, anding, loaded. Return to thoughtful-looking anchor.*

Italian Channel 3, RAI3 24 February 1991 7.00 p.m.
Topic is land war. Opens with CNN *film of battleship explosions, troops loading guns, tanks, artillery, jet fighters: each lasts about three-five seconds; about fifteen seconds of prisoners being taken; about fifty seconds of visuals, with its own sound (no other voice).*

Then the anchor comes on: he reads in studio about the land action and introduces their reporter's report for about thirty-five seconds. Then the reporter, Flavio Fusi (Servizio Di), provides the voice over CNN *film of tanks, prisoners, oil well fires, exploding gun-sight targets, a map of Kuwait and surrounding area, with American and Iraqi flags, and even one Italian flag, showing where they are. More visuals of big guns firing at night: this lasted about 1 minute zero seconds; then a cut to Schwarzkopf for about five seconds; visuals of prisoners, marines leaving helicopters around Kuwait city, lots of firing, trenches, battleships firing, about another minute. Then cut to another reporter, Fabio Cortese, from Baghdad, showing people walking, city life, presumably discussing the impact on everyday life; back to anchor for ten seconds; then voice over of what appears to be US network film of a reporter driving across the desert, looking at soldiers, equipment, with a voice-over by an Italian. Visuals of tanks, equipment in sand, apparently allied equipment, no* CNN *credit is given for this.*

Some of this was Italian film: an Italian reporter is shown on the scene doing a stand-up; interviews are shown with the reporter troops; reporter is shown eating with troops around a tank; shown driving through a sandstorm, it had also been raining. This lasted for about 3 minutes 30 seconds; then return to anchor.

Images had access because they constituted the news reality which, as usual, was quite different from other realities. According to one freelance reporter, John Alpert: '. . . the predominance of information coming to the American people were these music videos from Saudi Arabia of planes taking off in the sunset, bombs being lovingly loaded on to planes, and what happened on the other end of those bombs, we never saw'.

Then there was the Ameriva 'bunker' full of civilians that was bombed. It was justified by military officials because their information portrayed it as a command post, so it was hit. The numerous casualties were covered by the press, but not enough, according to some. At the bunker, the images and photos were shown: horrible pictures of burnt bodies, and children. They were sent to the West but they were not shown. Note how even images that had been passed by the Iraqi censors were not used by the American networks. The networks did discuss it, however. A partial transcript from ABC's *Nightline* illustrates how 'civilian deaths' became a special component of death, something which had received little coverage to this point in the war. Another point to keep in mind while reading the transcript is that 'information management' was acknowledged by the US reporters, on the one hand, while the military spokespersons cautioned against accepting claims from the managed Iraqi press!

Nightline – 13 February 1991

Voice-over (of BRIG. GENERAL RICHARD NEAL, *US Marine Press Information Officer in Riyadh) visuals of bombed-out civilian shelter in Baghdad]*

RN: *'It was a military target and it was struck as it was planned and as it was targeted.*

TED KOPPEL: *[voice-over as visuals continue] The Iraqis insist it was a civilian shelter. [Unidentified elderly Iraqi speaks at the shelter site]: I don't know why they hit children and. . . .*

TK: *But what if it was both? [What happens] when the lines between civilian and military targets are blurred during war? We'll examine that painful dilemma tonight. [Nightline music – graphics – verbal intro.]*

TK: *Today as the Gulf War entered its second month, what has seemed too often as a remote and bloodless battle took on a ghastly human face. There is no reason to doubt the word of US military commanders who insist that what was bombed in Baghdad today was an Iraqi command and control center. But the evidence is also overwhelming that hundreds of men, women and children had taken shelter in that building. And most of them were killed. Sometimes in war, civilians are targeted intentionally. The Germans did that during the Second World War when they aimed their V1 and V2 rockets at London and then when the Luftwaffe bombed Coventry. And by grim coincidence, it was on this day, forty-six years ago that more than 35,000 Germans died as the result of Allied bombing raids against Dresden. But in this war, the United States and its coalition partners insist that they are doing everything humanly possible to avoid civilian casualties. What still remains unanswered, however, is what will happen if Saddam Hussein deliberately insulates his remaining strategic targets by placing them in the midst of civilian centers. Or by sheltering civilians at military targets – as may have been the case today. We begin with this report from Nightline correspondent Jeff Greenfield. . . .*

Note: compilation of tape and narration; many voices/images are spliced together

RN: *From a military point of view – ah – nothing went wrong. The target was struck as designated.*

JG: *Four weeks after the Gulf War began, the United States came face-to-face with the real face of war. Not the images of pinpoint hits on buildings and bridges – not the high-tech wonders that blow-up only buildings – but the deaths of hundreds of civilians in the capital of the adversary. They died in a building bombed by American planes. A building described by Allied forces as a clear-cut military target – claimed by Baghdad as a civilian bomb shelter.*
[Unidentified Iraqi male in front of shelter (thirty-five to forty years of age] A lot of children [died], many women . . .
JG: *It was the kind of horror that sent Allied spokesmen into a day-long effort to explain what had happened. And to put responsibility for the dead and injured squarely back on Saddam Hussein. This morning, at the military briefing in Riyadh . . .'*
RN: *In fact, it was a command-and-control bunker. I can't explain if there were civilians in there, why they were in there.*
ABC reporter Barry Serafin alone in Riyadh briefing room
BS: *US military officials here in Riyadh fended-off inquiries all day long until the regular briefing. On camera and off, they took a hard line. They had radio transmission and photos, they said, showing that the Baghdad bunker was a legitimate military target.*
JG: *'At the White House, where the normal rules were suspended to permit on-camera coverage of press secretary Marlin Fitzwater . . .* MF: *We all know that Saddam Hussein does not share our value in the sanctity of life. Indeed, he time-and-again has shown a willingness to sacrifice civilian lives and property that further his war aims.*
Clip from Brit Hume, at night, in front of the White House
BH: *One idea that was considered was the release of the satellite information upon which the decision to bomb that facility was made. However the CIA, as it has in the past, vetoed that idea.*
JG: *In a speech by Defense Secretary Richard Cheney . . .* RC: *There is in Iraq a city called Ur, spelled U R. It is a city of significant archaeological interest. Satellite imagery obtained just this morning indicates that there are now two Mig 21_s – a combat aircraft of the Iraqi Air Force – parked right next to the pyramid.*
JG: *At a Pentagon briefing this afternoon, Captain David Harrington – Navy Defense Intelligence Agency:. . . .* DH: *The fact that it has a camouflage roof, the fact that it has a security fence around it – barbed wire.*
ARMY LT. GEN. TOM KELLY *Everythin' that we're seein' relative to this facility is comin' out of a controlled press in Baghdad.*
ABC PENTAGON REPORTER BOB ZELNICK *So the game of damage control became one of expressing the right tone over the deaths of civilians while suggesting that Saddam Hussein had no grounds to complain because of his own Scud attacks against civilians, suggesting even that maybe he had put Iraqis in danger by situating them in a military facility.*

CNN was not without its shortcomings and detractors, particularly in the early days of the war. Their control of the technology clearly gave them power to deny access to others. Alfonso Rogo, a reporter for *El Mundo/The Guardian*, had tried to use a telephone controlled by CNN and was not permitted; at one point he and Arnett were the only two western journalists in Baghdad. He asked Arnett to use the telephone, and Arnett would not permit it, to limit the competition.

From BBC2 The Late Show 20 March 1991:

ARNETT: *We were not serving as a link for the world press, we were CNN, and I would be similarly restrictive in the future with a foreigner, and I suspect someone else who had that competitive advantage would also be restrictive he, the other reporter, got angry and stormed off; if he had been in any way reasonable, I probably would have accommodated him, but, you know, if you're dying to use someone else's communications you'd better be nice about it.*

[Rogo stresses that it is unprofessional to claim, as CNN did, that they were the only Western journalists in Baghdad, and just wants to make the point that this was not true. He draws an analogy to the way the US, when they play baseball say, 'the world cup'; when they play football, the 'world match'. He sarcastically suggests that maybe there has been a mistake made in geography, that maybe they don't realise that Spain is part of the Western world.]

3: The ground war

The ground war was preceded by some concern and trepidation about blood being spilled, not only for the Iraqi 'others' but for the 'coalition' forces as well. Massive bombing runs were made to 'soften up' the opposition, especially their well-reported, via military spokespersons, claims about being dug-in etc., but there was little video provided of the actual bombing runs. It did not matter, since Department of Defense (DOD) film of 'carpet bombing' in Vietnam was available. Long-antici-pated by news analysts, the ensuing ground war was previously scripted as part of the war narrative, as though the third stage was significant to keep in mind while presenting the air war. Without doubt, the high-tech stardom of 'smart bombs' was compelling in its own right, but it was also given meaning and significance for what would come if it did not work – the ground war, in which machines killing machines would be substituted for more bloody bodies. What we continued to see, however, was still more graphics, maps, game plans; we were in the post-modern locker rooms of death!

Victories with little death were dealt to the world's audiences, directly, bypassing journalists, who were merely bit players at televised press conferences. Indeed, the occasional journalist who would challenge the frame leading a particular 'briefing', would be cast as conflictual, and even unkind by other reporters. Indeed, popular shows, e.g. *Saturday*

Night Live, performed skits demeaning journalists' behaviour. Journalists were expected to follow the rules of access or it could be denied, and most did. Schechter's (1992, p. 30) comments are instructive here:

> The few journalists who decided it was not their job to win a popularity contest nevertheless cooled their aggressive questioning at Pentagon press briefings as the winds of war boosterism started blowing through their news organisations. They began to feel isolated and out of step, especially after *Saturday Night Live* made journalists, not the generals, the target of their spoofs. According to the *New York Times*, once the Pentagon felt it had won legitimacy from such an unlikely source, it would not revise its media restrictions. The distinctions between entertainment programming and news further slipped away.

Comments from journalists I have interviewed from several countries are well represented in the remarks of some photojournalists who reflected on some of their war experiences, including those who relied on TV newscasts ('videographs') for their photos (BBC2 *The Late Show* 20 March 1991). A picture editor with *The Observer*, Tony McGrath, explained why they published a photo of the charred remains of an Iraqi soldier burned to death in his retreating vehicle: 'I tried to find a picture that . . . would hold up the story'. He says war is disgusting, terribly disgusting . . . we'd been watching eight weeks of a:

> 'brilliantly sanitised war; nobody was killed, nobody was injured. We saw a lot of destruction down camera gun-sights, Cruise missiles operating, but we never saw anybody die; . . . all of the pictures I saw were of equipment; not one of a body; not one of a wounded person; not one of a captured person. I just thought we can't allow this to pass without telling the people what happened . . . this [*referring to the photo*] is just one of the unfortunate people. It offends and it should.

4: Settlement

Victory was won, with several major tank battles, culminating in massive destruction and entanglements along major roadways. For both military and civilians. The resulting carnage was not shown, with the exception of a few celebrated cases (noted above) in British newspapers, and later in some documentaries. The negotiations received considerable attention, including asides of anger and frustration cast toward Kuwait, and the destruction of Kuwait City. Hussein was still alive, and was actively pursuing the rebels in the North, who, with US and coalition encouragement, revolted. But the political winds had shifted, and it was not in the coalition's interest to support them, so many thousands had fled, were stranded, and were being hunted down by the still sizeable remnants of Hussein's vanquished forces. Since journalists were not restricted from pursuing these events, hundreds, with cameras rolling, began to chronicle the human misery. The visual scenes of small children being buried by distraught parents appears to have eroded Bush's position, and the US and coalition forces intervened and provided food and supplies, as well as military protection for thousands of Kurds to immigrate into Turkey, where they were not wanted.

5: Postwar

Celebrations lasted longer than the war itself. Untold thousands of Iraqis and others were killed, but few coalition forces were. Indeed, several facetious estimates suggested that the number of pregnancies which had occurred on board naval vessels during the war exceeded US military deaths! President Bush had the highest voter-approval rating of any President in modern history. Generals were pursued to serve as political candidates, including future presidential contenders, senators and university presidents! Parades were everywhere and they were extensively covered, and heroism was won by having served 'in the sand'.

As with previous wars, however, 'midnight' came around, and with it questions about truth, purpose and 'where do we go from here'? Disconcerting information came forth, as with the previous wars, that **things were not as they were seen** and believed. The Patriot missiles that were celebrated for knocking out Scuds – and we had all seen this – really did not do so well, according to a Pentagon study, hitting, by some accounts, less than ten per cent of their targets! And the size of the Iraqi army and its numerous tanks turned out to not be so large after all. Moreover, the veterans, who were only months ago celebrated as heroes to whom 'your nation owes a debt of gratitude', were soon coming down with a wide range of ailments, maladies, infections, fevers, and emotional distresses, attributed by some to their having been subjected to unproven antidotes for poison gas. Of course, Hussein was still alive, and quickly was reported to have regained control, rebuilt armaments, was unco-operative with UN inspectors attempting to locate nuclear and poison gas stockpiles and resources, as well as pursuing, at this date, another threatening minority group – the Shi'ites – in the south. This time the news reports mimicked the infamous phrase 'line in the sand' of Desert Storm, by providing graphics of what we might term a 'line in the air', as the US-led coalition forces instituted a 'no-fly zone' over southern Iraq. The pictures, themes and sources had been carefully chosen, edited, and professionally presented throughout, but here we were again, facing similar problems with the 'Butcher of Baghdad'. Stay tuned.

There is also the issue about journalistic control, integrity, perspective and future in view of this discussion about access. One very significant thing that happened in the Gulf War that has not previously been noted is the way journalists accepted the guidelines and dictates of the military-sources, and actually became self-controlling! Despite reports in several countries about the restrictive guidelines which amounted to censorship of press activities, most journalists went along with the limits, and relied on the exciting pictures. There have been numerous reports about journalists who were 'turned in' by other reporters for breaking the rules, for taking advantage of the military guidelines, partly justified by the argument that this was hurting all reporters. What had begun as a severe limitation on journalists in Grenada had been normalised over a six-year period.

CONCLUSION

In sum, the Gulf War was a postjournalism production. Within the conceptual parameters set forth by the ecology of communication, *the Gulf War was a television product*. The TV coverage and, indeed, a good deal of the way in which it was conducted, reflects information technology, and particularly TV news formats. Information was set forth in good production terms, sources and journalists shared points of view about good work, and even though some journalists would have preferred to have more options to move about on their own, in the end it did not matter. The highest viewing audiences in history were achieved through this kind of postjournalism broadcasting. Given the revenue implications, world-wide TV news (and the journalists they pay) will no doubt be willing to work within such constraints again. This coverage has emerged from a more recent history of other conflicts and the resulting negotiations, developments and definitions set forth about public information.

More specifically:

1   The history of recent conflicts and wars e.g. Iranian hostage crisis, Falklands, Grenada, Panama, is important in understanding the approach used in the Gulf War. The challenge is to connect the information that is provided, i.e. content, with how the information is organised – from sources – to what it looks like.

2 The visual information was controlled on sight; domestically, the local 'angle' was used, but there was a problem with the Dover Air Force base 'services' for the dead, which received a good deal of visual coverage during Grenada and Panama, but not the Persian Gulf.

3 All three wars follow the change in individual attributions of evil and wicked, from Khomeini in Iran to Noriega in Panama to Hussein in Iraq.

4 The Gulf War was different because of the advanced technology and planning time; other wars had been featured as news reports, around certain facts or incidents, e.g. 'there was an invasion today'. The Gulf War was a 'real TV' event. *The military planners and the network people used much of the same technology and logic in planning-to-make-a-war and planning-to-cover-a-war.* The technology was rampant in conducting and planning this war. Satellites, lasers, fibre optics, micro-processors, video-screens, computer analysis (at data stations away from the immediate action). Strategically, logically and temporally, this war occurred in the way it did partly because of the way the previous two wars (Grenada and Panama) were not covered and planned. This war introduced a new kind of 'programming', with the closest approximation of a major sports event e.g. a Super Bowl.

5 Throughout the 'technological world', there was advanced planning for months (from August 1990 to January 1991). Scripts were written, scenarios were played out, sets were constructed, three-dimensional maps were developed for studio use, file (archival) film was dug up, computer graphics and simulations were constructed; DOD film was obtained; military and especially weapons experts were placed under contract by the networks; anchors learned before, and during the 'official' war, the language and euphemisms of the military; the news was given in military discourse. It was to be a news PROGRAMME.

6 Events reflect and are partially constituted by the discourse used in thinking, planning and conducting an event. This is partly what we mean when we speak of the 'frame' of an event, as illustrated by a news report. It is usually news sources that help frame events, and, in some instances, frame the process of choosing events. This is why sources use of media logic is important in order to understand the Gulf War.

7 The Gulf War was communicated differently. Journalists were not adversaries, but were important supporters. This time the newscast was framed from the standpoint of good television and media logic. However, the production of the event and the coverage were *reflexive*. It was a massive programme dominated by the technology and logic noted earlier. The military and the President were the real producers, and they had learned a lot from those other wars. The journalists would do the rest insofar as their dominant resource, the image, likeness, were

oriented to visual materials, which were controlled and limited; they knew this would happen, but they covered it anyway, because it was good television.

Our ongoing postjournalism project reveals some rather drastic inter-pretations and applications for future events and for the issue of access. A key element is that events are now mass mediated, and can be joined and spliced together through media logic and formats to produce a kind of extended programming. This extends even to criticism, perhaps my very words! TV coverage of wars have helped join different segments together into a coherent event. It is all grist for the logic of programming to borrow from established formats and genres in producing the fol-lowing.

WAR PROGRAMMING

a) Reportage and visual reports of the most recent war (or two);
b) anticipation, planning and preparing the audiences for the impending war, including 'demonising' certain individual leaders e.g. Noriega, Hussein;
c) coverage of the sub-segments of the current war, using the best visuals available to capture the basic scenes and themes involving the battle lines, the home front, the media coverage, the international reaction, anticipation of the war's aftermath;
d) following the war, journalists' reaction and reflection on various governmental restrictions, suggestions for the future (which are seldom implemented);
e) journalists' and academics' diaries, biographies, exposes, critiques and studies about the war, and increasingly the media coverage;
f) media reports about such studies, etc., which are often cast quite negatively and often lead to the widespread conclusion that perhaps the war was unnecessary, other options were available, and that the price was too high – all of this will be useful for the coverage of the next war;
g) for the next war, return to step 1.

ACKNOWLEDGEMENTS

Support for this project was partially provided by the Distinguished Research Award from the Graduate College of Arizona State University, 1990–91. In addition to my always-helpful colleagues Robert P. Snow and John M. Johnson, I gratefully acknow-ledge the work and suggestions of Dion Dennis and Gertrude Perlin who assisted in the collection and organisation of many of the materials which have directly or indirectly influenced my work on this project. The helpful assistance of journalists in the United States, United Kingdom, France and Italy are also acknowledged. Numerous professors at the Universities of Florence, Lecce, Rome, Paris, Bradford, and Glasgow also contributed to this project. In particular, Professors Henri Peretz (University of Paris), Luigi Spedicato (Lecce), Greg Philo (Glasgow), Paul Rogers, James O'Connell and Alan Bloomgarden (Bradford). Richard Ericson (University of British Columbia) proved to be a good listener and offered useful insights about cultural contexts.

PART FOUR

9

Television, identity and diversity in the United States and Canada

MARJORIE FERGUSON

INTRODUCTION

The 'melting pot' and the 'cultural mosaic' are metaphors often invoked to convey images of two very similar but very different societies, the United States and Canada. It has been said that North America is where 'two nations have evolved that are utterly alike in almost all their externals and yet are utterly unalike in their political cultures, as distinct from each other as the Germans and the French' (Gwyn 1985, p. 11). But it must also be said that there is an important caveat: if Canadians tend to emphasise the difference, Americans emphasise the similarities.

In this chapter I seek to explore how the definitions of national identity, embedded in the melting pot and the cultural mosaic, are reflected in the social value systems and political institutions of the US and Canada and how in turn these definitions impact on their broadcasting systems with respect to issues of media diversity.

Questions about who has access to which (or whose) media, and who dominates media content and controls its diversity are questions to ask across frontiers as well as within them. In the continental context of the US and Canada, such issues are dramatised by their 3500 miles of contiguous electronic frontier. For over seventy years, Canadian audiences have been bombarded (and mostly, quite happily so) with American radio and TV. And in addition to sharing much geography and media, both nations have in common other socio-economic and political conditions, e.g. democracy, peace, a market economy and relative prosperity. So it is perhaps all the more surprising to discover what they do *not* share by way of social values, political institutions, or broadcasting ethos. Divergences in the latter include legislation, regulation, promise and practice that are accented by political responses to growing cultural diversity more generally and multi-cultural TV audiences in particular.

The two countries, in economic terms, do comprise the world's largest trading partnership (some $190 billions Canadian in 1991): the US-Canada and North American Free Trade Agreements are predicated on that basis. Contrary to notions of continental (or global) homogeneity, the somewhat surprising fact is that Canada retains a considerable cultural distinctiveness despite its citizens' appetite for *Oprah, Married with Children* and American popular culture. Here government support for Canada's cultural industries arguably helps to maintain a public discourse reflective of Canadian lifestyles and communitarian values.

By the same token, the melting pot and cultural mosaic highlight issues of representativeness and diversity in broadcasting media content, just as the concentration of corporate media ownership highlight barriers to broadening of base media access, ownership and control. Canada's attempts to assert sovereignty over media industries that help construct and reconstruct a collective sense of 'Canadianness' is chalking up some modest successes (see e.g. Paul Audley and Associates, 1991). This interventionist model offers one that others, e.g. the European Community, may follow in attempting to foster local, regional or national media voices inside a global video marketplace.

Thus, ideas about the globalisation of culture that equate the transnationalisation of capital, markets and communication with Americanisation would predict that Canada and the US comprise a single, homogenous, continental entity. The cross-border picture is far more complex, multi-dimensional, and murky than this scenario suggests (Ferguson 1992; 1993). My point is that Canada offers a counter-case to mediacentric or technology-driven explanations about the pervasive power of television to determine culture, where the role of media in cultural formation can be over-extended. In Canada, as elsewhere, the omnipresence of American films and television does not break down the complexity of Anglo, Franco or multi-cultural identities or their media representations. The multi-dimensionality of identity based on, e.g. religion, language, gender, race or region is emphasised and inflected by electronic mediation of context, stereotypes, and symbols. It follows that the media's intimate connection to cultural construction and symbolic representation in late capitalist societies in no way lessens the acculturation process imposed by history.

From this premise flow these arguments. First, electronic media constructions and reconstructions can influence but do not necessarily shape the self-concepts of their media publics; and second, Canada offers a counter-case to assumptions about an undifferentiated, 'global-ised' culture based on consumption of common symbolic and material goods. It illustrates how such reductionist claims fail to stand up even on a single-continent basis.

ISSUES OF MEDIA AND DIVERSITY

Both Canada and the US were founded by immigrants and have developed increasingly polyethnic, multiracial cultures. As 'new' societies, both offer distinctive examples of the construction of 'imagined communities' (Anderson 1983) and 'invented traditions' (Hobsbawm and Ranger 1983) that have important consequences for media diversity, dominance and access.

McQuail (1992) in his analysis of media performance in democratic societies clarifies the concept of media diversity as extending beyond political theory. Today it is an end in itself, a broad principle open to a range of interpretation and manipulation: 'to which appeal can be made on behalf both of neglected minorities and of consumer choice, or against monopoly and other restrictions' (p. 142). National media systems differ in their emphasis on these policy goals, as will be shown with the US and Canada. Thus media diversity can refer to performance standards, pluralistic reflection, more audience channel choice, as well as diversity meaning access when media:

> 'make available' channels through which the separate 'voices', groups and interests . . . can speak to the wider society, express and keep alive their own cultural identity where relevant . . . can also help people to communi-cate among themselves, especially where sub-group members are widely scattered . . . the most essential conditions for effective access are: freedom to speak out; effective opportunity to speak (there being a sufficient number of independent and different channels); autonomy or adequate self-control over media access opportunities' (McQuail 1992, pp. 144–5).

Clearly, diversity as access includes not only freedom for non-domi-nant groups in society to communicate and be heard but also, by way of corollary, national autonomy or self-control over cultural industries and products. In markets inundated with imported (usually American) film, television and music, questions of national access become highly problematic. This is a situation that runs counter to the ideas of classical liberal democratic theory or a Habermassian public sphere where voices compete in the marketplace of ideas (see e.g. Curran 1991). Here the hollowness of much free market, 'free speech' rhetoric in media systems dominated by external and/or oligopoly domination is clear. As Keane (1991) has argued, such contradictions are endemic to market liberalism and their consequences mean that '. . . markets fail to guarantee the open expression and representation of opinions . . . [and] . . . also contradicts freedom of communication among a plurality of citizens' (p. 114).

It follows that media diversity can be interpreted either in terms of relative access between nations or between groups within a single state. Left exclusively to market forces in a media system overshadowed by American product, it is fair to say that without support for distinctive cultural industries most Canadians, eighty per cent of whom live within one hundred miles of the US border, would not realise to the extent they do either their complex, multi-faceted national identity or their communitarian cultural values and collectivist social priorities. Such characteristics differentiate them from their southern neighbours' fierce adherence to the foundationalist values of individualism, exceptionalism, market forces, and legal minimalism.

CULTURAL ETHOS AND NATIONAL IDENTITY

On both sides of the 49th Parallel difficult questions are being asked about 'who' or 'what' is American or Canadian, and what 'being' them means. There are no ready answers when such complex concepts and processes are at work. For instance, cultural ethos refers to the shared history, myths, symbols and social values that help define, and in turn are defined by, among other things, ambiguous notions of 'national identity' (see, e.g. Schlesinger 1991, 1993; Smith 1991). In the context of this chapter, national identity refers more to *who* is American or Canadian, rather than *what* being them implies – although both are interwoven.

Historically, Americans have devoted comparatively little attention to self doubt or northern neighbour comparisons. An insightful approach offered by Lipset (1990) emphasises the different history, cultural inheritance, core beliefs and 'organising principles' of the two nations. From the outset, he claims, Canada was Tory, conservative in the Euro-British sense of 'accepting of the need for a strong state, for respect for authority, for deference – and with the support of hierarchical state-supported religions'; America, on the other hand, was 'Whig and classically liberal or libertarian, doctrines that emphasise distrust of the state, egalitarianism and populism – reinforced by a voluntaristic and congregational religious tradition' (Lipset 1990, p.2).

More recently, the growing angst on the part of Americans about their own cultural cement is causing much public and private rethinking. Second thoughts about what the melting pot *means*, are dividing debates about political correctness, family values, gay rights, pre-life, pro-choice or 'owls versus jobs'. In what he calls the disuniting of America after almost two centuries of consensus, historian Arthur Schlesinger Jr. (1991) offers pessimistic conclusions:

> The escape from origins has given way to the search for roots. . . . The new gospel condemns Crevecoeur's visions of individuals of all nations melted into a new race in favour of an opposite vision: a nation of groups, differentiated in their ancestries, inviolable in their diverse identities. The contemporary ideal is shifting from assimilation to ethnicity, from integration to separatism (p. 2).

In Canada these kinds of anxieties have been around much longer, to the point where Canada, it is suggested, is the world's first postmodern nation[1]. If potential political and cultural fragmentation are definitional of that condition then officially bi-lingual, officially multi-cultural Canada is a prime candidate. (See for example, Cook, 1977, pp. 188–189) on Anglo-Canadians' inability to develop a secure and unique identity'). Confrontations over issues of collective, cultural and national identity have characterised bi-cultural, bi-lingual, Anglo-Franco debate for decades[2]. As Francophones seek to assert their cultural and political autonomy, and Anglophones search for their defining essence, hitherto they have provided dramatic contrast to their American neighbours' creedal certainties of divine destiny.

Canada's recent history of Anglo-Franco confrontation and constitutional impasse based on cultural nationalism(s) as well as its official bi-lingualism and multi-culturalism and potential for political implosion are interpreted by some as a threat to American hegemonic values (see e.g. Brookhiser 1992).

In socio-political terms, the different organising principles Lipset identifies are refracted through their respective constitutional guarantees: the American Declaration of Independence promises, 'life, liberty and the pursuit of happiness'; the Canadian Constitution promises 'peace, order and good government'. Thus the dominant ideas of Canadian public policy are stability, redistribution, equity, national identity, unity and regional diversity, as well as individual liberty (Doern 1984, p. 250). The dominant ideas of US public policy, on the other hand, reflect its 'loosely bounded culture', emphasising individual rights over collective responsibility, *laissez-faire* over government intervention, and assimilation over difference (Merelman 1982). Two policy areas that typify this opposition are those of health care and gun control, with universal care and strict handgun control found only in Canada.

Immigration and its impact on two nations founded by immigrants largely from Western Europe is a further area of American-Canadian similar lived realities but profound policy differences that have direct relevance for questions about media diversity and access. The large-scale inflow of migrants from Asia, Latin America and the Caribbean challenge earlier definitions of national identity and confront structures of cultural production and institutionalised power. This new cultural geography shakes the bases of federal democracy in Canada and ideas about melting-pot assimilation in the US as the divisive politics of identity, based on ethnicity, race, language, region, gender or religion are brought into play (see, e.g. Ferguson 1993; Gitlin 1991). Today, over a third of Canada's population is people whose ethnic origins are other than British, French or Native (Canada 1990, pp. 14–16). Recent projections for Canada's visible minorities, defined as 'non-white, non-Caucasian, non-aboriginal', forecast an almost one-in-five ratio by 2001, with major urban centres showing the largest rise; and in Metro Toronto, the old heartland of Anglo-Canada, projected to comprise half its population[3]. The US 1990 census reveals similar patterns of Afro-Caribbean, Asian and Hispanic large-scale immigration, showing just over ten per cent of migrants from Europe during the 1980s (US Bureau of the Census Table 9, 1991).

Despite sharing similar patterns of immigration, the two countries' responses to growing multi-culturalism supports my argument about the significance of differing values, institutions and organising principles for communication policies that bear directly on questions of media diversity and access. In the US the rhetoric of the melting pot reverberates still but is increasingly under siege, whereas in Canada, the cultural mosaic as citizenship has been constructed over three decades.

The story of Canada's multi-cultural enactments began with the 1960 Bill of Rights, the 1969 Official Languages Act, a 1971 Multi-culturalism Policy for integrating ethnic minorities into Canadian society, and much subsequent legislation, right through to the 1988 Multiculturalism Act and its 1991 follow-up creating a Department of Multiculturalism responsible for its implementation. (Official multi-culturalism, it should be noted, is not universally applauded, particularly among some descendants of the Anglo-Franco founding fathers.) Political capital, however, accrued from this policy from the outset, most notably and recently when multi-culturalism was adopted as a party plank by the populist Western Reform Party).

DIFFERENT ORGANISING PRINCIPLES; DIFFERENT BROADCASTING SYSTEMS

Assuming the economic imperative as self-evident, if politics, culture and technology are the Holy Trinity of Canadian broadcasting (Ferguson 1991) – PBS (Public Broadcasting System) notwithstanding – there is scant evidence to contradict the idea that the Holy Unity of American broadcasting is profit first and last. Not that Canada's private broadcasters are disinterested in the bottom line; most are highly profitable. The differences are of degree: degrees of regulation, accountability and enforcement in the public or private interest.

In confronting common problems of audience fragmentation, competing delivery systems, and new services, American and Canadian broadcasters predictably are responding in different ways and at different rates to growing cultural diversity in their audiences. Despite a decade of official commitment to deregulatory market forces, Canada's mixed, public-private broadcast economy is still regulated in the public interest to an extent totally foreign to the *laissez-faire* liberalism found in the US. And while the same questions can be posed either side of the border about media diversity and access, external cultural colonisation and internal cultural diasporas, the case studies below provide a selective, not a comprehensive, overview that highlights the regulatory agency, the public broadcaster and the private cable industry.

The US – television, diversity and access in the melting pot
The economic liberalism Lipset (1990) characterises as an American organising principle has shaped the US broadcasting system from the outset. In the 1980s a deregulatory Federal Communications Commission (FCC) accelerated away from decisions in the public interest that previously offered some measure of accountability with respect to media diversity, for example the abandonment of the Fairness Doctrine in 1988 (see, e.g. Davis 1992, pp. 124–5). Unlike Canada, discussed below, no legislation makes multi-culturalism a feature of American citizenship nor requires US broadcasters to reflect cultural diversity in programme content. The stance of the FCC is that minority access is covered by the licence holder's obligations to meet local community needs, a situation leaving considerable latitude in accountability.

The US – *public sector*

In the overwhelmingly private US system the Public Broadcasting System (PBS) averages only four per cent of the television audience, a rating that leaves it open to charges of elitism and 'social engineering'. In recent years financial backing from Congress (some $191 million in 1991) has been tied more closely to minority production and participation. For instance, the Public Telecommunications Act of 1988 requires a 'substantial amount' of the production money allotted to the Corporation for Public Broadcasting (CPB) be earmarked for 'producers of programming addressing the needs and interests of minorities' (CPB 1989, p. 1)[4]. The CPB responded with $800,000 for Asian, Native, African American and Latino consortia, and $3 million annually 1990–3 towards national minority programme production, reporting over 130 new minority programme initiatives two years later (CPB 1989).

But unresolved issues of media diversity and minority access remain:

1 striking a balance between 'inter-cultural' programming (where producers from cultural backgrounds make programmes that reflect differences between their own and other groups), and 'particularist' programming (where only members of the group being depicted are considered capable of its authentic reflection);
2 balancing 'broadly inclusive interpretations of 'social diversity' and specific efforts to redress the 'exclusion and exploitation of the racial and ethnic groups most strongly and most often discriminated against';
3 dividing scarce resources thinly over many projects or concentrating on a few promising ones (CPB 1991, p. 3).

The US – *private sector*

The subject of content guidelines for media diversity and multi-cultural representation is not on the agenda of the industry's National Association of Broadcasters (NAB). Given US broadcasters' vociferous commitment to the First Amendment, any content guidelines are interpreted as infringing their constitutional free press rights. What the NAB does do is attempt to increase minority employment levels in the broadcast industry, e.g. by supplying lists of recruitment sources (NAB 1991).

The history of the three major networks, CBS, ABC and NBC, is the story of seeking to maximise mass audiences by providing mainstream programming that offends few and appeals to many in order to sell mass, not minority, audiences to advertisers. There are signs that the Big Three gospel of the audiences is responding to demographic change and financial restructuring such as pay TV (see, e.g. McPhail 1992). On the other hand, the Capital Cities/ABC code of journalistic practice includes only a paragraph cautioning against misrepresentation based on 'race, religion, color, age, national origin, and sex' (Capital Cities/ABC Inc. 1989, p. 18).

Until recently, the growing diversity of media publics has tended to get lost in the ratings game. Network programmes generally are constructed around audience psychographics and demographics (e.g. *Murphy Brown*), rarely according to socio-cultural markers that define shared identities by ethnicity, region, language or whatever. CBS's *Northern Exposure* provides an exception. In Cicely, Alaskan multi-culturalism makes an interesting addition but is marginal to the central plot devoted to personal dramas and interaction. The programme also can be read as providing a model for a new melting pot that respects diversity based on distinctive behaviour or collective memory. The fourth network, Fox TV, has tackled programming for minority audiences with shows such as *In Living Color*, *ROC*, and *Martin*. While it is true that African-American actors star in such shows, the absence of Hispanic and Asian minorities on US TV and the cloning of formula primetime sit-com or talk-show formats hardly add up to programming diversity[5].

The US cable industry, like cablers elsewhere, can and does cater for small 'niche' audiences, e.g. all news, sports or film channels. But is this capacity applied to serving minority language or cultural television needs? Of seventy-six national video services, National Cable Television Association (NCTA) data indicate only nine dedicated to multi-cultural, minority or international television programming (NCTA 1992).

The Black Entertainment Television (BET) channel competes with all the mainstream English-language TV shows. BET reaches over one third of all US TV households and fifty-six per cent of cable households (Nielsen 1992) and audience data show that programmes featuring minority players and plotlines are the most popular (BET 1992). The African-American audience shows significant differences of TV usage. Not only do black households view forty-nine per cent more than 'all other' households (seventy-two hours during an average November week), but also women aged eighteen and over watched more TV than any other demographic group in black households, as did black non-adults aged two to seventeen watch fifty per cent more late TV than 'all other' non-adults (Nielsen 1991, pp. 1–2).

In contrast, the four Spanish language channels represented something of a 'foreign' language TV invasion. In the country that sells seven times more audio-visual product than its nearest international competitor (Britain) in the global market place, these channels beam novellas, talk shows, news and commentary from Spain, Brazil, Venezuela, Mexico to a potential audience of an estimated 24.5 million Hispanics. Media diversity in terms of foreign language programme provision yes, but media diversity in terms of access for Hispanic Americans? The evidence to date suggests otherwise[6].

For instance, Galavision/ECO Inc. is owned by Televisa, Mexico's largest telecommunications video entertainment conglomerate, and offers an interesting case of reverse cultural/media imperialism. Here a foreign-owned corporation is selling an international satellite television service to the Spanish-speaking diaspora that spreads from North Africa and Europe to North and South America – a phenomenon that is problematical for notions of 'Americanness'.

Canada – television, diversity and access in the cultural mosaic
To the extent that Canada maintains a distinctive broadcasting system from that of the US this is largely a consequence of four factors: a publicly-supported national broadcaster; drama production subsidies; 'Canadian content' quotas; and an active regulatory authority (see, e.g. Paul Audley and Associates 1991; Ferguson 1991; Lorimer and Wilson 1987). The reception of US TV signals expanded in the 1970s when Cancom satellite services intended to deliver television equity to the remotest northern regions also brought in the American 'three plus one' networks (NBC, CBS, ABC and PBS) as well as Canadian TV. With almost ninety-eight per cent of English-language drama imported, Canadian primetime is largely, and popularly, American primetime.

The preferential status Canada gives to its cultural industries is typified by insistence (prompted by Canadian nationalist opposition) that cultural industries be 'off the table' in the US-Canada Free Trade Agreement. Article 2012 of the Agreement defines cultural industries to include 'publication, distribution, or sale' of print media, and the 'production , distribution, sale or exhibition of film, video or music recordings and all radio, television and cable television and all satellite programming and broadcast network services' (US Congress 1988, p. 234).

Arguments about the economic and cultural benefits of production subsidies and 'Canadian content' quotas persist inside and outside Canada (with the US notably opposed at North American, EC and GATT levels). But so long as national media diversity is interpreted in terms of access for national products, in Canada the persistence of such voices is owed in large measure to such support strategies. In a cultural economy swamped with imported books, periodicals, films, records, radio and television, many Canadians view cultural production as more than an entertainment industry. Lorimer (1992, pp. 73–4), for instance, suggests they are the 'symbolic representation of ideas, realities and values-that-count' where government 'does not just *allow* for cultural expression, it *actively* fosters it' (emphasis in original)[7].

During the 1980s, for example, the Canadian Radio-television and Telecommunications Commission (CRTC), in regulating broadcasting in the public interest, addressed issues of multi-culturalism and media diversity in advance of the 1988 Act. In 1985 the CRTC issued new programme and employment guidelines for the broadcasting system to better reflect Canada's linguistic and multi-cultural diversity (CRTC 1985) and subsequently has issued decisions on native broadcasting policy, multi-lingual speciality programming and conventional over-the-air-ethnic broadcasting.

Canada – the public broadcaster

The battered flagship of Canada's mixed economy, public-private television industry is the bilingual national public broadcaster, the Canadian Broadcasting Corporation/Societie Radio Canada is charged under Section 3 of the 1991 Broadcasting Act '. . . that CBC programming should be predominantly and distinctively Canadian . . . contribute to shared national consciousness and identity . . . reflect the multicultural and multiracial nature of Canada' (Canada 1991, Section 3 (1m), p. 3). Parliament appropriates to the CBC between $8–900 million annually. For sixty years the CBC has helped construct and reconstruct a national public sphere and sense of Canadian consciousness and community (and not, as its critics aver, just by relying Stanley Cup playoffs).

It continues to serve regionally and nationally despite mission redefinitions, recurrent financial cuts and declining audiences. During the 1980s under the impact of new delivery systems and services audiences shrank. Between 1984–1985 and 1990–91 the English language audience fell from twenty-two to fifteen per cent, and the French from forty-four to twenty-nine per cent (CBC 1991b). Responding to the requirement of the Multi-culturalism and Broadcasting Acts, the CBC has added to its long-standing native languages Northern Service new initiatives such as monitoring French and English-language programme content and founding an Office of Equitable Portrayal in Programming (CBC 1991a).

A recent example of public policy support for broadcasting diversity is illustrated by the launch of Television Northern Canada (TVNC) in 1992 as a better cultural deal for Canada's scattered northern native peoples. Funded by $10 million over five years from the federal government and headed by a consortium of native peoples, educators, and broadcasters, TV Northern Canada is intended to provide northern native speakers with own-language communication and traditional-culture education (see, e.g. Curfoot-Mollington 1991; TV Northern Canada (1992).

Canada – the private sector
In the private sector, responses to the CRTC included detailed, comprehensive guidelines to shape programme content in accordance with cultural mosaic legislation from the Canadian Association of Broadcasters (CAB 1988). From the networks came declarations of good intent and codes of journalistic practice to avoid stereotyping and increase minority employment (e.g. CTV, 1990).

Like the US, the cable industry's technical capacity to narrowcast for minority language, culturally-diverse audiences results in new services. Canada is the more densely cabled: over four-fifths of television households have cable access and the availability of foreign language channels is increasing. Among seventeen local and national premium services, for example, six channels broadcast in French, eight in English, two in Chinese (Chinavision and Cathay International) and one, Telelatino, in Spanish and Italian (Canadian Cable Television Association, personal communication, 18 August 1992).

A further instance of private sector response to perceived new market opportunities is Canada's first multi-cultural off-air broadcaster, Toronto's CFMT-TV Channel 47 (owned and distributed on its Toronto cable system by Rogers Broadcasting Canada's media giant). Started up to meet the TV viewing needs of an increasingly linguistically and culturally diverse audience in the Toronto Metro area (e.g. it includes the largest Italian city outside of Italy) CFMTV provides programmes in sixteen languages. An example of the range its viewers can access are, *Italianissimo, Portugese Saturday*, Korean, Macedonian and Chinese *Journals*, all interspersed with mainstream US prime-time favourites.

Audience data reveal high viewer-levels for 'old country' programming. Italian speakers, for example, prefer their own language drama *Potere* to its American counterparts by over two to one (Rogers Broadcasting Company 1992). Such findings suggest there are a range of programme needs by minority groups not being met by the mainstream TV culture. Conversely, many of the 'own-language' shows, e.g. the Hong Kong variety show *Cantonese Super Saturday Night*, are clones of US formats and genres. What such findings also suggest is that country and language of origin are still important reference groups for immigrant cultural diasporas.

CONCLUSION

Questions remain, in the US, Canada, and elsewhere ...

In exploring media diversity inside the US and Canadian broadcasting systems, this chapter's arguments started from the premise that the power of electronic media to shape identity can be overblown: the forces of tradition, history, economy, and demography are also powerful predictors of collective definition and redefinition.

But issues of media diversity and questions about widening opportunities for minority and multi-cultural voices are contentious. Not only do they threaten existing structures of creative, economic and political control; they also raise the spectre of employment quotas – a favourite political stalking-horse. The issue of content representativeness – whether minority groups are depicted, and how they are depicted – also is a complex topic of debate. At the national level, without the requirements to show Canadian-made programmes it is doubtful if any national English voice would be heard outside the news and sports departments of Canada's broadcasters. At the group level, especially in the US, FCC guidelines about showing e.g. a percentage of Hispanic or Asian-American programming, would be laughed at or sued as contravening press freedom.

For communications scholars, however, several sociological and economic questions remain. First, is there sufficient evidence of audience demand for alternative voices to those of the mainstream TV culture to justify the cost of providing them? Second, what evidence is there that without large-scale public support of the CBC/SRC/TV Northern Canada variety, that indigenous cultural production – either national or minority – will get off the ground?

The US is a country rich in powerful symbols, myths and television imagery. All assume and reinforce a national identity based on cultural assimilation and homogeneity. Historically, immigrants come to the US because they want to become Americans, celebrating common badges and rituals of citizenship: the flag, the Constitution, Thanksgiving, et cetera. Recent experience suggests otherwise: immigrants come for the better life, while maintaining their ethnic and racial origins. One consequence is the de-massification of audiences and media as thriving cultural and communication diasporas multiply using a range of new and old technologies: satellites, telecommunications, camcorders and VCRs, often recycling 'old country' TV news and entertainment.

Although both countries share many of the same life-styles and conditions, noted above, their respective responses to issues of media diversity and access reflect the interaction between their separate organising principles and cultural mosaic and melting-pot ideologies. Inside their broadcast systems, the American stress is on employment, job training programmes and network codes of practice against minority stereotyping. Only PBS is charged with production diversity and minority representativeness. In Canada, policies are more explicit. Licensing conditions stress non-journalist, non-expert minority participation, availability of non-English language services, more explicit regulations about the depiction of visible minorities, including women and the disabled, as well as accountability to the CRTC.

What this comparison shows is not only the surprising extent of difference that persists across a continent-wide border despite sharing much the same television diet, but also the extent of cultural counterpull provided by country of origin inside societies that label themselves the cultural mosaic and the melting pot. Both Canada and the US illustrate how the media's role in constructing and reconstructing cultural and national identities remain multi-dimensional, interactive, and problematic.

To argue against the power of media and pop culture determinism as promulgated by postmodernists, media conspiricists *et al.* is in no way to denigrate the power of electronic media to shape our perceptions of self and society. Audio-visual media and consumption styles do impact, and visibly so, on our public and private discourses and identities, at the level of *surface* identities. Their capacity for longer-term permeation of *deep* identities based on kinship, language or religion remains a subject for future comparative research.

NOTES

1 For example, the conference theme of the British Association of Canadian Studies, asked 'Canada – the first postmodern state?', Cambridge, England, March 26–28, 1993.
2 This chapter concentrates on Anglo-Canadian identity debates as historically more problematic. Recent Franco-Canadian identity debates, on the other hand, although wrapped in the discourse of linguistic and cultural difference, in terms of *Realpolitik* are more about asserting political and economic power. See, e.g. Gotlieb (1992) and Dion (1988) for analyses of past and present predicaments.
3 As calculated in a study commissioned by the Race Relations Advisory Council on Advertising, *Toronto Star*, 30 May 1992, pp. A1–2.

4 Minority performers themselves are unhappy with some programmes perceived as stereotyping or caricaturing their group, see, e.g. 'Must blacks be buffoons?', *Newsweek*, 26 October 1992. Radio for black audiences is another story – see Arbitron (1992) – one regrettably beyond the scope of this chapter.

5 The extent of *local* off-air television for non-English speakers in the US has yet to be fully researched and may reveal more opportunities for local access and participation.

6 Conflicting audience data obscures the cultural orientations and national origins of those who actually watch Spanish-language TV. Are they American-born or immigrant Hispanics, and how can such differences be reliably measured when the US Census counts heads of households and market research individuals (Frase-Blunt 1992)?

7 For differing interpretations of Canada's broadcasting 'problems' and 'solutions', see e.g. Collins (1990); Lorimer and Wilson (1987); Raboy (1990); Smythe (1981). Collins, for instance, argues against cultural support and for market liberalism on the grounds that the separation of polity and culture are a 'new international norm': a conclusion open to challenge, not only in the Canadian context but also around the globe, given the current spate of neo-nationalising cultural entities.

10

Two types of freedom: broadcasting organisation and policy on both sides of the Atlantic

RICHARD COLLINS

Surprisingly little attention has been given to questions of access and control in discussions of UK broadcasting policy, with the notable exception of Heller (1978) and latterly the Peacock Report (Cmnd 9824 1986).[1] However the 1988 Broadcasting White Paper included the category 'popularity' among the policy goals for UK broadcasting. Even if true democratic control was not envisaged at least the White Paper's formulation suggested that the question of broadcasters' responsiveness to their audience had been considered. There are other straws in the wind which suggest that access, accountability and the interests of viewers and listeners are being accorded a new and higher priority in the policy debate. These include Channel 4's convening of a Broadcasting Accountability Forum in June 1992, the proposals for a 'Broadcasting Forum' (inspired by Colin Shaw, the Director of the Broadcasting Standards Council) and the growth in membership, influence and legitimacy of the Voice of the Listener and Viewer association.[2]

Why this interest in a hitherto neglected topic? Largely because of the belief that technological change has established unprecedented possibilities to establish a new relationship between broadcasters and viewers and listeners. Spectrum scarcity and the non-excludable 'public good' characteristics of broadcasting have effectively been abolished as a consequence of technological change. The development of digital transmission systems (which use spectrum more efficiently), communication satellites (which make usable for broadcasting frequencies which were formerly useless for broadcasting purposes) and pervasive establishment of cable and video cassette distribution of television signals (which do not use the radio frequency spectrum for the distribution of signals) have all mitigated spectrum scarcity. Moreover cheap encoding and decoding technologies have made broadcasting services excludable. They have thus made it possible to establish subscription and pay-per-view funding for broadcasting which promise (or threaten) to establish a broadcasting market which corresponds more closely to what neo-classical economic theory defines as a well-functioning competitive market than was formerly possible. In such a market, where there are no technological barriers to entry and in which a signalling system between consumers and producers can be established through price, viewers and listeners are able to ensure (at least in theory) that it is their preferences (rather than the corporate or political elites which have previously controlled broadcasting) which determine the shape and nature of the broadcasting system.[3] The new broadcasting technologies have therefore been claimed as 'Technologies of Freedom' (de Sola Pool 1983), though, as Golding and others have pointed out, resolution of the market failure which stemmed from spectrum scarcity and non-excludability has amplified rather than resolved inequalities in access to broadcasting services. Indeed Golding (1990) has argued that market theory is basically flawed because its presumption that society is constituted of basically equal individuals who are able to enter (and leave) markets on equal terms is false.

In the old broadcasting order, before the new technologies, spectrum limitation and non-excludability led to a general recognition of broadcasting as an instance of 'market failure'. If markets fail, then (but only then), political agencies should intervene to secure an efficient use of resources and the matching of supply to demand which well-functioning markets are deemed to do.[4] Thus, in a failed market such as broadcasting the reduction of the state to a 'nightwatchman' role is unlikely to serve the public interest: for failed markets require intervention if the public interest is to be served.

Yet political intervention in broadcasting markets is fraught with problems. Because broadcasting is widely credited by political authorities with unique powers, politicians are disinclined to establish mechanisms of access and accountability which render broadcasting genuinely independent of government. However democratic governments do not wish to exercise (or at least be seen to exercise) explicit and direct control of broadcasting. Indeed they have generally undertaken not to do so, notably by acceding to international conventions and treaties which guarantee (insofar as 'scraps of paper' can be said to guarantee anything) freedom of expression and freedom of access to information. Article 19 of the Universal Declaration of Human Rights and Article 10 of the European Convention on Human Rights are cases in point.

In consequence, broadcasters and government in western democratic societies have been fated to be locked together in a mortal embrace. Neither government or broadcasters have been able to renounce claims to independence from the other nor are either government or broadcasters able to be seen to exercise control over the other party. Political intervention in broadcasting markets (or, if the formula is preferred, governmental assumption of responsibility for broadcasting) therefore has fallen characteristically between the two stools of explicit intervention and explicit recognition of broadcasters' independence.[5]

But however difficult it has been to find a solid theoretical and institutional basis for political intervention in broadcasting in societies committed, even if not by a First Amendment and a Bill of Rights, to the independence of the media from government such intervention was long assumed to be necessary. However the perceived rationale for intervention – market failure – has been seen to be undermined by technological change. In consequence there has been a marked growth in advocacy of an augmented role for the market, and diminished role for the state, in the organisation of broadcasting.

PEACOCK AND PILKINGTON

In the UK these arguments have been made persuasively by libertarian democrats who have argued that a well-functioning broadcasting market, now possible thanks to technological change, will emancipate viewers and listeners from the choices hitherto imposed on them by broadcasters (and the state) and will enable a range of voices, formerly silenced in consequence of their exclusion from the system, to be heard. The linked rise in importance in discussion of UK broadcasting policy of the concepts of the market and the consumer interest can be dated from the publication of the Peacock Report in 1986. Peacock's emphasis on the importance of competition and the benefits of what one of the report's principal authors described as a 'sophisticated market system' (Brittan 1986, p. 1) is well known. What tends to be forgotten is the Peacock Report's arguments that the superordinate goals of broadcasting policy are to 'enlarge both the freedom of choice of the consumer and the opportunities available to programme makers to offer alternative wares to the public' (Cmnd 9824, p. 125).

Peacock's attribution of primacy to the viewer and listener was novel. For UK broadcasting policy has long been based on the supposition that viewers and listeners are vulnerable and that a chief role of the state in respect of broadcasting is to protect viewers and listeners from broadcasting, even if what they are to be protected from is what they themselves desire. As the Pilkington Report stated 'adopting the majority view . . . would be to mistake "what the public wants" . . . for the public interest' (Cmnd 1753 1962, para. 408). The creation of the Broadcasting Standards Council in 1988 reflects the continuing power of the underlying presupposition in UK broadcasting policy that viewers and listeners are vulnerable and require to be protected. As Samuel Brittan,[6] a leading member of the Peacock Committee, commented:

> 'in putting forward the idea of a free broadcasting market without censor-ship, Peacock exposed many of the contradictions in the Thatcherite espousal of market forces. In principle, Mrs Thatcher and her supporters are all in favour of de-regulation, competition and consumer choice. But they are also even more distrustful than traditionalist Tories such as Douglas Hurd of plans to allow people to listen and watch what they like, subject only to the law of the land. They espouse the market system but dislike the libertarian value judgements involved in its operation (Brittan 1987, p. 4).

By juxtaposing Peacock and Pilkington I have constructed the antinomy between market and the regulated/public service provision of broadcasting services which arose out of recognition of market failure as one between emancipation and restriction. Much in the actual organisation and practice of broadcasting in the UK exemplifies that opposition rather well. But state intervention in broadcasting has not been confined to the censorious kind of content regulation deprecated by Brittan. Content regulations (such as those which demand provision of children's programmes, adult programme genres undersupplied by the market such as education programmes, and programmes of national origin) have been established to stimulate production and dissemination of a wider variety of programmes than would otherwise be provided. More-over to suggest that the public service/market antinomy is synonymous with the antinomy between emancipation and repression grossly carica-tures the arguments advanced by proponents of public service broad-casting in recent years. Underpinning Blumler's (1992) arguments for public service broadcasting as a guarantor of diversity is a conception of broadcasting as an emancipation of the viewer through the provision of choice. So too with Garnham's (1990) support for public service broadcasting as a bearer of a contemporary public sphere and Mur-dock's (1990) advocacy of public service broadcasting as a counter-weight to the oligopolisation of broadcasting which he claims has fol-lowed the opening of broadcasting markets – or will. All these arguments for public service broadcasting are grounded very differently to those put forward by Pilkington. So different are the grounds of Blumler, Garnham and Murdock's arguments to those of Pilkington that there seems to be as much which unites contemporary proponents of market and public service provision of broadcasting services as separates them. In spite of the antinomy between market and public service models, it is clear that proponents of both models share a common goal: the emancipation of the listener and viewer. But although both sides invoke freedom they mean different things by it. They differ in particular in their allegiance to different institutional and organisational means through which the desired end is to be secured.

INTERNAL AND EXTERNAL DIVERSITY

The differences between proponents of public service and the market are crystallised in the relative priority given to different kinds of diversity. One side emphasises internal diversity (provision of a mixed programme schedule) and the other external diversity (choice between a plurality of channels). Each side of the debate is trying to convert a partial truth into a comprehensive truth, to make a necessary value a sufficient value.

Proponents of public service broadcasting (and/or exacting regulation of broadcasting markets) customarily argue that a market regime in broadcasting will diminish programme diversity because producers will have too little incentive to produce expensive (quality) programmes, broadcasters will have too strong an inducement to schedule for the highest common factor of audience tastes (and will thus exclude programmes which address the strongly held and distinctive interests of the plurality of 'publics' which are held to make up the audience for broadcasting). To ensure diversity in programmes and schedules ('internal diversity') advocates of public service broadcasting have customarily supported limits on the establishment of competing services. They have thus had the difficult and paradoxical task of arguing that diversity is best ensured by limiting the provision of services and through the inclusion of low rated, i.e. little-watched, programmes in the schedule. Whereas proponents of a broadcasting market have been on seemingly surer ground in arguing that diversity has been inhibited by restrictions on the establishment of new services. Yet there can be little doubt that a market based broadcasting regime will undersupply programmes to groups with little economic power, such as children, the elderly and subordinate social groups such as migrants and linguistic minorities.

// A striking example of this conflict between two conceptions of diversity (and the public interest) has unfolded in the European Community in recent years. This conflict also exemplified representative differences between market and public service conceptions of the public interest and how broadcasting should be organised to serve that interest. The principal protagonists in the conflict are the European Broadcasting Union, the 'club' of European public service broadcasters, and the Competition Directorate of the Commission of the European Communities, DG IV. The Competition Directorate has acted directly against the EBU in one important (and piquant) case[7] but the formal public combat between the EBU and DG IV is only the tip of the iceberg of a conflict which the Secretary General of the EBU described (interview 27 February 1992) as 'potentially fatal' to the EBU. Another EBU official (interviewed 24 February 1992) stated that the Commission's actions 'could lead to a catastrophic collapse of Eurovision'.

Essentially the Competition Directorate of the Commission regards most of the EBU's established working practices as anti-competitive. In its annual report (for the year 1989) DG IV described the European broadcasting market as one where 'a number of new, mostly commercial, broadcasters have entered the market, in competition with the established public broadcasting organizations ... the Commission has increasingly focused on the audiovisual media in recent years, from the standpoint of competition policy and stated that its main concern has been to keep markets open and to prevent or reduce barriers to market entry' (Commission of the European Communities 1990, p. 51). The message was unmistakeable and there was much in the EBU's behaviour that caused the Commission concern.

In 1990 the EBU explicitly confirmed its long-standing policy of denying membership of the Union to commercial broadcasters.[8] The EBU therefore appears to be a closed club which acquires exclusive rights to programming (notably sports rights) on behalf of its members, to be establishing barriers to entry to the broadcasting market for new commercial broadcasters by blocking their access to attractive programming. Furthermore, in the long-established exchanges of programmes (notably news, sports, live performances, music and a host of other programmes) via Eurovision between its members, the Union appears to cross-subsidise its membership and illegitimately advantage them *vis à vis* commercial rivals. Moreover the EBU members who benefit from these arrangements include not only obviously non-commercial broadcasters such as the BBC (almost alone among European broadcasters in receiving no advertising funding) but also profit-distributing advertising-financed broadcasters such as Radio Monte Carlo, TF1 and CLT. These broadcasters are difficult to distinguish, except in their historical origins, from the commercial broadcasters excluded from Union membership.

Yet, from the point of view of EBU members, the working practices, to which DG IV took exception, had served the public interest by enabling small and poor public-service broadcasters to give their audiences access to programming that would otherwise have been unaffordable. They have undoubtedly given all EBU members access to a tremendous pool of news coverage and other programming beyond the extent to which any single broadcaster, no matter how well-endowed, could aspire. These arrangements have kept weak public broadcasters from succumbing to commercial competition which has grown mightily in extent and power by giving them privileged access to programming without which they might simply have either gone out of existence or have been forced to change their programme schedules and reduce 'internal diversity'.

Clearly there is an unresolvable conflict between the principles on which the EBU was built and those espoused by the Competition Directorate. These differences, which are representative of the differences between the two sides in the broadcasting debate, are differences about the relative importance of two conceptions of freedom: negative freedom, 'freedom from' and positive freedom, 'freedom to'. These distinct concepts of freedom are explored in Isaiah Berlin's lucid essay 'Two Concepts of Liberty' (in Berlin 1969). Proponents of public-service broadcasting tend to invoke what Berlin called positive freedom, whereas proponents of the market tend to invoke negative freedom (Berlin 1969, *passim*). Neither conception of freedom is sufficient, both are necessary.

POSITIVE AND NEGATIVE FREEDOM

Berlin defines negative freedom (or liberty) as 'the area within which the subject . . . is left to do or be what he [*sic*] is able to do or be, without interference by other persons' whereas positive freedom (or liberty) is 'the source of control or interference that can determine someone to do, or be, this rather than that' (Berlin 1969, p. 121–2). The extent of negative freedom depends, Berlin (1969, p. 130) argues, on 'how many choices are open to me (though the method of counting these can never be more than impressionistic)'.[9] The extent of positive freedom ('the wish on the part of the individual to be his own master' (Berlin 1969, p. 131)) is limited by an individual (or a group's) capacity to achieve goals rather than by duress exercised by others. The distinction Berlin draws between positive and negative freedom, and which he feared might be seen to be excessively fine when applied to the case of an individual, becomes clearer once positive and negative freedoms are considered in relation to groups rather than individuals. Individuals may enjoy a high level of negative freedom but still be unable to realise to the maximum their potential for positive freedom whereas individuals may be better able to realise their individual potential for positive freedom by acting in concert with others.

Berlin further explores the social dimension in which freedom is realised or constrained. He considers humans to be interdependent (Berlin 1969, p. 124); the freedom of one is dependent on the degree to which others exercise their freedom. 'Freedom for the pike is death for the minnows' as he states. The negative freedom of one (or some) may (or may not) be diminished (or extended) by the exercise of positive freedom by another (or others) or vice versa. Berlin shows how the well-intentioned exercise of positive freedom by a group on behalf of its members (the coercion of 'men in the name of some goal – let us say, justice or public health which they would, if they were more enlightened, themselves pursue' (Berlin 1969, p. 132–3)) may become despotic. Yet although there may be a *potential* danger of despotism resulting from the exercise of positive freedom this will not necessarily be the case. The exercise of positive freedom cannot be devalued in relation to negative freedom because of a *potential* danger of harm. Nor too, Berlin argues, can the exercise of negative freedom be disqualified on the grounds that its exercise actually (or potentially) harms the capacity to exercise positive freedom. For if negative freedom is subordinated to positive freedom then 'Liberty, so far from being incompatible with authority, becomes virtually identical with it' (Berlin 1969 p. 148) or, put another way, 'sovereignty of the people could easily destroy that of individuals' (p. 163). Thus careful, circumstantial, judgement and action is required in order to optimise the total sum of freedom, positive and negative, realisable in any particular situation.

FREEDOM AND BROADCASTING

Negative communication freedoms are 'guaranteed' (insofar as agreements can guarantee anything) in a variety of declarations and treaties.

For example Article 19 of the Universal Declaration of Human Rights and Article 10 of the European Convention on Human Rights enshrine important aspects of negative communication freedoms. So too does the Treaty of Rome (EEC Treaty) from which the Competition Directorate of the European Community derives its powers. Indeed the Commission of the European Communities has defined the four fundamental freedoms of the European Community as negative freedoms: 'the free movement of goods, services, people and capital' (Commission of the European Communities 1992, p. 2). There can be no doubt that the re-regulation of European broadcasting during the last decade (notably through the European Community's Television Without Frontiers Directive, the successive actions of DG IV and the Council of Europe's Convention on Transfrontier Television[10] has significantly extended 'negative freedom' in broadcasting. Viewers have access to more services, broadcasters have more ready access to programme rights and to establishing service, and producers have better access to markets for the sale of programmes than before. The role of markets has increased and delivery of broadcasting services through competitive markets have delivered real benefits (notably new services) to consumers and to new broadcasters and programme suppliers (notably access to markets).

Yet these changes have done little to extend positive freedom. Notable examples of the measures taken to realise positive freedom are the institutions, regulations and subsidies put in place by individual states to ensure that certain classes of programmes are made available to viewers and listeners; measures such as quotas for national content, children's programmes, programmes for minorities and the like. Whether the institutional route taken to realise these goals is subsidy (such as Telefilm Canada's Broadcast Fund or the European Community's MEDIA programme), regulation (the European content quotas prescribed in the Television Without Frontiers Directive or the 'proper proportions' of UK/EEC content prescribed in the UK Broadcasting Act), or creation of public service broadcasters such as the BBC or Channel 4, the end sought is enlargement of positive freedom.

However certain cases of enlargement of positive freedom conflict with the enlargement of negative freedom. A striking example of such conflicts is apparent in the case of broadcasting content regulations. To take a particularly clear example of a general case; the requirement for a quota of national content, made in order to enlarge positive freedom, conflicts with the negative freedoms of broadcasters and consumers of broadcasts. For example, establishment of ethnic channels (serving diaspora minorities) in many countries would be incompatible with all but the least stringent of national content regulations. Given the inevitability of some trade-offs between negative and positive freedoms two questions arise. First, how can broadcasting be organised so that such conflicts are minimised? And second how are policy makers to decide what is the appropriate balance to strike between positive and negative freedoms?

In respect of the first question a mixed, market and public-service, broadcasting system seems likely to minimise the losses which follow the irreconcilability of positive and negative broadcasting freedoms. In respect of the second the answer must surely be to create a system which maximises choice for users and when, as inevitably any system must, choices have to be made, to ensure that those who make choices are accountable to users. Those who are accountable will, if prudent, therefore ensure that their choices are as close a proxy for users' choices as possible.

POLICY PROBLEMS

However both market and public-service based broadcasting systems face common problems. If the goal of broadcasting policy is to provide services which match consumer needs and desires two problems arise. First, how are services to be funded? Advertising finance is likely to deliver a system optimised to the needs of advertisers rather than audiences and subscription finance will exclude consumers and will thus lead to a welfare loss. In order to avoid these disadvantages two forms of public funding have been developed; either funding directly from the state budget (as in Canada for the CBC/Radio Canada) and from licence fees (as in most of Europe). However these two forms of funding are also objectionable: funding from the state budget because it makes broadcasters very vulnerable to political pressure from government (see Collins 1991), and funding from licence fees because it is a regressive form of taxation which, because it does not recognise differences in the licence payers' ability to pay, bears more heavily on the poor than on the rich. And, second, who is to decide, and on what grounds are they to decide, the number, character, and cost of services which are to be provided from public funding? If the answer is not to be that given by the Pilkington Committee (Cmnd 1753 1962) – regulation by Platonic Guardians – then a better signalling system between consumers and suppliers of broadcasting services is required. How can an effective signalling system between consumers and producers be established? The establishment of broadcasting markets in Western European states over the last decades has enabled audiences to send signals to service providers which formerly they were unable to do. Although the signalling systems provided by advertising and subscription-financed television are imperfect they are superior to those which formerly obtained. Just as the introduction of competition within UK television in the 1950s showed that viewers' desires for demotic, innovatory and entertaining programming had been undersupplied during the period of BBC monopoly so too has the introduction of competition in other markets. Notably the Netherlands, Italy and Germany have enabled Dutch, Italian and German viewers to send similar messages to their suppliers of broadcasting services.

Without competition there is real danger of service providers losing contact with their audience and transmitting programmes which satisfy broadcasters and elite opinion but not the majority of viewers. As Peacock noted (Cmnd 9824 1986, p. 41) less than half UK television viewers expressed themselves satisfied with a quasi-competitive (or as official rhetoric has it, competition for audiences but not for funding) broadcasting regime which has prevailed in the UK since the establishment of commercial television.

Granted a mixed broadcasting system, and a free-to-air system unvitiated by the welfare loss entailed by subscription broadcasting, the central policy problem is to ensure that the diversity supplied is the diversity wanted by viewers and listeners. Here the question the Peacock Committee proposed, 'How is the signalling system between viewers and broadcasters to be improved?', is central.

It is paradoxical, and unfortunate, that the question of satisfying consumers has most eloquently been raised in the UK context in the course of advocacy for 'a sophisticated market system' which cannot do so. Professor Peacock himself recognised that establishment of a 'pay-per-view' system, which would enable viewers to signal their desires and the intensity of their desires through the price system, entailed a significant welfare loss. Peacock stated that a table d'hôte broadcasting system might well be preferred to an à la carte system (Peacock 1986).

THE CONSUMER'S INTEREST

At a colloquium convened under the auspices of the Fulbright Commission it is particularly appropriate to draw comparisons between the organisation of broadcasting in the United States and in the United Kingdom. The distinctive broadcasting systems of the United Kingdom and the United States of America have assumed the character of models or 'ideal types', by reference to which broadcasting systems in other democratic societies are classified and understood. These different systems, each notionally part of a 'fourth estate' independent of other power centres in their respective societies, are distinguished one from the other by the differences in the relative importance each cedes to political authority and to competitive market relationships in the governance and organisation of broadcasting.

The long period of BBC monopoly (which lasted until 1955), established the 'UK model', the key elements of which were state funding for broadcasting,[11] vertically-integrated broadcasting organisations, universal access to broadcasting services, and broadcasting institutions founded on the linked beliefs that competition was destructive and audiences were vulnerable and needed protection. The US system, in contrast, was based on division between programme makers and broadcasters, on belief in the importance of competition, extension of service only so far as it was profitable to do so and the linked beliefs that the role of the state was to keep out of broadcasting and that the audience was able to look after itself. In fact, like many such models, closer examination reveals that the empirical bases of the types no longer (if they ever did) conform to the models which they notionally inspired. The state is no more absent from broadcasting in the USA than is the market from broadcasting in the UK.

However there is some truth in the conventional wisdom which sees the UK and US systems as opposites. Indeed broadcasting in the UK was developed *in opposition* to the trajectory established in the USA. Briggs, writing about the birth of broadcasting in the United Kingdom, observed 'American experience served as a warning throughout the whole of this period as is apparent in all the writings on radio on this side of the Atlantic' (Briggs 1961, p. 67). The US and UK have historically placed their emphases differently when choosing between these policy options. The US, partly because of fewer constraints imposed by spectrum scarcity, but more importantly because of a political culture less disposed than European political cultures to use the power of the state to realise 'positive freedom', has tended to opt for external diversity and has imposed fewer requirements on its broadcasters to provide internal diversity than has the UK. Moreover the US has placed less emphasis on maximising welfare than has the UK. Geographical extension of service to provide something very close to universal broadcasting service has been a central, and very costly, aspect of UK (and UK-type) broadcasting services, whereas broadcasting services in the USA have been geographically extended only so far as it has been profitable for broadcasters to do so. The UK has realised the 'positive freedom' of universal service via intervention, the USA instead chose 'negative freedom'. However, successive metamorphoses have brought broadcasting in the US and the UK closer and closer.

Within the new age of broadcasting an unresolved dilemma remains which is common to both broadcasting systems; how to match the broadcasting services offered to those demanded by consumers. Here there is an interesting difference between the US and the UK. The USA has a consumer/citizen movement which has vigorously represented consumer and citizen interests in broadcasting. Albeit under-resourced this movement in the USA mediates between consumers and producers and provides a signalling channel absent in the UK broadcasting system. A notable consumer body in the USA (but not the only one) is the Citizens Communications Center (founded in 1969). The CCC has, it states:

> represented public groups, both local and national, in legal proceedings before the Federal Communications Commission and in the courts. It has brought suits aimed at opening up the Federal Communications Commission to more civilian involvement. It has challenged the broadcast industry on its failure to provide equal opportunities in employment for all races and sexes. It has sought community responsiveness and diversity in programming and ownership in both broadcasting and cable (Citizens Communications Center 1979).

Both Canada and Australia,[12] but no European country, have consumer communication bodies comparable to those in the USA. However, though a UK group comparable to the CCC (and its Australian and Canadian equivalents) is desirable such a group could not, given the question of legal standing, take on a range of activities identical to those taken up by its American, Australian or Canadian counterparts. Yet though a UK consumer and citizen interest group would necessarily be different to its counterparts elsewhere the case for such a group and for more effective representation of the consumer interest in the UK can be quickly made.

THE CONSUMER INTEREST AND UK BROADCASTING

Potter (1988) has defined five criteria which require to be satisfied if the consumer's interest is to be adequately served; access, choice, information, redress and representation. If we assess UK broadcasting in terms of these criteria we find it wanting. Recent developments in

UK broadcasting have resulted in a worsening of *access* by all potential consumers to the full range of UK broadcasting services; whereas formerly all viewers had lawful access to all services if the licence fee was paid now some viewers are excluded by price both from new services and from access to programmes (such as soccer) to which they previously had access to. Moreover the establishment of Channel 5 on the lines proposed by the ITC will deny an estimated thirty per cent of the UK population access to the new service. Here we see a significant retreat from universal service which was formerly a central tenet of UK broadcasting policy.

Choice has been widened in the sense that some viewers now enjoy lawful access to a greater range of services than formerly (thanks to the establishment of satellite television). However some commentators fear a future reduction of choice in programmes (I know of no studies which have established that a loss of choice has in fact already taken place). This is notable in respect of programmes which have a poor ratio of returns in relation to costs, such as children's programmes, high-cost UK-produced drama and the like.

Information about programmes and services has probably been improved, thanks to the requirement that service providers must license publication of their programme schedules. But in other respects consumers are denied information that would assist them in making informed judgements about, and between, the services which they consume and for which they pay. Much audience research remains confidential, as do the grounds on which important regulatory decisions are taken (such as the allocation of franchises). The Chairman and Director General of the BBC declined to participate in the 1992 Voice of the Listener and Viewer 'Open Space' programme.

There are no satisfactory means whereby viewers and listeners can secure *redress* from the providers of broadcasting services, nor are there adequate means whereby they are able to *represent* their needs and desires to broadcasters and policy makers. Paradoxically, but not surprisingly, given the long-established conception in the UK of the consumer of broadcasting services as vulnerable, there is a plethora of 'guardians' charged with the representation of the users' interests. However these institutions have not been charged with assisting viewers and listeners to secure redress, or with enabling consumers of broadcasting services to represent their preferences.

A multitude of agencies are charged with serving the public and consumer interest (not always the same) in broadcasting: the Governors of the BBC, the Independent Television Commission, the Radio Authority, the Home Office, the Department of Trade and Industry, the Council of Europe, the European Commission, the Welsh Fourth Channel Authority, the Broadcasting Complaints Commission, the Broadcasting Standards Council and, arguably, Oftel and the International Telecommunications Union can all be enlisted as representatives of the consumer of broadcasting services. No less important are the suppliers of broadcasting services (and substitutes for broadcasting such as cable and video) to the consumer. Here too there are several agencies (and jurisdictions) involved: the BBC, the ITV companies, Channel 4, S4C, BSkyB and other satellite television programme companies, cable television programme companies, the Independent Local Radio companies and the 'additional' radio service providers, and anticipated new entrants to broadcasting – notably Channel 5 and National Commercial Radio. And, if we take as the unit of analysis the programme rather than the channel, the list increases to include agencies such as the Gaelic Language programme. As the Consumers Association stated 'there is a potential for confusion over which body to approach and over the effect that complaining and regulation will have' (Consumers Association 1991, p. 32). The Director General of Fair Trading's comment is as true of broadcasting as it is of Britain generally: 'A proliferation of regulatory bodies and regimes for different sectors of the economy requires some kind of rationalisation' (Director General of Fair Trading 1986, p. 11).

CONCLUSION

Three things are required for more effective representation of consumer and citizen interests in respect of broadcasting in the UK: definition of 'consumer rights' or entitlements in respect of broadcasting, assessment of whether (and if so how) the present arrangements for broadcasting in Britain must be changed for consumers to receive their entitlements and formulation and advocacy of whatever changes are judged necessary. Achievement of these goals will be possible only if the consumer interest is recognised and a UK body analogous to those established in other jurisdictions, notably the USA, is established.

It is to institutional change and creation of a consumer and citizen interest body to which we need to turn our attention if the goals of democratic control and wider access to broadcasting in the UK are to be realised. The creation of such an institution would be entirely in keeping with the establishment and enlargement of a public sphere in communications in the UK. It is not only through preservation and defence of established public service broadcasters that the viewer and listener interest and the establishment of a broadcasting public sphere can be served. Establishment of a UK CCC would be a move towards extending positive freedom in broadcasting.

ACKNOWLEDGEMENTS

Research for this paper was supported by the ESRC (Economic and Social Research Council) under research award R00023 2159. The author is grateful to the ESRC for its support, and to the Fulbright Commission and the Institute for Modern Cultural Studies at the University of Nottingham for the opportunity to participate in the Fulbright Colloquium of 1992. He also thanks Tom Gibbons, Elizabeth Jacka and Ralph Negrine for their helpful comments on this paper.

NOTES

1   But see also Madge (1989), Gibbons (1991) and McQuail (1992).
2   In comparison to other countries such as Australia and Canada what is most striking about the UK is the absence of grass roots, community/public broadcasting, initiatives.
3   For a representative general argument for competition as a guarantee of freedom and consumer sovereignty see Friedman and Friedman (1981).
4   It is important to note that this viewpoint is neither universally shared nor does it invariably correspond to historical experience. Many societies have experienced a state presence in economic activity *before* the establishment of markets. Indeed Australia never had communication and media markets prior to regulation.
5   A case in point was Leon Brittan's 1985 letter, formally written in his capacity as a private citizen but at a time when he held the office of Home Secretary, to the BBC to deplore the BBC's proposal to screen a 'Real Lives' programme in which leading members of Provisional Sinn Féin and the Ulster Democratic Unionist party were interviewed. This striking example from the United Kingdom of a generally unresolved contradiction can be paralleled with examples from other jurisdictions: Bob Hawke's dissatisfaction with ABC's reporting of the Australia's naval commitment to the Gulf war and Pierre Trudeau's discontent with Radio Canada's reporting of nationalist sentiment in Quebec come to mind.
6   Brittan is assistant editor and principal economic commentator of the *The Financial Times* and the brother of Sir Leon Brittan, formerly UK Home Secretary (and the minister who established the Peacock Committee) and latterly the Commissioner of the European Communities responsible for competition policy.
7   The Screensport/EBU Members case which was determined in 1991 (see OJ L 63/32–44 of 9 March 1991) stemmed from a complaint by the UK company W. H. Smith Television – WHSTV, (later ETN, European Television Networks) – and the principal investor in the satellite television channel Screensport. WHSTV complained that Eurosport (established by an agreement between the Eurosport

Consortium – a group of EBU member broadcasters including the BBC – and News International's company Sky Television), the satellite television sports channel (with which Screensport competed) infringed Community competition requirements and disadvantaged Screensport. The nub of the dispute was whether Screensport was improperly disadvantaged in the acquisition of rights to screen sports events by EBU member broadcasters with a stake in Eurosport.

The Eurosport Consortium argued in its defence that Sky Television was simply a sub-contractor to the Consortium and that the Eurosport channel did not constitute the anti-competitive arrangement that Screensport had alleged. Indeed the Consortium maintained that 'Eurosport enjoys the rights of an EBU member' and that the service has a 'public service character' (OJ L 63/38). The Commission rejected these propositions and argued that 'By contrast the viewing public has tended to associate Eurosport more closely with Sky' (OJ L 63/38) than with public service broadcasting. The Commission found in favour of Screensport's challenge to Eurosport. It judged that 'The joint venture agreements and all related contractual provisions . . . constitute an infringement of Article 85(1) of the EEC treaty' (Decision 19 February 1991 recorded in OJ L 63, 9 March 1991, p. 32–44). The piquancy of the case resides of course in the partnership between European public service broadcasters (including the BBC) and News International.

8 In the so-called 'Marino Charter', a comprehensive policy statement adopted by the EBU at its conference in Marino.

9 And on the degree to which the choices are realisable, how important they are relative to each other and what social constraints obtain in determining which choices are made.

10 The Council of the European Communities (1989) Directive on the co-ordination of certain provisions laid down by law, regulation or administrative action in Member States concerning the pursuit of television broadcasting activities (89/552/EEC, OJ L 298, 17 October 1989, p. 23–30).

Council of Europe (1989) European Convention on Transfrontier Television 5 May 1989, Council of Europe, Strasbourg.

Commission Decision of 15 September 1989 relating to a proceeding under Article 85 of the EEC Treaty (IV/31.734 – Film purchases by German television stations – OJ L 284/36–44, 3 October 1989).

Commission Decision of 19 February 1991 relating to a proceeding under Article 85 of the EEC Treaty (IV/32.524 – Screensport/EBU Members – OJ L 63/32–44, 9 March 1991).

11 The licence fee is a form of hypothecated ('earmarked') tax revenue. As is well known both the level of the licence fee and the proportion of the licence fee which is devoted to broadcasting are set by government. The relationship between BBC and government consequent on these arrangements was described in a *Financial Times* editorial as 'the corporation's longstanding supplicant relationship with government' (2 September 1992).

12 The Public Interest Advocacy Center in Canada and the Communication Law Centre in Australia.

PART FIVE

11

The Council of Europe's Convention on Transfrontier Television and the European Community Broadcasting Directive

JAMES MICHAEL

The truth of the matter is that in the contemporary world of electronics and jumbo jets news anywhere is news everywhere[1].

That quotation is from the *Spycatcher* case. In 1992 the European Court of Human Rights ruled that the United Kingdom had violated the rights of British newspapers by imposing a *temporary* injunction (although it lasted over a year) on publication of information from the book until the case was decided. The European Court of Human Rights found that the injunction violated the right to impart information after the book had been published in the United States, but not before.[2] The European Commission of Human Rights had found, by a margin of one vote, that the injunction was a violation before the book was published in the United States, and unanimously that the injunction violated the newspapers' rights after the book had been published in the United States.

Why begin a chapter in a collection on broadcasting, by quoting from a case that almost entirely involved book and newspaper publishing? The justification is that the case illustrates the continuing influence of the European Convention on Human Rights, and because the case centres on the question of whether 'prior restraint', even if temporary, violates the right to receive and impart information. Many of the issues likely to arise in the future regulation of broadcasting by European institutions will be about what broadcasting can be prevented, rather than whether punishment should be imposed after an offending broadcast. Although access to and control of broadcasting in the United States is still almost entirely a matter of US legislation and US constitutional law, it is impossible to discuss those aspects of broadcasting in the United Kingdom without considering the effect of European institutions. The European Convention on Human Rights and its interpretation by the European Commission of Human Rights and the European Court of Human Rights are fundamental; but equally fundamental is the law of the European Community as it is interpreted by the European Court of Justice.

THE TWO 'EUROPEAN COURTS'

Lawyers often illustrate the relative ignorance of journalists by pointing to newspaper reports of decisions by the European Court of Human Rights with headlines such as 'EEC Court Rules'. Some teachers of British Constitutional Law say that they fail any examination script that confuses the European Court of Human Rights with the European Court of Justice. The problem with this approach is that it sometimes is difficult to determine whether a student is very ignorant of the difference or well-read enough to know that the European Court of Justice does have some competence in human rights and the European Court of Human Rights does have some competence in economic regulation.[3]

The possibility of both courts ruling on the same activity, possibly with different results, has always existed, and there have been attempts to take the same grievance to both places. The landmark Italian broadcasting case, *Telebiella*, began with a reference to the European Court of Justice,[4] then became an application to the European Commission on Human Rights.[5] The restrictions imposed in Ireland on the communication of information about law and practice relating to abortion in other countries have now been tested under both the European Convention on Human Rights and the Treaty of Rome.

The European Court of Human Rights ruled that the Irish restrictions violated the right to receive and impart information under Article 10 of the Convention[6], while the European Court of Justice ruled that the restrictions did not raise a question of Community law because the publication of information about clinics in student newspapers was not advertising and so was not a commercial activity[7]. The two cases were slightly different on the facts, and the law in Article 10 of the Convention is different from that in Articles 59 and 60 of the Treaty of Rome, so the two findings did not clash directly. But if not clearly inconsistent, the two opinions do not co-exist easily. They were the first pair of cases before the two European Courts involving the limits of state regulation of the same (almost) activity, but they are unlikely to be the last. As a leading textbook says:

> The chances of such a coincidence, however, are not very great. Indeed if, in connection with the same factual situation, a case were to be brought before the Courts both in Strasbourg and in Luxembourg, in the two procedures different legal issues will probably be involved (van Dijk and van Hoof 1990, para. 2.4.4, pp.71–2).

Such overlapping competence is not only a matter of judicial jurisdiction but also legislative competence. Both the Council of Europe and the European Community have already taken parallel steps towards regulation in the fields of data protection and of broadcasting. In transfrontier television the European Community took the initiative with 'Television Without Frontiers' and then the Draft Directive, but the Council of Europe was preferred by a meeting of ministers responsible for the mass media in Vienna in December 1986. In the event, the two institutions produced the Directive on Television Broadcasting and the Council of Europe's Convention on Transfrontier Television almost simultaneously. Some day the two jurisdictions will apply different rules (or different interpretations of the same rules) to the same activity, even if it was avoided in the matter of abortion information.

Hypothetical illustrations of the overlapping competence of the European Court of Justice and the European Court of Human Rights often involve the right to receive and impart information, which is both a human right and often an economic activity. In a case that concerned broadcasting specifically, the European Court of Justice has ruled that restrictions on private broadcasting imposed by the Greek government violated the Treaty of Rome [8].

'PRIOR RESTRAINT' AND FREEDOM OF EXPRESSION

A few words about the history of 'prior restraint' may be useful, particularly in a collection concerned with British and American approaches. The notion that there should be no 'previous restraint', or at least that the legal balance should be very heavily weighted against it, is historically English, and is found nowhere in the words or jurisprudence of the European Convention (although it is an express provision of Article 13 of the American Convention on Human Rights, which was influenced in its drafting by the case-law of the US Supreme Court). In his *Commentaries* Blackstone defined the freedom of the press as an absence of prior restraint. 'The liberty of the press is indeed essential to the nature of a free state; but this consists in laying no previous restraints upon publications, and not in freedom from censure for criminal matter when published'. It is true that he was describing an absence of censorship by officials rather than judges, but the *American Cyanamid*[9] test of the 'balance of convenience', or maintaining the status quo, now makes temporary judicial restraint at the request of government relatively easy. In many media cases, the interlocutory injunction is effectively final because most news is extremely perishable, and a delay in publication of months or years is very nearly no publication.

The European Court of Human Rights' ruling that the temporary restraint on publication of *Spycatcher* information violated the Convention was the first time that it has distinguished between prior restraint and subsequent punishment, requiring a greater justification for prior restraint. It is clear from the language used by the Court that at least some of the judges were influenced by the way in which the US Supreme Court has developed the doctrine that there should be no prior restraint of the press or broadcasting. This is significant because the right to receive and impart information under Article 10 of the European Convention on Human Rights is the basic standard against which any European restriction on broadcasting must be judged, whether it is imposed by national law, European Community law, or even by the Council of Europe's own Convention on Transfrontier Television.

THE EUROPEAN CONVENTION ON HUMAN RIGHTS AND BROADCASTING

Article 10 of the Convention provides expressly for the licensing of broadcasting[10], but no significant cases were presented to the Commission or the Court until 1990. The first cases both involved restrictions imposed by Switzerland on the retransmission of broadcasts from other countries: one restriction was held to violate the Convention, and the other was held not to violate the Convention. In *Groppera Radio*[11] the Swiss government had prohibited the retransmission by cable of radio signals from an unlicensed station in Italy, mostly popular music programmes. Although the Commission had found that this violated Article 10, the Court ruled that the restriction was legitimate in regulating the allocation of broadcasting frequencies and to protect the rights of those who had been awarded broadcasting licences, especially as the restriction was imposed because of the source of the programmes rather than their contents. In *Autronic* the Swiss government had prohibited the retransmission of television signals from a Soviet satellite. The Swiss government argued that the Soviet satellite signal was telecommunications rather than broadcasting, and that they were not only justified but required to prohibit the retransmission of such signals because the permission of the Soviet government had not been obtained. The Commission found that this was a violation, and the Court agreed, saying that they would not distinguish between signals communicated to the general public in the 'footprint' of a direct broadcasting satellite and similar signals transmitted over a telecommunications satellite[12].

'COMMERCIAL SPEECH'

The case-law on regulation of broadcasting under the Convention does not give much clear direction as to what restrictions satisfy Article 10 and which are in breach of it. But there is another small but growing body of case-law on the right to receive and impart information that is also very relevant: restriction on 'commercial speech'. Many Council of Europe countries restrict broadcast advertising, with a dwindling number attempting to prohibit it completely. Satellite broadcasting is largely financed by advertising revenue, and the prospect of avoiding national restrictions on broadcast advertising is a powerful incentive. So, before moving on to the restrictions on advertising under the Transfrontier Television Convention and the Community Directive, it is worth considering what protection the Human Rights Convention provides to the communication of such information. In 1984 Anthony Lester and David Pannick argued that the Convention did protect commercial speech[13]. One of their opinions, that public authorities can only regulate the use of broadcasting licences for reasons that are given in Article 10, has since been upheld in *Groppera Radio*. But in *Markt Intern*[14] the Court (unlike the Commission) held that the protection of commercial interests justified an injunction stopping a bulletin from publishing information critical of a particular company[15]. The publication was not an advertisement, but the ruling seems to imply that regulation of speech affecting economic interests can be justified more easily than regulation of speech on political or artistic matters.

Broadcasting in most European countries has traditionally been public-service broadcasting, financed by a licence fee or some other source other than advertising. Many, but not all, countries have begun to allow some advertising-financed broadcasting. The question has often been asked whether a non-commercial monopoly on broadcasting is justified with the provision that Article 10 'shall not prevent States from requiring the licensing of broadcasting, television or cinema enterprises'. The Commission has begun to provide a clear answer to that question.

In September 1992 the Commission found that the refusal by Austria to license five private broadcasting stations violated Article 10 of the Convention[16] The first case was an application to operate an internal cable television system. The second, third, fourth, and fifth applicants had unsuccessfully sought licences for private radio stations, some commercial and some non-commercial. All were refused on the ground that only the Austrian Broadcasting Corporation was entitled by law to broadcast, and that this was in accordance with the provision of Article 10. The Commission found unanimously that there had been a violation in the case of the first applicant, and by a majority of fourteen votes to one that there had been a violation in respect of the other applicants. The case has been referred to the Court by the Commission, and seems likely to become one of the most important cases yet involving broadcasting regulation under the European Convention on Human Rights. If it is a violation of Article 10 for a state to refuse any applications for broadcasting licences other than the national monopoly, the next question is what grounds a state may justifiably rely on in refusing such licences.

THE EUROPEAN CONVENTION TO TRANSFRONTIER TELEVISION

The Council of Europe began to consider problems of transfrontier broadcasting in the 1960s, at first by the negotiation of various agreements relating to radio broadcasting. These will not be considered here, except to note that national restrictions imposed on those within the jurisdiction who were connected with 'pirate' broadcasters outside the jurisdiction were subsequently found by the Commission not to violate the Human Rights Convention. The leading case upheld the validity of criminal sanctions against the holders of car stickers advertising the then-prohibited Radio Caroline station[17].

The Steering Committee on the Mass Media, established in 1976, began the process of drafting Recommendations on Direct Broadcasting by Satellite for the Committee of Ministers that became the Convention on Trans-frontier Television. The Council of Europe's competence is largely in the fields of cultural affairs and human rights, while the smaller European Community's competence is in economic matters. But the communication of information and ideas is both the exercise of a human right and often an economic activity, and there has been a certain amount of competition and co-operation between the two overlapping groups of nations in exercising their authority to regulate. (Data protection is another such area.) The European Community's Green Paper on Broadcasting in 1984 concentrated the minds of the Council of Europe on the subject, and a meeting of the media ministers from Council of Europe countries in Vienna in 1986 decided that the Council of Europe should take the lead in drafting a Convention. The Convention was approved by the Committee of Ministers of the Council of Europe in May 1989 and opened for signature and ratification. (The European Community in turn was spurred into action, and its Directive took effect in October of that year.)

The essence of the Convention is to establish a television (it does not apply to radio) club with two basic rules: members will not allow broadcasts from their territory, or using their frequencies or satellites, to violate the standards of the Convention; and members will not restrict the retransmission in their countries of signals from another member. It is worth noting that most of the restrictions that may be imposed by a receiving country on transmissions thought to violate the standards of the Convention are on retransmission of signals. In other words, the Convention contemplates the large-scale reception of satellite signals by cable systems rather than individual dishes, and self-help measures in emergency breaches are to be directed against the retransmissions of signals by cable.

The Convention standards are entirely concerned with content, although the content regulation can be divided into programme standards and commercial aspects. Matters of ownership and control are not addressed, except in the very limited sense of exclusive control over major public events and programme origin. Article 9's provision on 'exclusive rights' over events of 'high public interest' is so vague as to be unenforceable, as is Article 10's provision to 'reserve for European works a majority proportion of their transmission time'. Only the provision in 10(4) prohibiting the transmission of cinema films for two years after release (unless agreed with rights holders) seems specific enough to be enforced.

Other programme standards in Article 7 range from a fairly abstract obligation to 'respect the dignity of the human being and the fundamental rights of others' to slightly more concrete duties to avoid indecency, pornography, undue violence or incitement to racial hatred. Items likely to 'impair the physical, mental, or moral development of children and adolescents' are not to be transmitted when they are likely to watch them. News is to be fairly presented.

The most specific programme standard is the right to reply which

Article 8 says must be given to 'every natural or legal person'. Unlike the equivalent in Article 23 of the Directive, this does not limit the right of reply to damaging assertions of incorrect facts.

Advertising and sponsorship standards are described in some detail in Chapter III, ranging from a general obligation to be 'fair and honest' to specific limits of fifteen per cent of daily transmission time to twenty per cent in any hour. The great debate over whether advertisements should be in blocks or at natural breaks ended in a compromise: they are to be 'between programmes' but may also be 'inserted during programmes' if the integrity of the programme and the interests of rights-holders are not prejudiced.

Sponsorship is specifically allowed, so long as it does not influence programme content. There are detailed limits on the advertising of particular products. This includes a ban on all tobacco advertising, which prompted a very specific possible reservation in Article 32, by which the United Kingdom may allow advertisements for cigars and pipe tobacco on terrestrial television. (In the event, the United Kingdom did not exercise this power, and the last television advertisements for such products were broadcast in October 1991.) Any state may also restrict retransmissions to comply with domestic limits on alcohol advertising. This reservation makes clear the essential effect of the Convention. States may regulate domestic broadcasting more strictly than the Convention allows (as in prohibiting advertising completely); but they may not restrict the reception and retransmission of Convention-standard material from other states party to the Convention. Only Article 16 makes advertisements that are directed at audiences other than those in the transmitting state subject to the rules of the receiving state. This was added at the insistence of the Netherlands. But the state regulation of domestic broadcasting is still, in theory at least, subject to the general requirements of the European Convention on Human Rights. And, as the Dutch government has learned, it is also subject to the rules of the Treaty of Rome, as interpreted by the European Court of Justice.

Disputes are to be resolved by conciliation by the Standing Committee, arbitration, or by self-help. Conciliation is the first step, with arbitration to follow if that fails. Self-help in the form of forbidding retransmission is allowed, but only for breaches of some standards. It is not available for breaches of the general quota requirements, failure to provide a right of reply, or transmission of unfair news.

The Convention is open to all members of the Council of Europe, members of the European Cultural Convention, and the European Economic Community. The Council of Europe has twenty-seven members (as of February 1993) with the admission of eastern European countries, and is likely to expand even more in the near future.

Articles 59–66 of the Treaty of Rome provide for the free movement of services within the Community, and the European Court of Justice made it fairly clear, in *Sacchi*[18], *Debauve*[19], and *Coditel*[20] that broadcasting is subject to Community law. In the *Dutch Advertisers* (or *Kabel Regling*) case[21] the Court ruled that a Dutch prohibition on retransmission of satellite advertisements sub-titled in Dutch violated the Treaty by discriminating in favour of the Dutch public advertising agency. As mentioned earlier, the Court has also ruled against Greek controls of broadcasting in the *Elliniki* case.

While the Court was establishing the principle that broadcasting was subject to Community competence, the Commission was considering the *Television Without Frontiers* Green Paper in 1984 and a Draft Directive in 1986. There is an interesting history of how proposals on copyright, radio, percentage quotas, and advertising came and went during the process that ended with the Directive that took effect in October 1989. The political process was that after the Council of Europe (of course including all Community) media ministers' decision in Vienna at the end of 1986 that the Council of Europe should lead, the content of the Directive had to follow. And so it did, with a final European Council meeting on Rhodes at the end of 1988 which decided that the rules should generally follow those of the Convention, dropping detailed percentage and timing requirements. Provisions on a right of reply and a ban on transmitting films for two years after release were adopted for conformity with the Convention (although not exact for right of reply). The controversial rising percentage of required European works (the definition of which was retained) was replaced by a duty to 'where practicable' reserve a majority of transmission time for them and an obligation to report. A more definite (although 'where practicable') obligation to reserve ten per cent of transmission time for independent producers was included.

As Community 'legislation' the Directive has no need to create a system of conciliation and arbitration like that in the Convention. It does provide for a rather more limited form of self-help in the Chapter III provision allowing states to prohibit retransmission of material seriously infringing the rules protecting minors or inciting to hatred 'on grounds of race, sex, religion, or nationality'. But the Directive requires at least two similar infringements in the twelve months preceding, with a warning of intention to prohibit retransmissions and a failure of amicable settlement within fifteen days, before the provisional suspension procedure can be used.

THE DIRECTIVE AND CONVENTION COMPARED

Although there was co-ordination in the drafting of the Directive and the Convention, there remain some interesting differences between them. The Directive is of more importance to those states which are members of the European Community. This is because the provisions of the Directive have direct application in national law, and because Article 27 gives priority to the provisions of the Directive by providing that '[p]arties which are members of the European Economic Community shall apply Community rules and shall not therefore apply the rules arising from this Convention except insofar as there is no Community rules governing the particular subject concerned'.

The Directive, in Article 24, provides that 'in fields which this Directive does not co-ordinate, it shall not affect the rights and obligations of Member States resulting from existing conventions dealing with telecommunications or broadcasting'.

In terms of subject matter, the Directive is much more comprehensive. Article 2 imposes obligations on each state regarding 'all television broadcasts transmitted by broadcasters under its jurisdiction', including those making use of a frequency or satellite capacity granted by, or satellite up-link situated in the state. By Article 3, the Convention, however, applies only to any television programme service transmitted within a state's jurisdiction 'which can be received, directly or indirectly, in one or more other Parties'.

Article 22 of the Directive requires states to:

take appropriate measure to ensure that television broadcasts by broadcasters under their jurisdiction do not include programmes which might seriously impair the physical, mental or moral development of minors, in particular those that involve pornography or gratuitous violence. This provision shall extend to other programmes which are likely to impair the physical, mental or moral development of minors, except where it is ensured, by selecting the time of the broadcast or by any technical measure, that minors in the area of transmission will not normally hear or see such broadcasts.

The Convention, on the other hand, seems to impose a stricter standard.

Article 7 of the Convention provides that 'all items of programme services . . . shall respect the dignity of the human being . . . in particular, they shall not . . . be indecent and in particular contain pornography'. It also provides, in language very similar to that of the Directive, that 'all items of programme services likely to impair the physical, mental or moral development of children and adolescents shall not be scheduled when, because of the time of transmission and reception, they are likely to watch them'.

The difference between the two is not only in the description of material to be prohibited, but in the possibility under the Directive of broadcasting such material by encryption. The Directive's only prohibition on pornography is for the purpose of protecting minors. It is possible to read the first sentence of Article 22 as containing a complete ban on pornography for that purpose, but it is also possible to argue that the ban is subject to the provisions of the second sentence, requiring broadcasters to protect minors by 'selecting the time of the broadcast or by any technical measure'.

The texts might be interpreted in various fora if the United Kingdom took action under the Directive or the Convention against 'Red Hot Dutch', a sexually explicit channel made available to British viewers in 1992, and reportedly available in 20,000 British households. Despite the name, the channel is now uplinked from Denmark, with programme material mostly from the United States. According to press reports, the channel was originally uplinked from the Netherlands. The Dutch authorities investigated after receiving complaints from the United Kingdom, and found that the channel was operating without a licence. When the operators applied for a Dutch licence it was refused. A spokesman for Continental Television, the Manchester company selling the decoder for use with the channel, was quoted as saying: 'We intend to move our uplink as and when we want. It may be in one country on Wednesday and another on Friday' (*The Times*, 9 December 1992, p.7).

The difficulty for the British authorities is that the channel is only available to those who have a suitable dish antenna and who buy a decoder to decrypt the signal. Article 2 of the Directive provides that a member state 'may provisionally suspend retransmissions of televisions broadcasts' if the conditions described earlier have been satisfied. Similarly, Article 24 of the Convention provides that 'the receiving Party may suspend provisionally the retransmission of the incriminated programme service'.

So neither the Directive nor the Convention provides expressly for any action by a downlink state to stop reception of objectionable programming other than suspending the retransmission of it. Article 2(2) requires that 'Member States shall ensure freedom of reception and shall not restrict retransmission on their territory of television broadcasts from other Member States for reasons which fall within the fields co-ordinated by this Directive', while Article 2(1) requires that each Member State shall ensure that all television broadcasts within its jurisdiction comply with the law applicable to broadcasts intended for the public in that Member State. The provision permitting prohibition on retransmission in the downlink state is 'without prejudice to the application of any procedure, remedy or sanction to the infringements in question in the Member State which has jurisdiction over the broadcaster concerned'. So although the United Kingdom is limited in its unilateral remedies to suspending retransmission, which is not effective against Red Hot Dutch because it is not retransmitted by any cable companies, it could request Denmark to take action to stop the uplink of any material in breach of the Directive's standards. If Denmark disagrees, the United Kingdom could take action against Denmark in the European Court of Justice.

If Denmark were to win the argument that the Convention does not prohibit the transmission of pornography by encrypted signals, the United Kingdom might then have a possible course of action under the Convention. The argument would be that 'as there is no Community rule governing the particular subject concerned', namely the transmission of pornography, that the Convention's stricter rules against the transborder transmission of pornography and indecent material, without any possible transmission by encryption, should apply.

The Convention, like the Directive, only provides that the downlink state may only take unilateral action by suspending retransmission. But this would not preclude the United Kingdom from communicating the alleged violation to Denmark under the provisions of Article 24(1), triggering the provisions for mutual co-operation under Article 19, conciliation under Article 25, and arbitration under Article 26. Conciliation would be under the auspices of the Standing Committee, on which the European Community is represented. If that did not succeed, the United Kingdom and Denmark could take their dispute to an arbitration tribunal outlined in the Appendix to the Convention.

All of these are possible courses of action that the United Kingdom might take under the Directive and the Convention. It has been reported that the British government is considering using the Broadcasting Act[22] to impose criminal penalties for providing the decoders (*The Sunday Times*, 31 January 1993, p.7). This plan reportedly has been approved by the European Community's Commissioner for audio-visual affairs as consistent with the provisions of the Broadcasting Directive about material that might seriously impair the moral development of minors. But the Commissioner is not the final interpreter of the Treaty of Rome and EC Directives. If such a prohibition order is put into effect, any legal proceedings to enforce it will almost certainly be referred to the European Court of Justice in Luxembourg.

BROADCASTING'S FUTURE IN EUROPE AND THE UNITED STATES

In the debate over the future of the European Community, 'federalism' has become a nearly-forbidden 'f-word' in the United Kingdom. But from a US perspective, events in Europe look remarkably like the United States of America in the early nineteenth century. From a legal point of view the main difference is in the overlapping jurisdictions of the Luxembourg Court in economic affairs and the Strasbourg Court in human rights: it is as if in the early history of the US the 'commerce clause' cases and Bill of Rights cases went to different Supreme Courts.

Broadcasting, as an economic activity and the exercise of a human right, inevitably involves both sets of European laws and institutions. Thus far, there has been no open conflict between them, but the potential for differences remains, despite efforts at co-ordination in the drafting of the Directive and the Convention. Perhaps, as the technologies of broadcasting and telecommunications converge, and as electronic communication of all kinds becomes an increasingly international activity, the experience of European institutions will prove useful in developing other regional institutions, and perhaps broader international ones. Europe may now be serving as a laboratory for responding to technological developments by testing the regulation of broadcasting by trans-national institutions, rather as the states of the United States have often been described as 'laboratories of democracy' in a federal system.

NOTES

1 Sir Nicholas Browne-Wilkinson, Vice-Chancellor, in *Attorney General* v. *Guardian Newspapers Ltd and others (No 2)* [1987] 3 All ER 316 at 332.
2 *Observer and Guardian* v. *United Kingdom*, 14 European Human Rights Reports 165.
3 For the first, see Edson and Wooldridge (1976); for the second, see the rapidly-increasing number of Strasbourg cases involving licences, Article 6 and Article 1 of the First Protocol.
4 Case 155/73, *Sacchi, Jur.* 1974, p. 409.

5   *Sacchi* v. *Italy*, Application No. 6452/74, 5 D&R 43 (1976).
6   *Open Door Counselling Ltd and Dublin Well Woman Centre Ltd and Others* v. *Ireland* [1991] 14 European Human Rights Reports 131.
7   *Society for the Protection of Unborn Children* v. *Grogan*, Common Market Law Review, December 1991.
8   *Elliniki Radiophonia Tileorassi – Anonimi Etairia*, decision of 18 June 1991, reported in [1991] ECR 2925.
9   [1975] AC 396.
10 'This Article shall not prevent States from requiring the licensing of broadcasting, television or cinema enterprises.'
11 28 March 1990 (14/1988/158/214).
12 Judgment of 22 May 1990, 15/1989/175/231, Application No. 12726/87.
13 'Advertising and Freedom of Expression in Europe'.
14 *Markt Intern Verlag GmbH and Beerman* v. *Federal Republic of Germany*, Application No. 10572/83.
15 Application No. 10572/83.
16 *Informationsverein Lentia, Jorg Haider, Arbetsgemeinschaft Offenes Radio (AGORA), Wilhelm Weber, and Radio Melody Ges. m.b.H* v. *Austria*. 9 September 1992.
17 Application No. 8266/78, decision of 4 December 1978, D.R. 16, p. 190.
18 155/73, *Italy* v. *Sacchi* [1974] ECR 409
19 52/79, *Procureur du Roi* v. *Debauve* [1980] ECR 833.
20 62/79, *Coditel* v. *Cine Vog Films* [1980] ECR 881.
21 352/85, *Advertisers' Association* v. *the Netherlands* [1989] 3 CMLR 113.
22 Section 177, 178.

12

Communications and access: pre-empting the debate – the role and strategies of Euro-media lobbies

MICHAEL PALMER

If, during the past year or so, you had attended a media industry conference about broadcasting in continental Europe, the chances are that one or several speakers would have referred to some new 'established' facts concerning broadcasting. First, the *caveats*, the qualifying phrases: the broadcasting industry is a sector with various private and public owner-operators with distinctive (although sometimes overlapping) roles for creators, artists, producers, and broadcasters – with the last mentioned, the licensed (or unlicensed) channel-operator often accused of exceeding the roles of programming and transmission to include in-house production. All the 'actors' – in the political science sense of the term – of the broadcasting industry are subject to a certain number of rules and regulations, laws, decrees and ordinances etc. These vary from country to country, although the EC Commission and to a certain, albeit lesser, extent, the Council of Europe, are cast by indstry executives in the role of the 'great leveller' (or, to simplify grossly, and use modern Eurospeak, that of the great 'harmoniser'). And, of course, there remain many national, regional and local variables due to all manner of factors.

With the caveats out of the way, the industry speaker can centre on his or her main point. '*Le train est en marche*', the die is cast, the Rubicon crossed. Broadcasting is a service industry: commercial factors apply here as much as in other industries which serve the public (howsoever the latter is defined). Media company executives even argue that while the state remains a more potent actor in broadcasting than in, say, the print media none the less, by and large, in the Europe of the 1990's, the broadcasting industry (or rather the environment in which it functions) has come of age. One may produce, buy and sell programmes, hire and dismiss personnel, invest in potentially attractive new media outlets and cut losses in other outlets – old and new – just like a commercial operator – a businessman, a tycoon, a mogul – in any other sphere of activity involving production, distribution and consumption. To simplify grossly, to cross journalese with graffiti-culture: in broadcasting nowadays as elsewhere, 'Adam Smith rules OK'. The profit motive underpins broadcasting as it does many other sectors of post-industrial economics and modern, that is bourgeois, civil society.[1]

Commerce, colonies and international warfare: while in Europe media company executives celebrate, to use a Thatcherism, 'the rolling back of the frontiers of the state', but continue to inveigh against the perceived dangers of EC 'meddlesome interventionism', the imagery and rhetoric used to describe international communications sometimes echoes points made (more brilliantly) by Hegel. For the German philosopher, international wars are means of distributing products without having to sell them. The US-led UN coalition against Iraq in 1991 off-loaded (and tested) allied military equipment, a new illustration of the old adage: 'the only way of giving something to someone without making him pay for it is to send it in the form of a bomb'. A major success of the US television industry of the 1980s, the Ted Turner CNN channels, received international recognition with its coverage of the US-Iraq conflict (the 'George and Saddam' show) from August 1990 onwards. The earlier financial difficulties of the company within the US ('the Turner junk bond saga') had been little covered in the European media trade press. For the victor, international war advances not only his military standing, but also the commercial prowess and appeal of companies – media corporations just like any other – that 'fly the flag'. Ted Turner's CNN channels gave a version – a commentary as well as a vision – of international news that was unashamedly (and, in may respects, understandably) American.

It was Hegel, also, who, in 1821, highlighted the role of colonies. Colonies serve to assuage conflicts within civil society by opening new markets or by discovering new sources of raw materials. Europe has been a 'new market' for US companies – and their advertising agencies – since the turn of the century, and for US media products for decades (as it has been, more recently, for Australian, Japanese and Brasilian TV products). The geopolitics of international communications change frequently and according to one's vantage-point. Who in Britain, say, other than the media professional, is likely to appreciate the importance of the US Hispanic TV-viewing public, and its apparent addiction to Mexican-originated programmes? Yet Hegel's analysis can still serve. The 'imperialism' of the English and American languages, cultural forms and even media personnel – the Australian-born, Oxford-educated and American citizen Rupert Murdoch, so long resistant to involvements in European countries whose languages he does not speak, illustrates the point – remaining a lodestone, a touchstone for debates about communication flows both within Europe – where suspicions of the UK as the US Trojan horse prove deep-seated – and beyond.

In the 1970s and 1980s, the 'cultural imperialism' and 'media imperialism' were part of the stock-in-trade of exchanges between their Third World accusers and the West, between the South and the North. The debate, involving heated exchanges within UNESCO, on a new world information and communication order (NWICO), transformed these slogans into the leitmotiv of international communications: the west and the northern hemisphere dominated the flow of media products. The title of a book published by the British scholar Jeremy Tunstall (1977) put the issue baldly: 'The media are American'. A distinct, but not unrelated, theme came to the fore in Europe during the 1980s. The EC Commission, sometimes building on work previously done by the mass media Committee of the Council of Europe, led attempts by governmental organisations to analyse the audiovisual media industry in Europe and to put the European media house in order. This echoed, in part, the concern voiced by media professionals, academics, and some politicians, in Europe at the growing hegemony of US 'media imperialism' within Europe, as elsewhere. There were many symbolic events in this confrontation: in the early days of the Mitterrand socialist (first) presidency in France, his culture minister Jack Lang spoke out repeatedly against the danger of what British commentators termed 'wall-to-wall Dallas'. But the symbolic issue *par excellence* was the debate over the EC Directive 'television without frontiers': finally adopted in 1989, and operational in various member-states since 1991, the directive was first issued in a draft form in 1986 and the process of its gestation was marked by an interim report (1983) and a green paper (1984). Throughout the 1980s, this issue gradually became a focal point for the expression of the concern of US and European, governmental and non-governmental organisations, about broadcasting, the advertising and media industries, and communication flows within Europe and beyond.[2]

'Warfare' (in Hegel's parlance) took the form of intense lobbying

preceding the agreements on the wording of texts whose adoption signi-
fied the taking of decisions and of the consequent, executive, action.
The 'TV without frontiers' issue exemplified this trait of international
communications: it was perceived to have all manner of implications –
commercial, industrial, political and cultural – by a wide range of
interested parties. To cite just two of them, from the USA: US trade
secretary Carla Hills opposed the EC directives, arguing that it would
generalise quotas on the import of audiovisual products of US-registered
companies. Jack Valenti, at the head of the influential trade association,
the Motion Picture Association of America (MPAA), briefed Carla Hills
and himself lobbied in Europe to remove the import provisions from
the Directive; since the 1930s, his association had opposed limits on
media import quotas imposed by various European nation-states.

Diplomacy, it is sometimes said, is the pursuit of warfare by other
means. Countries do not go to war over media issues as, say (or rather
as western international news media reported), Latin American countries went to war over a football match. But media politics, and the
geopolitical dimensions of the international communications industries
– themselves in constant flux – mean that lobbying, within and between
these industries, within and between governmental and non-governmental organisations in Europe, the US and across the world, has
grown, is increasing, and is likely to increase still further. Lobbying
often – but not always – results in compromises. Thus, in the case of
the broadcasting directive and the MPAA, it appears that Jack Valenti's
efforts were partly responsible for the decision that the import quotas,
while included in the EC directive, should be only voluntary. And, in
fact, US companies circumvent import quota restrictions by establishing
production subsidiaries within the EC.

Lobbying presupposes recognition. Governments and legislators in
western Europe now intervene less in the content, the funding and
running of broadcasting (than they did in the period of overt state
control). But, at local and regional, trans- or pan-European and international levels, governments and legislators, and the various regulatory
bodies that they have established (and whose independence may even
be protected by the constitution) remain the foci of the actions of
lobbyists. Recognition is all: access is the precondition to influence. To
cite a US example, taken from the print media: in the early 1980s the
ANPA (the main print media industry trade association) was registered
as a lobbyist by the US Congress. At first sight, this seemed to run
contrary to the tenets of the trade association. Indeed, in the past
newspaper publishers opposed such a move: a body devoted to the time-

honoured defence of the first amendment to the constitution – Congress shall make no law that restricts freedom of speech – should have no truck, no dealings, with the legislative power. Such a principled decision was untenable: legislation and executive action affect what is often presented as America's number two export industry, the movie and entertainment industry; dependent in part on the advertising revenue and consumer expenditure that underpin that industry, the press had no choice but to seek Congress registration as a lobbyist. At the time, the ANPA was particularly concerned to make its case heard on the issue of electronic publishing: it feared that advertising in the yellow pages of telephone companies ('telcos') would lead to other electronic information services, and siphon advertising revenue away from the press. A lobbyist seeks access – to Congress, say – as much to learn what is afoot, as to put his own case across.

In the 1980s, partly as a result of EC and CoE debates over broadcasting directives and conventions,[3] communications media trade associations increased their representation in European bodies based in Brussels and Strasbourg, Luxembourg and Geneva. It has been observed that European lobbyists in general, as a *genus proprius*, have been slow to organise their collective representation by, say, the EC Commission.[4] The importance of effective representation in Brussels and other European 'capitals' has clearly risen over the past decade. But it is worth recalling that in 1961, four years after the EC was founded, a trade associations was formed to ensure that EC Commissioners heard newspaper publishers' associations (NPA's) views on such industry matters as duty-free newsprint import quotas. CAEJ – la Communauté des Associations des Editeurs de Journaux, representing the NPAs of the (then) EC member-states – was itself an offshoot of FIEJ – the International Newspaper Publishers' Association (of which the American ANPA is a member). In European broadcasting, the European Broadcasting Union (EBU–founded 1950) originally represented only state or public service channel organisations. Partly because of the success of Eurovision and of other instances of the pooling of resources by member-organisations, EBU became a 'broad church', with members and associate members from outside Europe *per se* – TV channel operators from North Africa and Israel, for example. A body specialising in professional, legal, and technical matters, the EBU was somewhat reluctantly obliged to assume a more political role in the early 1980s, when the EC Commission argued that it was entitled under the Treaty of Rome (1957) to include broadcasting within its remit governing the free circulation of goods, services, persons and capital throughout the Community: broadcasting is a service industry. The EBU defended the viewpoints of national public-service broadcasters at a time when pan- or trans- European broadcasting appeared increasingly probable and when most of the first such broadcasters were private sector operators – the first version of Rupert Murdoch's Sky Channel, for instance, began in 1982. During the 1980s, also, the linked but distinct phenomena of the liberalisation, deregulation, and privatisation of broadcasting modified the context in which the EBU operated. Spain, for instance, had no national public service TV channels but private sector channels proliferated; in France the main TV channel, TF1, was privatised in 1986–87, and a rival private channel, la Cinq, argued that the EBU could hardly continue to exclude other private channels from a club whose public service ethos had already been 'polluted' by the presence of the privatised TF1.

In short, the changing political, economic and technical circumstances of broadcasting in Europe led to the emergence of new lobbies. Associations attentive to the need for a better representation of major private sector broadcasters were launched. The Association of Commercial Television came into being in 1989: members included Britain's (then) ITVA, TF1 of France and Sat1 of Germany, while the Italian, Silvio Berlusconi of Fininvest, was ACT's first president, 'dedicated to both free competition and quality in broadcasting'. His words – 'every product is improved by competition' – could have been echoed by Rupert Murdoch, whose News Corporation was a member of another recent European grouping. Set up in 1991, the European Publishers' Council (EPC) also had as founder-members Prisa (Spain), Burda (Germany), Mondadori (Italy) and Elsevier (Netherlands). Print media groups across Europe, like private sector broadcasters, found it judicious to have a new body to forcefully present the case to 'the Eurocrats' – to adopt a polemical simplification that they sometimes use in unguarded moments.

Such terminology, of course, may appear somewhat Manichean, indicative of a 'them' and 'us' mentality. What, elsewhere, we have called 'Euro media lobbying' (Tunstall and Palmer 1991, Ch. 4) is, in fact, a singularly more complex and subtle process. To cite one example: launched in 1980, the European Advertising Tripartite (EAT) is a 'veritable alliance for action', i.e. a lobby. It represents, at the European level, all the actors of the advertising industry, and is an umbrella organisation grouping trade associations representing advertisers, advertising agencies, advertising media, and national tripartites of the three. From EAT literature and presentations, it is apparent that the lobbying of others is accompanied by 'the education' of the trade associations that form the lobby. To appreciate how the EC works, and the complex relations between Council of Ministers, Commission and Parliament – not to mention the different policy areas, and thoughts of various EC Commissioner – is to show that the Commission, for instance, is not necessarily 'anti-advertising'. The climate of opinion prevailing in the Commission in 1992 differs markedly from that current in the 1970's when the Commission initiated proposals that ultimately led to the directive on 'misleading advertising'.

Lobbying at various levels requires, of course, the co-ordination of effort and the pooling of information. During the 1986–89 broadcasting directive debate, the UK trade associations, members of EAT, put their views to the UK ministers responsible for broadcasting. These were partly taken on board by the UK minister discussing in Council of Minister meetings the Commission's proposed directive and the European Parliament's amendments. At Strasbourg and Brussels, EAT representatives met European Parliamentarians and co-ordinated the information exchange process. Euro-media lobbying, in short, requires concerted action at both the national and European levels, and involves monitoring and briefing ministers, commissioners and parliamentarians, and monitoring judgments by the judiciary – by, for instance, the European Court of Human Rights (Strasbourg) and the European Court of Justice (Luxembourg). Lobbying, therefore, involves the marshalling of strategic data (that often the industry is best placed to provide), and presentation 'nous' or know-how, in various committee-rooms and at pre-lunch drinks, or post-prandial coffee.

Media lobbying also involves, on occasion, campaigns directed at 'public opinion' – sometimes via the press. In Britain, over the past year, the Newspaper Publishers' Association (NPA) ran a campaign comprising full-page ads in quality newspapers: 'People read newspapers' was the theme; the aim, however, was to remind advertisers of the advantages of pricing ads in print media rather, say, than in television.[5] Frank Rodgers, chairman of the NPA and managing director of *The Daily Telegraph*, is also president of the European Publishers Council. This EPC also seeks to defend the newspapers as an advertising medium against rival commercial media and, above all, against 'Eurocrats'. Its public posturing, however, has been less aggressive than that of some of the other lobbies fearful of EC Commission 'machinations'. In early 1992, British quality papers carried full-page ads[6] containing texts in English and French refuting arguments used by 'Brussels' in order 'to ban the advertising of tobacco', the ads cited a Canadian court judgment of 1992 whereby bans on advertising were deemed to be 'a form of censorship and social engineering'. These ads were placed by the Tobacco Advisory Council, an association funded by the tobacco industry, which is concerned at the success of measures limiting the promotion of its products.[7] Advertising-funded media in general, and the various advertising industry trade associations, all actively oppose any EC (or other) 'threats to commercial speech'. Direct marketing and data protection are two related areas where different advertising, promotion and information interests lobby in recent months against proposed EC measures.[8]

It is often argued that, as a result of the debate over 'television without frontiers', the EC Commission established that it was legitimate that the Community have a 'broadcasting policy'. It was sometimes pointed out – in Brussels, Strasbourg, and elsewhere – that the economic and cultural aspects of broadcasting required that it could no longer be left to the sole competence of individual member-states. Furthermore – as some commentators added – not only did different national laws, rules and regulations lead to all manner of discrepancies and variations but frequently they were not applied. Indeed, the international nature of broadcasting and other communication flows, and of multi-media trans-national operators such as Time Warner and Bertelsmann, Murdoch and Berlusconi, meant that only European or international bodies or 'observatories' might monitor and assess them with any degree of precision. The 'TV without frontiers' debate, some argue, shows that American and Japanese rhetoric about the dangers of 'Fortress Europe', in communications as elsewhere, should not prevail: broadcasting policy was an area where the EC must 'get its act together', otherwise US telefilms, Australian or Brazilian soaps, and Japanese cartoon films etc. would increasingly 'dominate' European TV screens. As the number of TV channels increased in and across Europe – according to one (Saatchi) estimate, the number rose tenfold, 1980–90 – the perceived shortage of programme material (*'la pénurie des programmes'*), required that the EC act, or so some 'Eurocrats' argued.

The analysis and proposals formulated in 1990 by the EC commissioner responsible for the audiovisual sector, Jean Dondelinger (1990; Hott 1990), were thought to suggest possible answers. Here, I shall only highlight some political aspects of these proposals. Two metaphors – 'triptych' and 'rules of the game' – encapsulate the analysis, diagnostic and policy recommendations the document contains. The latter shows that, in terms of supply and demand, Europe's audiovisual distributors (including TV channel operators) remain dependent on cheap imported material. It proposes both specific measures and a 'conceptual' framework for such measures, intended to foster Europe's audiovisual production industry. Broadcasters, by this token, are to do less in-house production, and commission more programmes from independent producers.

The point I would highlight here concerns the activities of trans-national multi-media operators: Murdoch and Berlusconi, Bertelsmann and Hersant, and other European or international groups. The very idiosyncrasies and diversity of these 'media moguls' makes it difficult to treat them as all of a kind. At the same time, many such trans-national operators are past masters in using material acquired on one side of the Atlantic (or Pacific) for use in their media assets in various national or pan-European markets in 'the old continent'. Dondelinger notes that the governments of individual EC member states are not best-placed to assess the intricacies of the operations of trans-national media groups:

> Whereas the activities of media operators have increasingly assumed a European dimension, the response to the effects these may have, in certain cases, on pluralism has, for the time being, not gone beyond national limits. National legislation, existing or planned, could be circumvented and would not therefore be convenient to guarantee pluralism in all cases (Dondelinger 1990).

Trans-national multi-media operators are often one – if not several – step(s) ahead of measures that national legislators or governments may take to curb their actions. The Dondelinger analysis has not been followed by action with respect to any trans-national group. In laying down 'the rules for the game', 'Eurocrats' tend to lay emphasis rather on the distinction between broadcasters and producers, and the assistance given to the latter. It was not European Community actions that caused the severe difficulties experienced between 1990 and 1992 by several multi-media groups that straddle, in varying degrees, the Atlantic: the rescheduling of the debts of his News Corporation groups by Rupert Murdoch; the demise of Robert Maxwell and the break-up of most of his group, MCC; the imprisonment of the Italian financier Giancarlo Parretti, who had previously acquired control of the US studios, Metro Goldwyn Meyer and United Artists, and had sought to acquire France's Pathé Cinema; and the debts of France's Hachette group, present in North and Latin America as well as in France, where it was forced to close down the loss-making television channel, la Cinq. Commercial factors (including sales and advertising revenue), marketplace reasoning, the volatility of international finance and of increasingly deregulated stock exchanges, are likely to remain the decisive factors affecting the houses of cards built by 'media moguls'.

At first sight, therefore, it seems that US parlance – 'let the market-place decide' – seems more pertinent than, say, German experience: Germany's Cartel Office has, on occasion, forced the major media groups not to expand beyond certain limits in certain areas.[9] In the United States, of course, the Federal Communications Commission has acted similarly. Since 1940, for instance, the FCC limits the number of radio stations that can be controlled by a single firm. None the less, the phrase 'regulatory capture' – referring to the sympathetic attitude shown by regulators to the key actors of industries that they are supposed to regulate – appears to have a longer track-record in the United States than in Europe.

Prescriptive rather than restrictive measures are probably the most that should be expected of the EC 'media policy' and at a time in European history when political and economic liberalism remain in vogue. In most west European nation-states, the prevailing climate favours self-regulation by the various actors of the communications industry. Conservative politicians say as much in Britain as in France: in 1990 Douglas Hurd, the minister responsible for broadcasting policy, argued that the planned new regulator body, the Independent Television Commission would apply 'a lighter touch' than its predecessor, the Independent Broadcasting Authority. In 1992 in France, opposition spokesman Alain Madelin praised the virtues of self-regulation and criticised the existing over-regulation of broadcasting. Programme quotas, for example, stifle existing TV channels, and contributed, he claims, to the closure of la Cinq (*Stratégies*, 6 July 1992). In Europe, as in the States, industry actors – by their very nature – rail against regulation and legislation and urge 'let the market place decide'.

Despite some of the provisions of the Dondelinger proposals, and occasional appeals for the existence of a Euro-wide broadcasting regulatory authority, Europe appears set on what might be termed a policy of subsidiarity in communications policy as elsewhere. National governments – and broadcasting ministers in particular – are unlikely to allow the EC Commission to tackle wholesale the complex issues involved say, in the operations of trans-national multi-media groups (communication flows, programme imports, concentrations of ownership, minority holdings, and so on). At the same time, ministerial reorganisation suggests that national governments are attempting to put their own communication policy-making house in better order. The past history of ministerial reorganisation suggests that some changes may prove cosmetic and a response to short-term party political factors: the communications portfolio has suffered from being the plaything of many different ministries and departments trade and industry, commerce, education and foreign affairs, telecommunications and defence, space and the interior (or Home Office). In France, in the Bérégovoy government appointed in April 1992, the same minister was responsible for both the education ministry on the one hand, and for the culture and communications portfolio on the other. More significantly, since 1981, a junior or delegate ministry for communications has worked alongside the minister for culture. In Britain, in 1992, the creation of a new ministry for National Heritage saw broadcasting and print media policy at last removed from the Home Office. Too many fingers in the communications pie: the number of ministerial actors involved, at the level of national governments, does not help clarify matters in dealings with the EC Commission, where three commissioners at least are concerned by communications policy.[10] While bothersome, this multiplicity (and possible mismatch) of public policy actors sometimes eases the task of private sector trade associations. And media moguls and their like find it that much easier to remain a step ahead of any potentially restrictive measure that might emerge from a cumbersome and slow-moving public policy machine of apparatus.

In an article entitled 'Why EC legislation threatens press freedom', the chairman of the European Publishers Council argued thus:

> There is much evidence that, far from limiting pluralism, the beneficial effects of concentration of ownership within and between different media have led to an increasing diversity of information sources. So long as no organisation has a monopoly of any particular media, publishers should remain free to expand – which will lead to increased choice for consumers of news and entertainment' (Rogers 1992).

This argument, it seems, is winning the day.

NOTES

1 In Germany, the expression that denotes 'civil society' may also be translated as 'bourgeois society'. Marx, in his critique of Hegel, who coined the term 'civil society', makes much of this ambiguity. These points are made by the French philosopher François Chatelet (1992, p. 186). On the relevance of the term (and its genesis) for communication studies see Habermas (1986).

2 In May 1988 François Mitterrand stood for re-election as President of the French Republic: in his election manifesto, he wrote disparagingly of the existing broad-

casting regulatory body – the CNC set up by the liberal-conservative Chirac administration – and proposed the creation of a new body, which might be enshrined in the constitution. See Palmer and Tunstall (1990).

3   The European Community Broadcasting Directive, the Council of Europe's Conventions on Trans-frontier Television, both finalised in 1989.

4   Some estimates put the number of accredited representatives or lobbyists in Brussels at 3000. See Andersen (1992) and Gardner (1992).

5   An example: *The Financial Times* of 9 June 1992 carried a full page advertisement: half the page reproduced the advertisement for a product called 'Ibulieve' in newspapers: '. . . In May 1991, Ibulieve was launched solely in the national press. Within three months it had become brand leader in its sector. . . . The printed word works where television can't. . . . People read newspapers'.

6   'Brussels now has no excuse for ignoring the facts' *The Sunday Times*, 1 March 1992.

7   The Tobacco Council, as well as advertising and marketing industry trade associations, opposes the proposed EC Directive that 'would ban tobacco advertising throughout the EC'.

8   One industry fear was that curbs on tobacco promotion would be followed be EC bans on alcohol advertising and directives that would threaten advertising and marketing of financial services, food labelling, motor vehicles, distance selling, data protection and children's toys. Following a meeting in March 1992 with the European Publishers Council, the EC Commission president was reported to have said 'tobacco is a special case . . . "Subsidiarity" will be used more and more, and the EC will intervene less and less'. See: 'Smoke signals emerge on EC tobacco curbs', *The Financial Times* 19 March 1992; Rogers (1992, p. 13).

9   It has been argued both that the Office prevented the Springer group from conquering the Munich newspaper market, and that limits placed on expansion within printed markets in Germany encourage such groups to expand into domestic broadcasting and become commercial broadcasters, and to expand abroad. Similar arguments are used to explain the expansion outside France of the Robert Hersant group (in Spain, Belgium, Hungary, Poland, Czechoslovakia). They do not convince: see Tunstall and Palmer (1991).

10 According to some EC sources, the commissioners most directly concerned with the formulation of communications policy include those responsible for the following sectors: foreign relations and commercial policy; research and development, telecommunications and information industries; competition policy; the internal marker; audiovisual and cultural affairs, information and communication; budget policy. See Jorna (1991).

Of course, 'communications policy' is a specious term, a house with many mansions. It ranges, for example, from the proposed directive on tobacco advertising, to the directive on the future norms for D2 MAC Packet audiovisual transmissions and to high-definition television.

The twenty-three directorates-general of the EC prepare briefs for commissioners (and have dealing with lobbyists) on all manner of issues. In the communications policy area, there is perhaps more a concern with fashioning structures, and assisting innovation than in becoming embroiled in discussions concerning media content or communications software. For example, the 'rules for the game' prescribed in the 1989 EC broadcasting directive – despite protests to the contrary – are relatively minimalist.

13

Government and broadcast media in France

JEAN-CLAUDE SERGEANT

The French broadcasting system has traditionally been notorious for its reliance on government's guidance and authority. In 1973 President Pompidou went down in history when he exclaimed that the ORTF – the French broadcasting corporation of the time – was the 'voice of France'. Since those days France has had no fewer than four reforms of broadcasting and admittedly no other European country with the possible exception of Italy has experienced such an in-depth revamping of its broadcasting system over the last decade.

Whereas in 1980 French television meant three state-owned channels, by 1992 French viewers could choose between six different channels, four of them commercial. But the system is still evolving since the frequency made available through the demise of La Cinq was allocated to a new Franco-German public channel – ARTE – which went on the air at the end of September 1992. Yet, if the increase in the number of private channels has limited the scope for intervention by the government in the functioning of TV broadcasting, one is tempted to suggest that government control over TV operators remains potent, albeit in a more subdued way than before 1981.

Identifying the reasons for such an enduring influence is no easy task; among them one would mention in particular the specificity of the French system of government in which most powers are concentrated in the hands of the president. Structural reasons, particularly the role of the successive broadcasting watchdogs set up since 1982 must also be taken into consideration as these regulating bodies have taken an increasing importance over the years.

Such bodies are the latest manifestations of a long tradition of government control over broadcasting which began in 1949 with the Deferre Act which set up the RTF (Radiodiffusion et télévision françaises). At the time broadcasting meant almost exclusively radio which was available to about 25 million listeners through about seven million wireless sets. The French broadcasting corporation was run by a board on which sat representatives of the government, as well as of the staff, and of various economic and cultural organisations. The chairman of the board was directly appointed by the Council of Ministers and was directly answerable to the Information minister. This seemed to be a perfectly proper practice since, according to François Mitterrand who was a member of the government in 1948–49 'the government feels quite logically that it is the representative of the French nation because it enjoys the confidence of a majority of representatives in the National Assembly and has hus the duty to articulate the will of the nation' (quoted in Montaldo 1974).

The control of the state over broadcasting was further strengthened in 1953 when on the occasion of the vote over the appropriation bill for the RTF the government first spelt out the concept of state monopoly in programme making which was to remain on the statute book until 1982. The effective management of radio and television required however an increased functional autonomy which the government eventually granted in 1959 and 1964. This was reflected in the change of name of the RTF. The new Office de radiodiffusion et télévision françaises (ORTF) had very much the same status as a British corporation, although the role of the Ministry of Information was in no way diminished as the unrest in May 1968 demonstrated.

Broadcasting House on the right bank of the Seine was identified as the stronghold of the government's absolute rule over public broadcasting, which journalists and broadcasting workers hoped to bring down by staging endless marches around the circular broadcasting building which had become a new intellectual Bastille. After restoring law and order, the government reaffirmed its control over the ORTF by purging it of its more militant members. President Pompidou, who had succeeded General de Gaulle in 1969, did not prove any more liberal than his predecessor in his handling of broadcasting policies despite his commitments in the election campaign. He opposed the significant relaxation of the government's controlling power which Prime Minister Chaban-Delmas had introduced as part of his 'New Society' programme. Chaban had decided among other things to suppress the Information Ministry and to set up an independent news and current affairs unit for each of the two public channels. In his memoirs, he recalls: 'I am not far from believing that the plot to remove me from the highest office in the State machine found its origin in the decision

I took in 1969 to appoint Pierre Desgraupes at the head of the news and current affairs unit at the first channel' (Chaban-Delmas 1975, p. 374). Desgraupes, who had pioneered current affairs programmes in the early 1960s, was generally considered as an unreliable maverick in the corridors of power and Chaban had to twist Pompidou's arm before Desgraupes' appointment was accepted.

In the meantime, Chaban-Delmas was preparing the dismantling of the ORTF which had become an unwieldy and ineffective monster. This reform was actually carried out by Giscard d'Estaing and Chirac shortly after the presidential election of 1974. Seven autonomous companies were carved out of the ORTF, three of them corresponding to the former ORTF TV Channels. However, the state monopoly over production and transmission was in no way repealed while the chairman of each of the new companies was to be appointed for three years by the cabinet, very much along the traditional lines. What was new was the decision to define for each of the companies a brief detailing of its duties and obligations which was to be officially endorsed by parliament.

If one can argue that Giscard's reform of public broadcasting was largely inspired by his will to make TV channels more market conscious, it is hardly disputable that his attempt failed and only resulted in more duplication and increased competition between the channels, which started to woo audiences as never before. By 1982, the total number of staff employed by the state broadcasting companies stood at 17,600 – that is fifteen per cent more than the ORTF employed before its dismemberment. Besides, the state broadcasting companies were increasingly felt to be inadequate channels for the expression of alternative political views at a time when the combined forces of the left were gaining in influence in the country . Numerous so-called 'free radios' started to spring up in clear defiance of the monopoly, the culminating episode in this desperate fight for extended freedom being the prosecution of Radio Riposte run by the Socialist party headed at the time by François Mitterrand. State TV and radio companies were seen as the mouthpiece of the government – so much so that the crowds which celebrated the victory of the Socialist candidate in Bastille Square in May 1981 were chanting slogans demanding the demotion of two notorious TV journalists.

Very much in the same flamboyant vein, Georges Fillioud, the newly-appointed Communication Minister introduced the presentation of his Broadcasting Bill at the Assemblée nationale by the following quip which has remained famous until this day: 'Away with censorship, welcome freedom'. And indeed, the 1982 Broadcasting Act can be considered as a landmark in the history of French public radio and television. Not only did it proclaim the end of the state monopoly in programme making but it also constituted the first concrete step towards severing the all-too-visible links between the political power and public broadcasting.

In practice, the government divested itself of its substantial powers of control in favour of a High Authority which was to act as a watchdog but also as 'the custodian of the independence of public broadcasting.' The nine wise persons designated by the President of the Republic, the President of the Assemblée Nationale and the President of the Senate were to ensure pluralism, fairness and balance in the programmes. They also had to see to it that the public service missions ascribed to the state-run radio and TV companies were properly fulfilled. However the more sensitive role of the High Authority lay in the allocation of frequencies to radio broadcasters and local TV companies and above all in the appointment of the heads of the public broadcasting companies. This was the single most important departure from tradition and in that respect the High Authority managed to preserve its independence in spite of the inevitable pressure from the government to secure the appointment of their favoured candidates.

Where the High Authority was less successful was in the enforcement of its decisions regarding the allocation of frequencies to the new independent local radios which tended to ignore transmission power specifications with the result that some of the national public stations in the FM band could not be heard properly. When the Authority tried to correct excesses with whatever limited powers the law had equipped it with, its stern warnings were often overlooked, as in 1984 when NRJ, threatened with extinction because of repeated breaches of the rules managed to turn the tables on the High Authority by calling a very large crowd of vocal youngsters into the Paris streets. The government abstained from supporting the Authority through fear of antagonising a clientele which would hardly have forgiven them the demise of the first round-the-clock pop and rock music station.

Additionally, the High Authority made itself unpopular among programme comptrollers for a tendency to meddle with programmes on account of alleged breaches of fairness and impartiality rules. If, on the whole, the stop-watch remained the main instrument of measurement of the largely mythical concept of balance and neutrality, the High Authority was suspected of developing a code of practice which all TV journalists and programme makers would have to apply.

Despite this schoolmasterly approach to TV ethics, the air of change

on the screen was unmistakable. Those were the days of such programmes as *Moi je* and *Droit de réponse* which explored entirely new
avenues in the field of documentary programmes and live debates. In
particular, the deliberately provocative tone of Michel Polac, the producer of *Droit de réponse*, provided a sharp contrast to the hitherto benign
and insipid debates that French television had supplied.

One year after the setting up of the High Authority, sixty-two per
cent of the viewers felt that French TV had either 'quite changed' or
'changed a lot', but an equal proportion, not necessarily the same,
considered that the change had been for the worse (*Télérama*, 2 February
1983). A slightly less impressive majority (fifty-eight per cent) admitted
they hardly liked or did not like at all what they saw on the screen. If
the changes in programme schedules did not go down well with the
public, the increased political diversity one could sense in the news
programmes did not escape the viewers, forty-three per cent of whom
agreed that TV provided for the expression of all political opinions,
while thirty-five per cent maintained that TV was government biased.
And yet not many people were prepared to give credit to the High
Authority for the unprecedented freedom which had pervaded television.
Only thirty-eight per cent of the viewers considered that the High
Authority as an adequate mechanism to guarantee the independence of
TV, against twenty-seven per cent reporting an opposite opinion, while
thirty-five per cent preferred not to commit themselves.

It would be exceedingly naive to describe the High Authority as
an ideal regulating body. Admittedly, the government had retained a
considerable influence over the institution, yet the efforts of the High
Authority under the chairmanship of Michèle Cotta, an experienced
journalist, precluded the return to the previous situation where governments could impose their will on powerless TV chiefs.

The new right-wing majority which emerged from the 1986 general
election framed a new broadcasting bill with a view to enlarging the field
of competence of the projected regulating body and to implementing the
privatisation of TF1, the oldest and most popular of the three public
TV channels. The brief of the new statutory regulator called CNCL
(Commission nationale de la communication et des libertés) also
included the renegotiation of the franchises that the government had
granted to two commercial channels, La 5 and M6 in 1985.

Nearly 200 hours of debates (the longest debate over a bill ever
recorded since the beginning of the Fifth Republic) were devoted to the
bill which triggered off 1,800 amendments and a motion of no confidence
as well as a reference to the Constitutional Council, the French equiva-

lent of the Supreme Court. The controversial bill was denounced by the left opposition as a typical product of the government's free-market philosophy. On the other hand, the bill strengthened rather than reduced the powers of the new regulating body whose mission was defined in broadly similar terms to those of the former Authority. This included safeguarding the free expression of all views, ensuring the citizens' access to free communication as well as the defence of the French language. But the main task of the Commission – a less impressive name than that of High Authority – was to implement the first article of the new Act which ensured that:

> the installation and the use of telecommunications systems is free, such freedom being only limited by a number of constraints: the protection of defence communication networks, the respect of private persons' freedom and property and the necessity of allowing for the articulation of all bodies of opinion.

The membership of the Commission was increased in order to provide the necessary expertise in the field of telecommunications for instance, but also to tone down the political overtones that the previous system of appointment had created. Thus a representative of the written press was added to the number of people appointed by the three presidents, as well as a member of the Académie française and a representative of the TV programme makers. On the whole, the thirteen members of the CNCL did not handle their various tasks any less seriously than the former High Authority. The vast majority of the 1,800 independent local radios we now have in France got their franchise from the CNCL which also, as a result of a public hearing, awarded TF1 to the Bouygues company, which had no previous media interest, when pundits had predicated that the channel would fall into the lap of Hachette. Additionally, the CNCL attributed the fifth channel to the Hersant-Berlusconi team while the sixth went to the Luxembourg-based CLT.

But the CNCL opened themselves to criticism when they appointed as chairmen of the two public TV channels two personalities whose sympathy for the Gaullist party was well-known. Besides, one of its members, who incidentally represented the Académie française, got involved in a legal case over the breach of the rule which forbade members to receive fees or salaries while serving on the CNCL. So much so that President Mitterrand was prompted to comment in an interview to a magazine that the CNCL had lost every right to respect. For his part Jack Lang, who had been Minister for Culture in the previous government, suggested that the CNCL had betrayed the hopes that the 1982 Broadcasting Act had raised adding that the respectable acronym CNCL had come to mean '*Commission nationale des censeurs de la liberté*' (*Le Monde*, 8 January 1987).

The 1988 presidential and general elections which confirmed Mitterrand as President and brought back a left-wing majority to the Assemblée nationale heralded the winding up of the CNCL. Determined to put an end to the see-saw exercise which had become a ritual with each change of majority, Mitterrand refused to re-nationalise TF1 as a number of socialists and broadcasting trade-unionists had encouraged him to do. He was aware that the regular revamping of the broadcasting system induced cynicism among the public. One poll among others published in December 1988 confirmed the general feeling of distrust about the alleged independence of the CNCL, fifty-four per cent of the respondents stating that that body had not been independent of the government while a slightly larger proportion doubted that the organism which was to replace it would enjoy more autonomy (*Stratégies*, 12 December 1988).

In his campaign manifesto – the 'Open Letter to Every French Citizen' – Mitterrand had suggested that the broadcasting regulating body should be enshrined in the constitution,[1] but by 1988 the more urgent task was to dispose of the CNCL. Yet, instead of introducing a wholesale reform of the system the new Prime Minister, Michel Rocard, was content to modify and adjust the 1986 Act through a new law passed in January 1989. The law provided for the replacement of the CNCL by the CSA (Conseil supérieur de l'audiovisuel) while nine members were appointed in the same way as those of the former High Authority. As with the High Authority, the chairman was to be chosen from among the members by the President of the Republic, which paved the way for the accusation that the chairman was but 'the mouthpiece of the Elysée' that is of the President himself (Guilhaume 1991, p. 242).

After setting up the CSA, the government introduced in mid-1989 a bill which allowed for the appointment of a joint chairman for the two public channels in order to co-ordinate their efforts in responding to the increased competition which had resulted from the privatisation of TF1 and the establishment of two new commercial channels. The appointment was to be made urgently by the CSA after hearing the six candidates who had applied for the position. Much to the annoyance of the government, the CSA chose Philippe Guilhaume, a professional with considerable experience who was at the time running the public TV production company SFP, but who happened to be no friend of the socialists. The Communications Minister lost no time in conveying to the newly-appointed superchairman, as he was called, the message that the government would fight him in every possible way. Indeed, Philippe Guilhaume realised very quickly that he could not run public television effectively without the full support of the government which was also the cash provider of the system. Half way through his term, Guilhaume resigned and was promptly replaced by Hervé Bourges, one of the previous unsuccessful candidates who had more impeccable political credentials.

If after this original political gaffe the CSA has toed the line by appointing unfailingly to the head of the various state-run broadcasting companies people who were known to be sympathetic to the left. The CSA has also managed to prove its mettle in the field of regulation where CSA members have fulfilled their mission with fastidious zeal and increasing independence. Recent examples include the FF 30 millions fine (the largest ever imposed on a broadcaster) inflicted on TF1 for ignoring its commitment concerning quotas of French language programmes to be broadcast in prime-time. Also, in August 1992, the CSA advised the government not to go ahead with their projected TV commercial campaign advocating a 'Yes' vote in the Maastricht referendum, as such a campaign would have been in breach of a 1990 Act forbidding TV and radio commercials of a political nature. The government decided to abide by the recommendation of the CSA and to scrap the campaign in order to avoid getting involved in a dispute with the leaders of the 'Campaign for a No vote' group.

In its latest annual report, the CSA emphasised the necessity to move gradually from a prescriptive and authoritarian role to a more flexible regulatory position which would take into account the specificity of each individual TV company and adjust the programmatic constraints accordingly. Thus the CSA has been instrumental in the redefinition of the concept of prime-time, which may not mean the same for a mainstream general public TV channel as for a smaller youth-oriented channel such as M6. Besides, the CSA managed to convince the government to defer until 1 January 1992 the implementation of the quotas of programmes of French and European origin, this concept having been considerably enlarged as a result of the CSA's recommendation on the subject.

At the same time, the CSA finds itself in the uncomfortable position of an authority obliged to enforce rules which it did not contribute to framing. Those applying to advertising or the relationships between producers and broadcasters are defined by the 1989 Act, whereas a strictly autonomous body ought to be able to exercise its judgement more liberally in those areas where the CSA's pronouncements are bound to affect the operators. The fact that such views are now expressed by former members of the CSA (Balle 1993, pp. 52–3) reflects the uneasy situation in which the institution finds itself. Yet those who advocate a larger share of autonomy for the CSA accept that an autonomous administrative body, even of the regulatory kind, implies some contradiction in terms. After all, the State Council (Conseil d'Etat), the highest administrative court in the country, can always reject a ruling of the CSA and it has not infrequently been consulted by the CSA and its predecessors before making a decision. For instance, the CNCL asked the Council to decide whether a film shown on television could legitimately be described as erotic. Thus, the CSA is constantly obliged to look over its shoulder when applying its detailed and sometimes inhibiting set of rules which it has no statutory power to adjust to specific circumstances. Assessing the broadcasting scene in its latest report, the Senate Finance Committee summed up the ambivalent position of the CSA in the following terms: 'The CSA can make appointments and apply sanctions but is unable to contribute to the shaping of the policies' (Sénat no. 86 1992, p. 387).

However, it would seem that the current government is now more willing to listen to the considered advice of the regulatory body while at the same time retaining a considerable power of control over public television. Obviously the most important means of control lies in the discretionary power of the government to propose an increase in the licence fee, or occasionally to bring it down, as the Chirac government actually did in 1987. The proceeds of the licence fee being notoriously insufficient – even added to the advertising revenues that public TV channels are allowed to collect[2] – it is up to the government to mop-up public TV's deficit with supplementary grants appropriated by parliament. One of the controversial issues in this field is the decision of the government to exempt a number of people in the lower income bracket, old age pensioners mainly, from the payment of the licence fee. This represents a deficit of about FF2 billion for the public TV channels for which government only partially compensates. Public-service programme constraints such as provision of religious programmes, consumer awareness programmes, access for political parties etc., also result in increased costs that commercial channels do not have to bear. If the remit of public channels is defined by the law, the government requires additionally those channels to commit themselves to fulfil specific 'sets of objectives' which are far more stringent. For example, the two public channels must commission a given proportion of their production to the

SFP, the state-funded production company. The creation of La Sept, the cultural channel now incorporated into ARTE provides another example of government interference with the management of public television. The channel was originally broadcast by satellite and made available to cable subscribers who were few and far between. In order to enlarge the audience of the cultural channel which had become a pet project of the government, it was decided to show the Sept programmes on FR3 during the Saturday afternoon and evening slots. In a similar vein, and against the advice of the CSA, the government imposed the allocation of the evening *tranche* on the recently-vacated fifth channel to the new Franco-German ARTE which started to broadcast on 28 September 1992.

The considerable power wielded by the President of the Republic in the choice of the members who sit on the CSA has already been alluded to, and while it is generally accepted that M. Mitterrand has little interest in broadcasting, there is evidence to suggest that some of the more momentous decisions which have recently affected French broadcasting have been taken by the President and endorsed by the government subsequently. The creation of Canal Plus in 1984 and of two commercial channels in the following year was initiated by François Mitterrand and imposed on reluctant cabinet members. Similarly, the right for local radios to accept advertising was granted in 1984 after pressure had been applied by the presidency.

Other examples could be cited to suggest that broadcasting has now become in France the preserve of the president alongside international affairs. This is probably the side-effect of a political system which confers in practice absolute power to the president, who is seen as the keystone of the constitution. The confrontational attitudes of the political parties over the broadcasting issue may also be interpreted as the consequence of an election system which reinforces polarisation between political forces and leaves little room for consensus. Quite appropriately Hervé Bourges, the current joint chairman of the two public channels denounces 'this archaic warfare waged by two camps on behalf of values inherited from the nineteenth century'.

Television in France is still largely seen in terms of power and political influence rather than in terms of provision of quality programmes to the public. However, a growing concern over programmes and professional ethics is currently articulated by a small number of viewers' associations. With a limited membership they try to promote a dialogue between professionals and the public (MTT) or to turn viewers into discriminating consumers of television programmes (Les Pieds dans le PAF). It is doubtful whether their action has had much impact on either broadcasters or viewers but things may change. The latest of these associations, Carton Jaune TV, set up in June 1992 by lawyers, intends to launch more effective actions and recently sued a popular news anchorman of TF1 over a faked interview with Fidel Castro.

The increasing blurring of the frontier between reality and fiction, including in news programmes, has reached an alarming proportion as a result of the alleged taste of the public for sensationalism pandered to by all the TV channels locked in deadly competition, with the notable exception of ARTE. The 1986 Broadcasting Act provided that programmes, including news programmes, were to be fair and reflect pluralism (Art. 28). Breaches of this provision could be punished by the broadcasting regulator, but apart from ensuring political balance at election time neither the current Authority – nor its immediate predecessor for that matter – did much more than wag a reproachful finger at the offenders for fear of antagonising TV operators who often feel, above all in the commercial sector, that they would be better off without the CSA.

Part of the problem of the CSA stems from its inability to assert its moral authority over broadcasters who see it as an impediment to the full play of the market forces or, even worse, as the transmission belt of the government of the day. In the opinion of the Senate's Committee rapporteur:

> The government's incapacity to provide the broadcasting system with an organism recognised as fully independent and vested by the State with the statutory powers which should regulate such an important sector as broadcasting reflects the lack of maturity of our country in this highly sensitive area' (Sénat no. 86, 1992, p.387).

In other words, the reluctance of successive governments to renounce their ingrained hands-on approach to broadcasting seems to be a national feature inherited from centuries of Jacobin rule. If this be the case, the British system with its allegedly superior mixture of professionalism, independence and restraint will long remain the explicit and inaccessible model of the domestic critics of broadcasting *à la française*.

NOTES

1   The proposal, which had been kept under wraps for the last four years, has recently been revived by President Mitterrand in his constitutional reform package (Letter to the Presidents of the Assemblée nationale, the Senate and the Conseil constitutionnel 30 November 1992).

2 Advertising revenue represents about thirty per cent of the budget of French public broadcasting.

Bibliography

Adler, P. (1981), *Momentum: a Theory of Social Action*, Beverly Hills, Sage.

Alali, O. and Eke, K. (eds) (1991), *Media Coverage of Terrorism: Methods of Diffusion,* London, Sage.

Alexander, Y. and Latter, R. (eds) (1990), *Terrorism and the Media: Dilemmas for Government, Journalists and the Public*, Washington, Brassey's.

Alexander, Y. and Picard, R. G. (eds.) (1991), *In the Camera's Eye: News Coverage of Terrorist Events*, Washington, Brassey's.

Altheide, D. L. (1985), *Media Power*, Beverly Hills, Sage.

Altheide, D. L. (1987) 'Format and symbols in TV coverage of terrorism in the United States and Great Britain', *International Studies Quarterly*, XXXI, pp. 161–76.

Altheide, D. L. and Snow, R. L. (1979), *Media Logic*, Sage, Beverly Hills.

Altheide, D. L. and Snow, R. L. (1991), *Media Worlds in the Postjournalism Era*, Hawthorne NY, Aldine de Gruyter.

Amnesty International (1989), *United Kingdom: Investigating Lethal Shootings: the Gibraltar Inquest*, AI Index: EUR 45/02/89 (April), London, Amnesty International.

Andersen, C. (1992), *Influencing the European Community*, London, Kogan Page.

Andersen, R. (1988), 'Visions of instability: US television's law and order news of El Salvador', *Media, Culture and Society*, X, 2, pp. 239–64.

Anderson, B. (1983), *Imagined Communities: Reflections on the Origin and Spread of Nationalism*, London, Verso.

Arbitron (1992), *Black Radio Today. For the 1990s*, New York, Arbitron Information on Demand.

Ascherson, N. (1992), 'How the BBC invented the sound of the nation', *The Independent on Sunday* 6 September, p. 21.

Axtell, R. E. (1985), *Do's and Taboos Around the World*, New York, John Wiley & Sons.

Balle, F. (1993), 'En finir avec l'hypocrisie', *Médias Pouvoirs*, XXIX, January.

BBC (1989), *Guidelines for Factual Programmes*, London, BBC Information.

BBC (1992), *Extending Choice: the BBC's Role in the New Broadcasting Age*, London, British Broadcasting Corporation.

Berlin, I. (1969), *Four Essays on Liberty*, Oxford, Oxford University Press.

Berrigan, F. (ed.) (1977), *Access: Some Western Models of Community Media*, Paris, Unesco.

Black Entertainment Channel (1992), personal communication from BET research, September 1992, Rosslyn, Va, BET.

Blumler, J. G. (ed.) (1992), *Television and the Public Interest; Vulnerable Values in Western European Broadcasting*, London, Sage.

Blumler, J. G. and Nossiter, T. (eds) (1991), *Broadcasting Finance in Transition*, New York, Oxford University Press.

Blyskal, J. and Blyskal, B. (1985), *PR: How the Public Relations Industry Writes the News*, New York, Macmillan.

Bolton, R. (1990), *Death on the Rock and Other Stories*, London, W. H. Allen/Optomen.

Bonnechère, M. (1988), *The Gibraltar Inquest on the Deaths on 6 March 1988, of the Irish Nationalists Mairead Farrell, Daniel McCann and Sean Savage: the IADL Judicial Observer's Report*, Brussels, International Association of Democratic Lawyers.

Bower, T. (1991), 'Maxwell and the strong-arm of the law', *The Guardian*, 9 December 1991.

Braithwaite, J. and Fisse, B. (1987), 'Self-regulation and control of corporate crime', in Shearing, C. and Stenning, P. (eds), *Private Policing*, Beverly Hills, Sage.

Bridson, D. (1971), *Prospero and Ariel*, London, Gollancz.

Briggs, A. (1961), *The History of Broadcasting in the United Kingdom*, Oxford, Oxford University Press.

Briggs, J. and Peat F. D. (1990), *The Turbulent Mirror: an Illustrated Guide to Chaos Theory and the Science of Wholeness*, New York, Harper and Row.

Brissett, D. and Snow, R.P. (1993), 'Boredom: where the future isn't', *Symbolic Interaction*, 16, 3, pp. 237–256.

Brittan, S. (1986), 'Bird's eye view of Peacock', in *The Financial Times*, 5 July 1986, p. 1.

Brittan, S. (1987), 'The fight for freedom in broadcasting', *Political Quarterly*, 58, pp. 3–23.

Brittan, S. (1991), 'Towards a broadcasting market: recommendations of the British Peacock Committee' in Blumler and Nossiter (eds) (1991).

Brookhiser, R. (1992), 'Canada might get interesting', *Time*, March p. 78.

Brown, M. (1988), *BBC Bush House Newsroom Guide and Style Book*, London, BBC.

Burns, T. (1979), 'The organization of public opinion,' in Curran, J. *et al.* (eds), *Mass Communication and Society*, Beverly Hills, Sage.

Cabinet Office (1982), *Cable Systems: a Report By the Information Technology Advisory Panel*, London, HMSO.

Cable Authority (1986), *Annual Report and Accounts*, London, Cable Authority.

Canada (1990), *Multicultural Canada: a Graphic Overview*, (Cat. No. C196–48/1990), Ottawa, Minister of Supply and Services.

Canada (1991), *Statutes of Canada Chapter 11*, (Bill (- 40), Ottawa, Minister of Supply and Services.

Canadian Association of Broadcasters (CAB) (1988), *A Broadcaster's Guide to Canada's Cultural Mosaic. Programming Opportunities and Community Relations*, Ottawa, CAB.

Canadian Broadcasting Corporation (CBC) (1991a), 'The multicultural mosaic in CBC programming', *Parliamentary and National Community Relations Committee Report*, Ottawa, CBC.

Canadian Broadcasting Corporation (CBC) (1991b), *How People Use Teleivision: a Review of Broadcasting Habits*, Ottawa, CBC Research.

Canadian Radio-television and Telecommunications Commission (CRTC) (1985), *A Broadcasting Policy Reflecting Canada's Linguistic and Cultural Diversity*, (Public Notice CRTC 1985–139), CRTC, Ottawa.

Capital Cities/ABC Inc. (1989), *Programme Standards* (15 May), Los Angeles, Capital Cities/ABC Inc.

Carey, J. (ed.) (1987), *Media Myths and Narratives*, Newbury Park CA, Sage.

Carriere, K. and Ericson, R. V. (1989), *Crime Stoppers: a Study in the Organization of Community Policing*, Toronto, Centre of Criminology, University of Toronto.

Carter, M. (1991), 'Television limbers up for a sponsored run', *Marketing Week*, 11 March pp. 20–1.

Chaban-Delmas, J. (1975), *L'Ardeur*, Paris, Stock.

Chatelet, F. (1992), *Une histoire de la raison*, Paris, 'Points' Editions du Seuil.

Cheong, K. and Foster, R. (1989), 'Auctioning ITV franchises' in Hughes, G. and Vines D. (eds), *Deregulation and the Future of Commercial Television*, Aberdeen, Aberdeen University Press.

Chibnall, S. (1977), *Law-and-Order News*, London, Tavistock.

Chomsky, N. (1989), *Necessary Illusions: Thought Control in Democratic Societies*, London, Pluto.

Citizens' Communications Center (1979), *Summary of Accomplishment*, mimeo.

Cm 517 (1988), *Broadcasting in the 1990s: Competition, Choice and Quality*, London, HMSO.

Cm 2098 (1992), *The Future of the BBC: a Consultation Document*, London, HMSO.

Cmnd 1753 (1962), *Report of the Committee on Broadcasting* (the Pilkington Committee), London, HMSO.

Cmnd 6753 (1977), *Report of the Committee on the Future of Broadcasting*, London, HMSO.

Cmnd 8866 (1983), *The Development of Cable Systems and Services*, London, HMSO.

Cmnd 9284 (1986), *Report of the Commiittee on Financing the BBC* (the Peacock Committee), London, HMSO.

Cockerell, M., Hennessy P. and Walker, D. (1985), *Sources Close to the Prime Minister: Inside the Hidden World of the News Manipulators*, London, Macmillan.

Cohen, A. A., Adoni, H. and Bantz, C. R. (1990), *Social Control and Television News*, Newbury Park CA, Sage.

Collins, R. (1990), *Culture, Communication and National Identity: the Case of Canadian Television*, Toronto, University of Toronto Press.

Collins, R. (1991), 'Between two broadcasting acts: Canadian broadcasting policy and the public sector', *British Journal of Canadian Studies*, 6, (2), pp. 319–39.

Commission of the European Communities (1990), *Nineteenth Report on Competition Policy*, Luxembourg, Office for Official Publications of the European Communities.

Commission of the European Communities (1992), *The European Economic Area; European File*, Luxembourg, Office for Official Publications of the European Communities.

Condon, W. S. (1978), 'An analysis of behavioral organization', *Sign Language Studies*, 13, pp. 285–318.

Consumers' Association (1991), *Broadcasting in the 1990s; the Policy Issues from a Consumer Perspective*, mimeo.

Cook, R. (1977), *The Maple Leaf Forever; Essays on Nationalism and Politics in Canada*, Toronto, Copp Clark Pitman.

Corner, J. (1991a), 'Documentary voices' in Corner, J. (ed.) *Popular Television in Britain: Studies in Cultural History*, London, British Film Institute.

Corner, J. (1991b), 'The interview as social encounter' in Scannell, P. (ed.) *Broadcast Talk*, London, Sage.

Corner, J. (1991c), 'Meaning, genre and context: the problematics of "public knowledge" in the new audience studies', in Curran J. and Gurevitch M. (eds) (1991).

Corner, J. and Richardson, K. (1986), 'Documentary meanings and the discourse of interpretation' in Corner J. (ed.) *Documentary and the Mass Media*, Edward Arnold, London; reprinted in Corner J. and Hawthorn J. (eds.) (1993), *Communication Studies: An Introductory Reader (fourth edition)*, London, Edward Arnold.

Corner, J., Richardson, K. and Fenton, N. (1990), *Nuclear Reactions: Form and Response in Public Issue Television*, London, John Libbey.

Corporation for Public Broadcasting (CPB) (1989), *Final Report and Recommendations of the Task Force on National Minority Programming*, Washington, DC, CPB.

Couch, C. (1990), *Constructing Civilizations*, Greenwich, CT, JAI Press.

Couch Jr., C. (1989), *Social Processes and Relationships: a Formal Approach*, Dix Hills, NY, General Hall Inc.

Council of the European Communities (1989), *Directive on the coordination of certain provisions laid down by law, regulation or administrative action in member states concerning the pursuit of television broadcasting activities*, 89/552/EEC, OJ no. L 298. 17 October 1989. pp. 23–30.

CPB (1991) *Making a Difference. A Report to the 102nd Congress, 1st Session on Public broadcasting's Services to Minorities and Other Groups*, Washington, DC, CPB.

Cran, B. (1989), 'Death of a terrorist', *Frontline*, WGBH Boston for the PBS network.

Crelinsten, R.D. (1987), 'Terrorism as political communication: the relationship between the controller and the controlled', in Wilkinson, P. and Stewart, A. (eds), *Contemporary Research on Terrorism*, Aberdeen, Aberdeen University Press.

Crilly, A. 1988, *Mother Ireland*, Derry Film and Video Workshop, 1 Westend Park, Derry.

Crissell, A. (1986), *Understanding Radio*, London, Methuen.

Csikszentmihaly, M. (1990), *Flow: the Psychology of Optimal Experience*, New York, Harper & Row.

CTV News, Features and Information Programming (1990), *Journalistic Policy*, Toronto, CTV Television Network.

Curfoot-Mollington, M. (1991), 'How does satellite television affect small linguistic societies?', paper presented at the conference of the International Council of Education Media, Reykjavik, Iceland.

Curran, J. (1990), 'The new revisionism in mass communication research: a reappraisal', *European Journal of Communication*, V, pp. 135–64.

Curran, J. (1991) 'Rethinking the media as a public sphere; in Dahlgren, P. and Sparkes, C. (eds) *Communication and Citizenship: Journalism and the Public Sphere in the New Media Age*, London, Routledge.

Curran, J. and Gurevitch, M. (1991), *Mass Media and Society*, London, Edward Arnold.

Curtis, L. (1984), *Ireland: the Propaganda War*, London, Pluto.

Curtis, L. (1989), *Briefing: Update: Incidents Following the Broadcasting Ban on Ireland*, Information on Ireland, PO Box 958, London W14 0JF.

Davis, F. (1973), 'Crime news in Colorado newspapers', in Cohen, S. and Young, J. (eds), *The Manufacture of News*, London, Constable.

Davis, R. (1992), *The Press and American Politics: The New Mediator*, New York, Longman.

Dayan, D. and Katz, E. (1992), *Media Events: the Live Broadcasting of History*, Cambridge, Mass., Harvard University Press.

De Bens, E. and Petersen, V. G. (1992), 'Models of local media development', in Suine, K. and Treutzchler, W. (eds), *Dynamics of Media Politics*, London, Sage.

de Sola Pool, I. (1983), *Technologies of Freedom*, Cambridge, Mass., Belknap Press of Harvard University Press.

Derry Film and Video Workshop (1988), *Press Release, 1 November*, Derry Film and Video, 1 Westend Park, Derry.

Dion, L. (1988), 'The mystery of Quebec', *Daedalus*, 117, (4), pp. 283–317.

Director General of Fair Trading (1986), *Annual Report of the Director General of Fair Trading 1985*, London, HMSO.

Ditton, J. and Duffy, J. (1982), 'Bias in newspaper crime reports: selected and distorted reporting of crime news in 6 Scottish newspapers during March 1981', *Background Paper Number 3*, Glasgow, Department of Sociology, University of Glasgow.

Doern. (1984) 'Beyond the integration question: dominant ideas in Canadian public policy', in Pammett, J. and Tomlin, B. (eds) *Integration Question: Political Economy and Public Policy in North America*, Don Mills, Ontario, Addison-Wesley.

Dondelinger, J. (1990), *EC Commission: Communication from the Commission to the Council of Ministers and Parliament on Audiovisual Policy*, Brussels, 21 February 1990, COM (90) 78 final.

Dorfman, A. (1983), *The Empire's Old Clothes*, New York, New Pantheon.

Douglas, T. (1993), 'Toothless ITC's crunch time', *Marketing Week*, 5 March, p. 23.

Doyle, A. (1992), 'The news media and corrections', unpublished paper, Centre of Criminology, Toronto, University of Toronto.

Dreschel, R. (1983), *News Media in the Trial Courts*, New York, Longman.

Dussuyer, I. (1979), 'Crime News: a study of 40 Ontario newspapers', Toronto, Centre of Criminology, University of Toronto.

Edson, W. R, and Wooldridge, F. (1976), 'European Community law and fundamental human rights: some recent decisions of the European Court and national courts', in *Legal Issues of European Integration*, Europa Institute, Kluwer, Deventer, Europa Institute.

Elliott, P. (1972), *The Making of a Television Series*, London, Constable.

Elliott, P. (1977), 'Reporting Northern Ireland: a study of news in Britain, Ulster and the Irish Republic', *in Media and Ethnicity*, Paris, UNESCO.

Epstein, E. (1974), *News from Nowhere*, New York, Vintage.

Epstein, E. (1975), *Between Fact and Fiction*, New York, Vintage.

Ericson, R. V. (1989), 'Patrolling the facts: secrecy and publicity in police work', *The British Journal of Sociology*, XC, 2, pp. 205–26.

Ericson, R. (1991a), 'Mass media, crime, law and justice: an institutional approach', *British Journal of Criminology*, XXXI, pp. 219–49.

Ericson, R. (1991b), 'Why law is like news': paper to the British Society of Criminology, York, July.

Ericson, R. V., Baranek, P. M. and Chan, J. B. L. (1987), *Visualizing Deviance: a Study of News Organization*, Milton Keynes, Open University Press; Toronto, University of Toronto Press.

Ericson, R. V., Baranek, P. M. and Chan, J. B. L. (1989), *Negotiating Control: a Study of News Sources*, Milton Keynes, Open University Press; Toronto, University of Toronto Press.

Ericson, R. V., Baranek, P. M. and Chan, J. B. L. (1991), *Representing Order: Crime, Law and Justic in the News Media*, Milton Keynes, Open University Press; Toronto, University of Toronto Press.

Eron, L. (1992), *Report of the American Psychological Association Commission on Violence and Youth*.

Featherstone, M. (ed.) (1990), *Global Culture: Nationalism, Globalization and Modernity*, London, Sage.

Ferguson, M. (ed.) (1990), *Public Communication; The New Imperatives*, London, Sage.

Ferguson, M. (1991), 'Politics, Culture and Technology: the Holy Trinity of Canadian Broadcasting', in Blumler and Nossiter (eds) (1991).

Ferguson, M. (1992), 'The mythology about globalization', *European Journal of Communication*, 7, pp. 69–73.

Ferguson, M. (1993), 'Invisible divides: culture and communication in Canada and the US'. *Journal of Communications*, 43 (2), pp. 42–57.

Fishman, M. (1980), *Manufacturing the News*, Austin, University of Texas Press.

Fiske, J. (1987), *Television Culture*, New York, Methuen.

Fiske, J. (1989), 'Moments of television: neither the text nor the audience', in Seiter E. *et al.* (1989).

Fisse, B. and Braithwaite, J. (1983), *The Impact of Publicity on Corporate Offenders*, Albany, NY, State University of New York Press.

Frase-Blunt, M. (1992), 'Who watches Spanish language TV?', *Hispanic*, November, pp. 26–7.

Fraser, N. (1992), 'The frames people play', *The Sunday Times*, 20 September.

Friedman, M. and Friedman, R. (1981), *Free to Choose*, New York, Avon.

Gardner, J. (1992), *Effective Lobbying in the European Community*, Dordrecht, Kluwer Law and Taxation Publishers.

Garnham, N. (1990), *Capitalism and Communications*, London, Sage.

Garofalo, J. (1981), 'Crime and the mass media: a selective review of research,' *Journal of Research in Crime and Delinquency*, XVIII, pp. 319–50.

Giddens, A. (1984), *The Constitution of Society*, Cambridge, Polity Press.

Gibbons, T. (1991), *Regulating the Media*, London, Sweet and Maxwell.

Gitlin, T. (1987), 'Prime-time ideology: the hegemonic process in television entertainment', in Newcomb, H. (ed.) *Television: the Critical Review*, New York, Oxford University Press.

Gitlin, T. (1991), 'On the virtues of a loose cannon', *New Perspectives Quarterly*, 8, 3, pp. 53–5.

Glasgow University Media Group (1976), *Bad News*, London, Routledge and Kegan Paul.

Glasgow University Media Group (1982), *Really Bad News*, London, Writers & Readers.

Glasgow University Media Group (eds) (1993), *Getting the Message*, London, Routledge.

Gleick, J. (1987), *Chaos: Making a New Science*, New York, Viking.

Goffman, E. (1963), *Behavior in Public Places*, New York, The Free Press.

Golding, P. (1990), 'Political communication and citizenship: the media and democracy in an inegalitarian social order', in Ferguson (ed.) (1990).

Golding, P., Murdock, G. and Schlesinger, P. (1986) *Communicating Politics*, Leicester, University of Leicester Press.

Gosling, M. (1991), 'Anomalies in the unbanning of "Mother Ireland" ', letters page, *The Guardian*, 20 April.

Gotlieb, A. (1992), 'A staggering act of protest by Canadians', *Washington Post* 3 November, p. 19.

Graber, D. (1980), *Crime News and the Public*, New York, Praeger.

Graef, R. (1991), 'Remit or cash: an epic duel from Channel 4', *The Independent* 28 August, p. 3.

Groombridge, B. (1972), *Television and the People*, London, Penguin.

Guilhaume, P. (1991), *Un Président àbattre*, Paris, Albin Michel.

Gunter, B. (1987), *Television and the Fear of Crime*, London, John Libby.

Gwyn, R. (1985), *The 49th Paradox. Canada in North America*, Don Mills Ontario, Totem Books.

Habermas, J. (1986), *L'espace public*, Paris, Payot.

Hall, E. (1983), *The Dance of Life*, Garden City, Anchor/Doubleday.

Hall, S., Critcher, C., Jefferson, T., Clarke, J., and Roberts, B. (1978), *Policing the Crisis: Mugging, the State and Law and Order*, London, Macmillan.

Hallin, D.C. (1987), 'Hegemony: the American news media from Vietnam to El Salvador, a study of ideological change and its limits', in Paletz. D. (ed.), *Political Communication Research: Approaches, Studies, Assessments*, Norwood, NJ, Ablex.

Harris, L. (1987), *Inside America*, New York, Vantage.

Hauge, R. (1965), 'Crime and the press,' in Christie, N. (ed.), *Scandanavian Studies in Criminology I*, Tavistock, London.

Heller, C. (1978), *Broadcasting and Accountability*, London, British Film Institute.

Henderson, L., Miller, D., and Reilly, J. (1990), *Speak No Evil: The British Broadcasting Ban, The Media and the Conflict in Ireland*, Glasgow, Glasgow University Media Group.

Henry, G. (1992a), 'ITV current affairs shows "must deliver" ', *The Guardian*, 6 May, p. 3.

Henry, G. (1992b), 'ITV chiefs "moguls of Mammon placing profits over quality" ', *The Guardian* 9 October, p. 6.

Herman, E. S. and Chomsky, N. (1988), *Manufacturing Consent: the Political Economy of the Mass Media*, New York, Pantheon.

Herman, E. (1986), 'Gatekeeper versus propaganda models: a critical American perspective,' in Golding P., Murdock G., and Schlesinger P. (eds) (1986).

Higson, A. (1986), 'Britain's outstanding contribution to film', in Barr, C. (ed.) *All Our Yesterdays*, London, British Film Institute.

Hobsbawm, E. J. and Ranger, T. (eds) (1983), *The Invention of Tradition*, Cambridge, Cambridge University Press.

Höijer, B. (1990), 'Studying viewers' reception of television programmes: theoretical and methodological considerations', *European Journal of Communication*, V, pp. 29–56.

Holland, J. (1989), *The American Connection: US Guns, Money and Influence in Northern Ireland*, Swords, Co. Dublin, Poolbeg.

Hott, T. (1990), 'European commission plans single market for film and television', *Screen Finance*, 7 March 1990.

Howitt, D. and Cumberbatch, G. (1989), *A Measure of Uncertainty: the Effects of the Mass Media*, London, John Libbey.

Humphreys, P. (1990), *Media and Media Policy in West Germany: the Press and Broadcasting Since 1945*, Oxford, Berg.

Independent Television Commission (1990), *Draft ITC Code of Programme Sponsorship* (October), London, Independent Television Commission.

Isaacs, J. (1989), *Storm Over 4: a Personal Account*, London, Weidenfeld and Nicholson.

Jacka, E. (1992), 'Remapping the Australian television system', paper delivered to the Cultural Industries Seminar Series, CIRCIT, Melbourne, 17 June.

Jacobs, J. (1977), *Stateville*, Chicago, University of Chicago Press.

Jacobs, J. and Brooks, H. (1983), 'The mass media and prison news' in Jacobs, J.(ed.), *New Perspectives on Prisons and Imprisonment*, Ithaca, NY, Cornell University Press.

Jay, P. (1984), 'Electronic publishing', in Jay, P. *The Crisis for Western Political Economy and Other Essays*, London, Andre Deutsch.

Jorna, K.C. (1991), 'The European Commission's regulatory framework for commercial television', London, Advertising Seminars International.

Keane, J. (1991), *The Media and Democracy*, Oxford, Polity Press.

Kellner, D. (1991), 'The "crisis in the Gulf" and the mainstream media', *Electronic Journal of Communication*, 2, (1).

Kingsburg, B. (1981), 'Complaints against the media: a comparative study', *Canterbury Law Review*, I, p. 155.

Kitchin, H. (1989), *The Gibraltar Report: Inquest into the Deaths of Mairead Farrell, Daniel McCann and Sean Savage*, London, National Council for Civil Liberties.

Kitzinger, J. (1990), 'Audience understandings of AIDS media messages: a discussion of methods', *Sociology of Health and Illness*, XII, 3, pp. 319–35.

Kitzinger, J. (1992), 'Focus groups: methods or madness?', paper presented to ESRC conference *Challenge and Innovation: Methodological Advances in AIDS Research*, 14–15 May, 1992, Harrogate.

Kitzinger, J. (1993), 'Understanding AIDS: media messages and what people know about Acquired Immune Deficiency Syndrome, in Glasgow University Media Group (eds (1993).

Kitzinger, J. and Miller, D. (1992), ' "African AIDS": the media and audience beliefs', in Aggleton P., Davies P. and Hart, G. (eds), *AIDS: Rights, Risk and Reason*, London, Falmer Press.

Kleinsteuber, H. (1992), 'The global village stays local', in Suine, K. and Treutzchler, W. (eds) *Dynamics of Media Politics*, London, Sage.

Knight, G. and Dean, T. (1982), 'Myth and the structure of news', *Journal of Communication*, Spring, pp. 145–61.

Kundera, M. (1980), *The Book of Laughter and Forgetting* (trans. M. H. Heim), New York, Knopf.

Laqueur, W. (1978), *Terrorism*, London, Abacus.

Leapman, M. (1987), *The Last Days of the Beeb*, (revised edition), London, Coronet.

Levine, J., *et al.* (1973), 'Subway behavior', in , Birenbaum, A. and Sagarin E. (eds), *People in Places*, New York, Praeger.

Leonard, G. (1978), *The Silent Pulse*, New York, E. P. Dutton.

Likierman, A. and Taylor, A. (1992), 'Government departmental reports: pointers to the future', *Research Report 29*, Chartered Association of Certified Accountants, London.

Lipset, S. (1990), *Continental Divide: the Values and Institutions of the United States and Canada*, New York, Routledge.

Lorimer, R. (1992), 'TV, radio, books, film: government support for culture', *Social Policy*, 23, (1), pp. 73–9.

Lorimer, R. and Wilson, D.C. (eds) (1987), *Communications Canada: Issues in Broadcasting and New Technologies*, Toronto, Kagan and Woo.

Macdonnel, D. (1986), *Theories of Discourse*, Oxford, Blackwell.

McDonnell, P. (1988), *100% American*, New York, Posiedon.

McLeod, J., Kosicki, G. and Pan, Z. (1991), 'On understanding and misunderstanding media effects', *in* Curran and Gurevitch (eds) (1991).

McLuhan, M. (1964), *Understanding Media: the Extensions of Man*, New York, McGraw-Hill.

McNair, B. (1988), *Images of the Enemy*, London, Routledge.

McPhail, T. (1992), 'Population shift plus pay-per-view: the new dynamics of American TV', *Intermedia*, 20, (6), pp. 22–4.

McQuail, D. (1992), *Media Performance*, London, Sage.

Madge, T. (1989), *Beyond the BBC*, Basingstoke, Macmillan.

Melucci, A. (1988), 'Social movements and the democratisation of everyday life' *in* Keane, J. (ed.) *Civil Society and the State: New European Perspectives*, London, Verso.

Melucci, A. (1989), *Nomads of the Present: Social Movements and Individual Needs in Contemporary Society*, London, Hutchinson Radius.

Mercer, D. (1987), 'The media on the battlefield' in Mercer, Mungham, and Williams (1987).

Mercer, D., Mungham, G. and Williams K. (1989), *The Fog of War*, London, Heinemann.

Merelman, R. (1982), *Making Something of Ourselves: On Culture and Politics in the United States*, Berkeley, CA, University of California Press.

Meyrowitz, J. (1985), *No Sense of Place: the Impact of Electronic Media on Social Behavior*, New York, Oxford University Press.

Meyrowitz, J. (1991), 'First the word . . . now the image' in *Human Concerns*, Fall, pp. 4–5.

Miles, P. and Smith, M. (1987), *Cinema, Literature and Society*, (Chapter 6 'John Grierson and the documentary film movement'), London, Croom Helm.

Miller, D. (1991), 'The media on the rock: the media and the Gibraltar killings', in Rolston, B. (ed.) (1991).

Miller, D. (1993), 'The Northern Ireland Information Service: aims, strategy, tactics', *in* Glasgow University Media Group (eds) 1993.

Miller, D. (forthcoming), *Don't Mention the War: Northern Ireland, Propaganda and the Media*, London, Pluto.

Moloney, E. (1991), 'Closing down the airwaves: the story of the broadcasting ban', in Rolston, B. (ed.) (1991).

Montaldo, J. (1974) *Dossier ORTF 1944–74*, Paris, Albin Michel.

Morley, D. (1980), *The "Nationwide" Audience, Structure and Decoding*, London, British Film Institute Publishing.

Morrison, D. E. (1992), *Television and the Gulf War*, London, John Libbey.

Morrison, D. E. and Tumber H. (1988), *Journalists at War*, Newbury Park CA/London, Sage.

Mungham, G. (1987), 'Grenada: news blackout in the Caribbean', in Mercer, D., Mungham G. and Williams, K. (1987).

Murdock, G. (1990), 'Redrawing the map of the communications industries: concentration and ownership in the era of privatization' in Ferguson (ed.) (1990).

Murdock, G. (1991), 'Patrolling the border: British broadcasting and the Irish question in the 1980s', *Journal of Communication*, XCI, 4, pp. 104–15.

Murdock, G. (1992a), 'Citizens, consumers and public cultuure', in Skovmand, M. and Schroder, K. C. (eds) *Media Cultures: Reappraising Transnational Media*, London, Routledge.

Murdock, G. (1992b), 'Selling the silver: British commercial television after the franchise auction', *Media Perspektiven* 4/92.

Murdock, G. (1992c), 'Embedded persuasions: the fall and rise of integrated advertising', in Strinati, D. and Wagg, S. (eds) *Come on Down? Popular Media Culture in Post-War Britain*, London, Routledge.

Murdock, G. and Golding, P. (1989), 'Information poverty and political inequality: citizenship in the age of privatised communications', *Journal of Communication*, 39, (3), pp. 180–95.

Murray, R. (1989), 'Fordism and post-Fordism' *in* Hall, S. and Jacques, M. (eds), *New Times: the Changing Face of Politics in the 1990s*, London, Lawrence and Wishart.

National Association of Broadcasters (1991), *Diversity in Broadcasting; Actions Toward Better Business*, Washington DC, NAB.

National Cable Television Association (NCTA) (1992), *Cable Television Developments; Directory of Top 50 MSOs; Directory of Cable Networks*, 16, (58), NCTA, Washington DC.

Nielsen (1991), 'Television viewing among Blacks', *Nielsen Media Research Notes*, Jamuary, p. 2.

Nielsen (1992), *Nielsen Home Video Index: Monthly Universe Estimates*, New York, Nielsen.

Norton-Taylor, R. and Pallister, D. (1992), 'Saddam, the spies and the supergun', *Guardian*, 7 March 1992.

Oakley, G. (1990), 'Opening up the box' *in* Willis, J. and Wollen, T. (eds.) *The Neglected Audience*, London, British Film Institute.

Paletz, D., Ayanian, J. and Fozzard, P. (1982), 'Terrorism on TV news: the IRA, the FALN and the Red Brigades', in Adams W. C., *Television Coverage of International Affairs*, Norwood, NJ, Ablex.

Paletz, D. and Schmid, A. (1992), *Terrorism and the Media: How Researchers, Terrorists, Government, Press, Public, Victims View and Use the Media*, Sage, Newbury Park CA/London, Sage.

Palmer, M. and Tunstall, J. (1990), *Liberating Communications: Policy-making in France and Britain*, Oxford, Blackwell.

Parenti, M. (1991), *Make Believe Media: the Politics of Entertainment*, New York, St Martin's Press.

Paul Audley & Associates (1991), *Film and Television Production in Canada: Trends to 1989 and Projection to 1995*, Toronto, Paul Audley & Associates.

Paulu, B. (1981), *Television and Radio in the United Kingdom*, London, Macmillan.

Peacock, A. (1986), 'Television Tomorrow', paper presented to the Conference of the International Institute of Communication, Edinburgh. (Revised version published as 'Technology, the political economy of broadcasting', *Intermedia*, 14, (6), pp. 35–7).

Philo, G. (1990), *Seeing and Believing: the Influence of Television*, London, Routledge.

Porter, V. and Hasselbach, S. (1991), *Pluralism, Politics and the Marketplace*, London, Routledge.

Postman, N. (1984), *Amusing Ourselves to Death*, New York, Viking.

Potter, J. (1988), 'Consumerism and the public sector: how well does the coat fit?', *Public Administration*, 66, (2), pp. 149–64.

Raboy, M. (1984), *Movements and Messages: Media and Radical Politics in Quebec*, (trans. D. Homel), Toronto, Between the Lines.

Raboy, M. (1990), *Missed Opportunities: the Story of Canada's Broadcasting Policy*, Montreal, McGill-Queen's University Press.

Reith, J. C. W. (1924), *Broadcast Over Britain*, London, Hodder and Stoughton.

Rifkin, J. (1987), *Time Wars*, New York, Henry Holt and Company.

Robinson, J. and Levy, M. (1986), *The Main Source: Learning from Television News*, Beverly Hills, Sage.

Rock, P. (1986), *A View from the Shadows*, Oxford, Oxford University Press.

Rogers, F. (1992a), 'Address to the European Print Medium Symposium May 1992', London, Advertising Seminars International.

Rogers, F. (1992b), 'Why EC legislation threatens press freedom', *The European* 5 March.

Rogers Broadcasting Company (1992), *Channel 47 Television*, Toronto, Rogers Broadcasting Company.

Rolston B. (ed.) (1991), *The Media and Northern Ireland: Covering the Troubles*, London, Macmillan.

Royal Commission on Newspapers (1981a), *The Newspaper and Public Affairs*, Research Studies on the Newspaper Industry, Ottawa, Supply and Services Canada.

Royal Commission on Newspapers (1981b), *Newspapers and their Readers*, Research Studies on the Newspaper Industry, Ottawa, Supply and Services Canada.

Royal Commission on Newspapers (1981c), *Final Report*, Ottawa, Research Studies on the Newspaper Industry, Ottawa, Supply and Services Canada.

Rudin, M. (1985), ' "At the Edge of the Union" – censorship and constitutional crisis at the BBC', *Journal of Media Law and Practice*, VI, November, pp. 277–300.

Said, E. (1993), *Culture and Imperialism*, London, Chatto and Windus.

Schechter, D. (1992), 'The Gulf War and the death of TV news', *The Independent*, January/February, pp. 28–31.

Schiller, D. (1986), 'Transformation of news in the US information market,' in Golding, P., Murdock, G. and Schlesinger, P. (eds) (1986).

Schiller, H. (1989), *Culture, Inc.: The Corporate Takeover of Public Expression*, New York, Oxford University Press.

Schiller, H. (1991), 'Not yet the post-imperialist era', *Critical Studies in Mass Communication*, 8, (1), pp. 13–28.

Schlesinger, A. M., Jr. (1991), *The Disuniting of America*, Whittle Direct Books, Knoxville, Tenn.

Schlesinger, P. (1987), *Putting 'Reality' Together: BBC News* (second edition), London, Methuen.

Schlesinger, P. (1989), 'From production to propaganda?' *Media, Culture and Society*, XI, pp. 283–306.

Schlesinger, P. (1991), *Media, State and Nation: Political Violence and Collective Identities*, London, Sage.

Schlesinger, P. (1993), 'Wishful thinking: cultural politics, media and collective identities in Europe', *Journal of Communication*, 43, (2), pp. 6–17.

Schlesinger, P., Dobash, R. E., Dobash, R. P. and Weaver, C. K. (1992), *Women Viewing Violence*, London, British Film Institute.

Schlesinger, P., Murdock, G. and Elliott, P. (1983), *Televising 'Terrorism': Political Violence and Popular Culture'*, London, Comedia.

Schudson, M. (1993), 'Watergate: a study in mythology', *Columbia Journalism Review*, May/June 1992, pp. 28–41.

Screen Digest (1991a), August 1991, pp. 177–83.

Screen Digest (1991b), September 1991, pp. 201–8.

Seaman, W. (1992), 'Active audience theory: pointless populism,' *Media, Culture and Society*, XIV, pp. 301–11.

Seiter, E. *et al.* (1989), *Remote Control: Television, Audiences and Cultural Power*, London, Routledge.

Sénat no. 86 (1992) *Rapport d'information fait au nom de la Commission des Finances, du*

Contrôle budgetaire et des Comptes économiques de la Nation sur la situation audiovisuel en 1992 (Rapport Cluzel).

Shaw, D. L. and McCombs, M. E. (1977), *The Emergence of American Political Issues: the Agenda-Setting Function of the Press*, St Paul's, Minn., West Publishing.

Sigal, L. (1973), *Reporters and Officials*, Lexington, Mass., D.C. Heath.

Simmel, G. (1971), *On Individuality and Social Forms*, (ed. D.N. Levine), Chicago, University of Chicago Press.

Singer, B. (1986), *Advertising and Society*, Don Mills Ontario, Addison-Wesley.

Smith, A. (1992), 'Cash Prizes', *New Statesman and Society*, 27 November p. 47.

Smith, A. D. (1991), *National Identity*, Harmondsworth, Middx, Penguin Books.

Smyth, D. (1981), *Dependent Road: Communication, Capitalism, Consciousness and Canada*, Norwood, NS, Ablex.

Stone, C. (1975), *Where the Law Ends: the Social Control of Corporate Behavior*, New York, Harper and Row.

Taggart, B.J. (1992), 'The Development of cable television in the United States and the United Kingdom and a projection for the growth of the medium in Britain', unpublished PhD, University of Strathclyde, Glasgow.

Taylor, P. M. (1986), 'The semantics of political violence', in Golding, P., Murdock, G. and Schlesinger, P. (eds) (1986).

Taylor, P. M. (1992), *War and the Media: Propaganda and Persuasion in the Gulf War*, Manchester, Manchester University Press.

Television Northern Canada (1992), *Television Northern Canada: the Vision Becomes a Reality*, Ottawa, Television Northern Canada.

Tomlinson, J. (1991), *Cultural Imperialism*, London, Pinter Publishers.

Tuchman, G. (1978), *Making News*, New York, The Free Press.

Tunstall, J. (1977), *The Media Are American*, London, Constable.

Tunstall, J. and Palmer, M. (1991), *Media Moguls*, London, Routledge.

TV Choice (1989), *The Irish Question*, TV Choice, 80 St Martin's Lane London WC2N 4AA.

Tweedie, J. (1988), *The Gibraltar Inquest Report: a Report into the Deaths of Mairead Farrell, Daniel McCann and Sean Savage, Gibraltar Coroner's Court, September 1988*, Inquest, London.

Twitchell, J. B. (1992), *Carnival Culture: the Trashing of Taste in America*, New York, Columbia University Press.

US Bureau of Census (1991), *Statistical Abstract of the United States: 1991* (3rd edition), US Bureau of the Census, Washington DC.

US Congress (1988), *US-Canada Free Trade Agreement*. 100th Congress, second session, House Document 100–2/6, US Government Printing Office, Washington DC.

van Dijk, P. and van Hoof G. J. H (1990), *Theory and Practice of the European Convention on Human Rights* (2nd edition), Deventer, Kluwer.

Voumvakis, S. and Ericson, R. V. (1984), *News Accounts of Attacks on Women: a Comparison of Three Toronto Newspapers*, Toronto, Centre of Criminology, University of Toronto.

Ward, K. (1984), 'Ulster terrorism: the US network news coverage of Northern Ireland 1968–1979', in Alexander, Y. and O'Day, A. (eds), *Terrorism in Ireland*, London, Croom Helm.

Williams, R. (1977), *Marxism and Literature*, Oxford, Oxford University Press.

Williams, R. (1989), *Raymond Williams on Television: Selected Writings*, Toronto, Between the Lines.

Windlesham and Rampton, R. (1989), *The Windlesham/Rampton Report on 'Death on the Rock'*, London, Faber and Faber.

Woodward, W. (1988), 'America as a culture (1): some emerging lines of analysis. America as a culture (II): a fourfold heritage', *Journal of American Culture* 11, (1), pp. 1–32.

Young, H. (1992), 'Devious paths from the secrets maze', *The Guardian* 14 May.

Index